CHRISTIE'S

Review of the Season 1987

Louis XVI porcelain and ormolu guéridon
The top mounted with a large Sèvres plaque, the painting attributed to Bouillat *père*, the gilding by Vandé
The plaque 16½ in. (41.7 cm.) diameter
Sold 17.6.87 in London for £121,000 ($193,600)

CHRISTIE'S

Review of the Season 1987

Edited by Mark Wrey
and Susanna Spicer

PHAIDON · CHRISTIE'S
OXFORD

Distribution through Phaidon · Christie's Ltd., Littlegate House, St. Ebbe's Street, Oxford OX1 1SQ

British Library Cataloguing in Publication Data

Christie's review of the season.——
  1987
  1. Art —— Periodicals
  705   N1
  ISBN 0-7148-8054-X

Distribution in USA and dependencies by Salem House, 99 Main Street, Salem, NH 03079

Design and layout by Normal Ball, Logos Design, Datchet, Berkshire

Phototypeset in Compugraphic Baskerville by J & K Hybert, Maidenhead, Berkshire

Printed and bound in the Netherlands by Drukkerij Onkenhout b.v., Hilversum

Endpapers: Four of nine original pen and ink drawings by Lewis Carroll illustrating scenes from *Alice's Adventures in Wonderland*, c.1865: (front) *The Lobster* and *The Duchess;* (back) *The Mad Hatter's Tea Party* and *The Mock Turtle.* Sold 3.12.86 in London for £187,000 ($266,101), a record auction price for a manuscript relating to children's literature.

All prices include the buyer's premium where applicable. The currency equivalents given throughout the book are based on the rate of exchange ruling at the time of sale.

Contents

Foreword

CHARLES ALLSOPP

Over the past twenty-five years the turnover of the two international auction houses has risen almost inexorably; in the case of Christie's from some £3 million in 1962 to nearly 200 times that figure, £581 million, in the season under review here. This rise, and the records that go with it, have been greeted for the most part with enthusiasm in the press, to whom our thanks and those of our shareholders are due, but sometimes with a degree of indulgent cynicism in other circles 'more and more being paid for less and less'.

What the pages of this book will show, however, is that 1986/7 was not only a good year for Christie's but for the fine art and auction market as a whole. We are fortunate in having been asked to sell major works of art in almost every field, from drawings by Barocci to cars by Bugatti and the entire contents of houses. The international market is a discerning one and at the highest level it has been at its strongest. Record prices have been paid not only for pictures but for silver, jewellery, gold boxes, art deco and modern furniture, cars, sculpture, musical instruments, sporting memorabilia and wine. In that last category the record was broken by a bottle of Chateau d'Yquem bottled for the architect of the American constitution, Thomas Jefferson, whose bust by Houdon also made a record price, fittingly in our New York rooms.

In England the contents of Keddleston, Nostell Priory and Weston Park were finally settled on the nation, and where no such solution existed country house sales were organized; Great Tew in Oxfordshire, which saw the beginning of the enormous enthusiasm for Bullock furniture, and Sheringham Hall in Norfolk which, with its Gillow sofa, started the season off so well. Successful house sales were also held in Lexington, Kentucky, and Newport, Rhode Island, in the United States, and in Scotland, Ireland, and Italy.

Sales of 19th-century pictures were, of course, exceptional, with the two great van Goghs and Manet's Impressionist masterpiece *La Rue Mosnier aux Paveurs*; the 20th century had its 'greats' too – Derain at his Fauve best, Modigliani at his most sensitive and Giacometti at his most mysterious – as well as the vigour of Francis Bacon and the style of Sam Francis.

The more conservative eye could enjoy Constable's *Flatford Lock and Mill*, Gainsborough's *Colonel Jonathan Bullock* and Zoffany's *Rosoman Family*, and here I would like to pay tribute to the underbidder on that picture, Mrs Vivien Duffield, who instead of dwelling on her disappointment immediately gave the money she didn't spend on her own collection to the Tate Gallery to enable the gallery to buy Constable's *The Opening of Waterloo Bridge*. Another masterpiece by Constable, one of the great artist's own favourites and twice a previous record breaker at auction at Christie's, *Stratford Mill*, often called *The Young Waltonians*, found a permanent home at the National Gallery, thanks once more to the 'acceptance in lieu' procedure.

1987 was a notable year for the sale of Old Master drawings. The fiercest critic of the art market could not fail to be touched by the beauty of Barocci's *Madonna del Popolo* from the Chatsworth Collection or the sureness of line in Rembrandt's drawing, *The Ramparts near the Bulwark beside the St. Anthoniespoort*, from the same collection.

The strength and purpose manifested in the Rembrandt could also be found in Giambologna's bronze statue of Mars and in the Roman statues from Marbury Hall. These were just two of the important sales of sculpture during the year.

If in the fine arts, sales of paintings, drawings and sculpture this season were exceptional, they were no less so in the field of the decorative arts. It was not, though, a year for the purists' taste in furniture, the giltwood sofa at Sheringham set the scene for the season, and the Palmella Suite by Bullock sold in London in June sealed it; Chippendale survived! His name was associated, albeit generically, with the second most expensive piece of furniture sold during the season, the Philadelphia dressing-table, and of course with the contents of Nostell Priory, but it was the gilded and exotic which caught the popular eye; the imagination of Bullock, the striking yellow and ivory lacquer of the George I secretaire-cabinet and Daniel Quare clock, the amazing Boulle desk from Knole, the Louis XVI mounted commode and guéridon and the coolly elaborate architectural grate by Thomire, the last four lots sold in the remarkable French furniture sale of 17 June.

More exotic still was the Frederick the Great snuff box sold in Geneva last autumn and also in Geneva, plainer though still in gilt, the beautiful German astronomical table clock. Sales of jewellery, too, had an exotic flavour: the Cartier chimera bangle in coral, emerald and diamond, the lovely 'Pelegrina' pearl and the purple-red diamond which exceeded the previous best price per carat for a diamond by over seven times. In silver, Lamerie's remarkable *épergne* set a new record, Lamerie's own extravagance added to *en plus* in the 19th century. There was one lot for the purist, the ewer and dish made for Lord Warrington by James Shruder. Decorated only with armorial engravings it was a perfect example of restrained good taste. Not dissimilar but in porcelain and again decorated with coats of arms, was a rare Meissen tea service made for Christian VI of Denmark; it was amongst the best of many good lots of porcelain.

At Christie's we are very proud of our record in preserving the nation's heritage – hackneyed though that phrase has become – and during 1986/7 that record, as Christopher Ponter's article on pp.12-13 will further show, was amply upheld. Demonstrably the best Old Master picture to change hands during the year was van Dyck's portrait of Thomas Hanmer; described by the diarist John Evelyn as, 'one of the best he ever painted', it will remain at Weston as the property of the nation. Not far away in Birmingham the public will be able to enjoy Matthew Boulton's fascinating sidereal clock, and, as already mentioned, Constable's *Stratford Mill* has gone to the National Gallery. This should give us all cause for great satisfaction and allay the fears 'that everything is going abroad'.

Christie's were also pleased to have been able to join with Enterprise Oil in sponsoring the centennial exhibition of the New English Art Club in the Great Rooms last September. The exhibition was extremely well-received by the critics and showed off British painting over the past 100 years to good advantage. During the year we were happy to have supported numerous charities associated with the arts and to have held a more than usually high number of charity auctions. Two in particular deserve a mention here: the first for two causes which Christie's have supported for over a quarter of a century, Youth Aliyah and Save the Children Fund; the second for an entirely new but tragically deserving cause, the Aids Crisis Trust. This auction was graced by the presence of Her Royal Highness the Duchess of York and was splendidly supported by the fine art and fashion trades of both England and America; as a result it raised £250,000.

The Hon. Charles Allsopp taking the sale of van Gogh's *Sunflowers* in Christie's Great Rooms, 30.3.87

The 1986/7 season was full, varied and successful – it was, though, made exceptional by the sale of van Gogh's *Sunflowers* and the huge price paid for this painting. Twice since the war pictures have fetched sums of money which have broken by far all previous records. Rembrandt's *Aristotle Contemplating the Bust of Homer* made $2,300,000 in 1961 at the old Parke Bernet Galleries on Madison Avenue, and Velazquez's *Juan de Pareja* 2,200,000 guineas at Christie's in 1970. The *Sunflowers*, like the Rembrandt and the Velazquez, was a masterpiece and showed what could be achieved by a sale at auction, pushing even higher the possible price of a work of art.

Two other pictures sold during the season should be mentioned. The *Rue Mosnier aux Paveurs* showed how good an Impressionist painter Manet could be. That Manet was a great painter is happily beyond doubt, that he was a great Impressionist painter is less certain; he painted and exhibited with the Impressionists but he was for the most part much more concerned with composition and subject-matter than, as Monet was, with the study of light, the essential point of Impressionist painting. The *Rue Mosnier* however, is a brilliant evocation of light and space – no reproduction can do it justice – it is a painting that shimmers. The sun rakes across the street through the gaps in the buildings on the left, catching in the foreground the shoulders of the road-menders bent over the paving-stones, the middle ground is in shadow and then a stream of light brightens the distant end of the rue Mosnier and the street that crosses it. The figures and the architectural details are more suggested than drawn, mirrors to reflect light. If you

SIR ANTHONY VAN DYCK
Flemish 1599–1641
Portrait of Sir Thomas Hann
Oil on canvas
Accepted in lieu of tax bu
remaining at Western Pa

Exhibition celebrating the centenary of the New English Art Club, held in Christie's Great Rooms, September 1986. Sponsored by Enterprise Oil

wanted a picture to explain Impressionism you could do much worse than choose the *Rue Mosnier*.

Van Gogh was a Post-Impressionist but he too was passionately interested in light. It was in search of the perfect light that he moved to Provence and took up residence in Arles. Amongst the pictures he painted during his short stay there was the *Pont de Trinquetaille*. This picture is discussed in detail later in this review so suffice it to say that when I saw the picture twenty years ago in the Kramarsky family apartment it made a deep and lasting impression which was reinforced when it appeared, after exhibitions in Tokyo and Hong Kong, in London for sale this summer. Its price was only bettered by the *Sunflowers*.

To have had these three pictures and everything else which follows within a single season is lucky indeed. The thanks of all of us at Christie's are due to our vendors for their trust, our buyers for their continued support, particularly the fine art trade with whom I hope we have ever friendlier relations, for their continued support and from the board of Christie's to our staff all over the world who have worked so hard to achieve such remarkable results.

Negotiated Sales

CHRISTOPHER PONTER, LL.B.

Of the various negotiated sales during the year, by far the most significant was the transfer of the most important work by Constable still in private hands. *Stratford Mill on the Stour*, sometimes known as *The Young Waltonians,* was one of Constable's 'six-footers' - a series of major exhibition pictures of scenes on the River Stour - and was regarded by the artist as one of the finest of all his paintings. In his own words, it was grander than *The Hay Wain*, which it now joins in the National Gallery. On the three previous occasions this painting had appeared in Christie's saleroom it had achieved record prices, and at £10 million it now becomes the most expensive individual item acquired through the acceptance in lieu of Capital Transfer Tax procedures.

During the cataloguing of the house sale at Elveden, our attention was drawn to a remarkably well-preserved archive of Suffolk manuscripts of the first importance, particularly cartularies and other documents relating to religious houses in Suffolk. Much of this extensive material, formerly in the hands of Suffolk antiquaries of the 17th and 18th centuries, was assembled by Sir Thomas Phillips between 1829 and 1859, and was acquired from his trustees in 1914 by the 1st Earl of Iveagh. We were pleased to negotiate the private sale of this archive to the Suffolk County Record Office for the sum of £250,000.

La Place Clichy by Renoir, a charming portrait of a young woman, precisely drawn against the coloured blur of Parisian passers-by, was formerly part of the Courtauld Collection, and its negotiated sale to the Fitzwilliam Museum, Cambridge, for the sum of £1 million has ensured its permanent retention in the United Kingdom.

Originally made for the Old Library at Powderham Castle, Devon, the fine pair of architectural bookcases by John Channon of Exeter (dated 1740) are the only fully documented examples by him and have become the touchstone for all Channon attributions. Their continued association with Powderham is now secured as they have been purchased by the Victoria and Albert Museum, with the aid of a grant of £465,000 from the National Heritage Memorial Fund.

One of the outstanding exhibits at the recent Washington exhibition was one of the most brilliant of Hilliard's early miniatures (*c.*1571–4), that of Robert Dudley, Earl of Leicester, set against a unique silver background. This miniature formed part of an important group which originally came from Penshurst Place, including another Hilliard of Mary Sidney, Countess of Pembroke, a Hilliard of a gentleman (*c.*1580–5), an Isaac Oliver of Robert Devereux, 2nd Earl of Essex, and a portrait of Mary Dudley, Lady Sidney, attributed to Levina Teerlinc (*c.*1575). Given to the 2nd Earl of Harcourt (1736–1809), they remained in that family until the recent death of the 2nd Viscount Harcourt, and have now been accepted in lieu of Capital Transfer Tax. It is the family's wish that these miniatures be allocated to the national collection but no final decision has been taken at the time of writing.

Thought by historians to have been lost or destroyed, there existed among the contents of Great Tew Park in Oxfordshire an exceptionally important George III ormolu sidereal clock, made by Matthew Boulton and John Fothergill in 1744 (see p. 16). Sidereal time represents

JOHN CONSTABLE
British 1776–1837
Stratford Mill on the Stour
Oil on canvas
50 × 72 in. (127 × 182.9 cm.)
Now in the National Gallery, London

the star time, and the sidereal day being four minutes shorter, it results in one extra day in a sidereal year. Sent to St. Petersburg in 1776 in the hope that it might be purchased by Catherine the Great, it did not find favour, and fortunately it returned to Boulton's factory at Soho, Birmingham, some eleven years later. Almost exactly 200 years later, it has now been accepted in part payment, to the extent of £440,000, of the heavy tax liability arising on the death of Major Robb of Great Tew Park.

Group of Penshurst miniatures:
Attributed to Levina Teerlinc: *Mary Dudley, Lady Sidney*
Nicholas Hilliard: *Robert Dudley, Earl of Leicester*
Nicholas Hilliard: *Mary Sidney, Countess of Pembroke*
Isaac Oliver: *Robert Devereux, 2nd Earl of Essex*
Nicholas Hilliard: *An Unknown Gentleman*

PIERRE-AUGUSTE RENOIR
French 1841–1919
La Place Clichy
c. 1880
Signed
Oil on canvas
25½ × 21 in. (65 × 54 cm.)
Now in the Fitzwilliam
Museum, Cambridge

George III documentary ormolu planispheric-
projection sidereal clock
By Boulton and Fothergill
1774
35 in. (89 cm.) high
Now in the Birmingham City Art Gallery

Pictures

SPINELLO ARETINO
Italian 1330(?)–1410
The Crucifixion
Oil on gold ground panel
11¼ × 31¾ in. (28.5 × 80.5 cm.)
Sold 10.7.87 in London for £187,000 ($299,200)

CRISTOFORO MUNARI
Italian 1667–1720
Still Life with Musical Instruments, Fruit and Parrot
Oil on canvas
45 × 44½ in. (114 × 113 cm.)
Sold 27.5.87 in Rome for L.138,000,000 (£64,186)

GIOVANNI ANTONIO CANAL, IL CANALETTO
Italian 1697–1768
The Grand Canal, Venice, looking North-west from the Campo Santa Sofia
Oil on canvas
$23\frac{1}{2} \times 37$ in. (59.7 × 94 cm.)
Sold 12.12.86 in London for £572,000 ($819,104)

MATTIA PRETI
Italian 1613–99
Saint John Chrysostom
Oil on canvas
96 × 74 ½ in.
(244 × 189 cm.)
Sold 10.7.87 in
London for £209,000
($334,400)

BARTOLOMÉ ESTEBAN
MURILLO
Spanish 1618–82
The Virgin and Child
Oil on canvas
$40\frac{3}{4} \times 32\frac{1}{2}$ in.
(103.5 × 82.5 cm.)
Sold 10.4.87 in
London for £638,000
($1,030,370)
Record auction price
for a work by the artist

LUCAS CRANACH I
German 1472–1553
Charity
Signed with the serpent device
Oil on canvas
19½ × 13 in. (49.5 × 33 cm.)
Sold 10.7.87 in London for
£242,000 ($387,200)

SIMON VOUET
French 1590–1649
Saint John the Evangelist
Oil on canvas
29⅛ × 23¼ in. (74 × 59 cm.)
Sold 12.12.86 in London for
£60,500 ($85,910)

CLAUDE-JOSEPH VERNET
French 1714–89
A Mediterranean Inlet at Sunrise
Oil on canvas
Signed and dated 1775
$25\frac{3}{4} \times 38\frac{3}{8}$ in. (65.5 × 97.5 cm.)
Sold 10.7.87 in London for £198,000 ($316,800)

JEAN-BAPTISTE LALLEMAND
French 1710–1805
The Château de Montmusard near Dijon from the West
Signed 'Lalmand'
Oil on canvas
35 × 46¼ in. (89 × 117.5 cm.)
Sold 10.7.87 in London for £165,000 ($264,000)

FRANS HALS
Dutch 1580–1666
A Girl singing, with *A Boy with a Viol* on the reverse
Both signed with monogram
Oil on panel
$7\frac{1}{4} \times 7\frac{1}{4}$ in. (18.4 × 18.4 cm.)
Sold 13.1.87 in New York for
$572,000 (£385,000)

EGLON HENDRICK VAN
DER NEER
Dutch 1634–1703
*A Lady attended by a
Negro Page and a
Maidservant*
Signed
Oil on canvas
31¼ × 25¾ in.
(79.4 × 65.5 cm.)
Sold 12.12.86 in
London for £143,000
($203,060)

JAN VAN DE CAPELLE
Dutch 1624–79
Shipping in a Calm
Indistinctly signed with monogram
Oil on panel
24½ × 32¼ in. (62.2 × 83.2 cm.)
Sold 13.1.87 in New York for $990,000 (£668,017)

PHILIPS WOUWERMANS
British 1619–68
A Riding Party taking Refreshment
Signed with monogram
Oil on canvas
26 × 32 in. (66 × 81.2 cm.)
Sold 13.1.87 in New York for $462,000 (£308,000)
Record auction price for a work by the artist

JAN DAVIDSZ. DE HEEM
Dutch 1606–84
Still Life with a Portrait Miniature of the Artist
Signed and dated 1628
Oil on panel
12 ¾ × 16 in. (32.5 × 40.5 cm.)
Sold 10.4.87 in London for £308,000 ($497,420)

MELCHIOR D'HONDECOETER
Dutch 1636–95
A Cock and a Hen, a Golden Oriole, Shovelers, a Wigeon, a Goosander, a Smew and other Ducks in a Wooded Landscape
Signed and dated 1681
Oil on canvas
47 × 56¼ in. (119.5 × 143 cm.)
Sold 10.7.87 in London for £176,000 ($281,600)
From the collection of the late Lord Wolverton

ADRIAEN COORTE
Dutch 1685–1723
Wild Strawberries with
Strawberry Blossom in a
Chinese Blue and White
Wanli Bowl
Signed and dated 1704
Oil on canvas
11¾ × 9 in.
(29.8 × 23 cm.)
Sold 20.5.87 in
Amsterdam for
D.fl.603,200 (£177,412)
Record auction price for
a work by the artist

LUDOLF BAKHUIZEN
Dutch 1631–1708
The Frigate Princes Maria, flying the Standard of Prince William of Orange, getting under Way in a Stiff Breeze
Signed 'L. BAKF' and inscribed
Oil on canvas
42¾ × 62⅝ in. (108.5 × 159 cm.)
Sold 10.4.87 in London for £308,000 ($497,420)

JOHAN ZOFFANY, R.A.
British 1733–1810
Group Portrait of Thomas Rosoman, his wife Mary, and their three children Thomas, Maria and Sussannah, with a black and white dog, on the Thames at Hampton, with the Shakespeare Temple in the garden of David Garrick's house in the background
Oil on canvas
40 × 50 in. (101.6 × 127 cm.)
Sold 24.4.87 in London for £880,000 ($1,426,480)
Record auction price for a work by the artist

JOSEPH WRIGHT OF DERBY, A.R.A.
British 1734–97
Penelope unravelling her Web
Oil on canvas
40 × 50 in. (101.6 × 127 cm.)
Sold 24.4.87 in London for £495,000 ($802,395)

THOMAS GAINSBOROUGH, R.A.
British 1727–88
Portrait of Lieutenant-Colonel
Jonathan Bullock of Faulkbourn Hall,
in the Uniform of the East Essex
Militia
Oil on canvas
89½ × 60 in. (227.3 × 152.4 cm.)
Sold 24.4.87 in London for
£1,100,000 ($1,783,100)
Record auction price for a work
by the artist

SIR JOSHUA REYNOLDS, P.R.A.
British 1723–92
*Portrait of Lord de Ferrars, in the Uniform of the
15th King's Light Dragoons*
Oil on canvas
94 × 56½ in. (238.7 × 143.5 cm.)
Sold 21.11.86 in London for £297,000
($417,879)

JOHN FREDERICK HERRING, SEN.
British 1795–1865
The Earl of Chesterfield's filly 'Industry', with W. Scott up, and 'Caroline Elvina', with C. Edwards up, in a Paddock
Signed and dated 1838
Oil on canvas
27½ × 35½ in. (69.8 × 90.2 cm.)
Sold 24.4.87 in London for £154,000 ($249,634)

GEORGE STUBBS, A.R.A.
British 1724–1806
Stallion and Mare, traditionally called 'Jupiter and Mare'
Signed
Oil on canvas
39¾ × 50 in. (101 × 127 cm.)
Sold 17.7.87 in London for £418,000 ($668,800)
From the collection of Sir Martyn Beckett, Bt., M.C.

JOHN CONSTABLE, R.A.
British 1776–1837
Flatford Mill from the Lock
Oil on canvas laid down on board
6 × 8½ in. (15.2 × 21 cm.)
Sold 24.4.87 in London for £242,000 ($408,492)
This sketch is one of a group of five made by Constable between 1810 and 1811 which culminated in the view of *Flatford Lock and Mill* illustrated opposite. In this sketch, as in the other studies, a lock keeper is seen operating the lock gates. In the final painting, this figure does not appear; instead a young fisherman in a yellow waistcoat is seen leaning by the entrance to the lock.

JOHN CONSTABLE, R.A.
British 1776–1837
Flatford Lock and Mill
Oil on canvas
$26 \times 36\frac{1}{2}$ in. (66×92.7 cm.)
Sold 21.11.86 in London for £2,640,000 ($3,714,480)
Record auction price for a work by the artist
By order of the beneficiaries of the estate of K. Clark Morris
Constable drew and painted Flatford lock many times. This view is taken from the south bank beside the lower lock gates, looking downstream, with the miller's house and part of the mill itself on the left. The painting was exhibited at the Royal Academy in 1812.

RICHARD PARKES BONINGTON
British 1801–28
The Palazzi Manolesso-Ferro, Contarini-Fasan and Venier-Contarini on the Grand Canal, Venice
Oil on board, stamped with the name of Mr Davey of Newman Street
14½ × 18¾ in. (36.8 × 47.6 cm.)
Sold 24.4.87 in London for £374,000 ($606,254)
Record auction price for a work by the artist

SIR EDWIN HENRY LANDSEER, R.A.
British 1802–73
A Portrait of Neptune, the Property of William Ellis Gosling, Esq.
Signed with initials and dated 1824
Oil on canvas
60 × 79 in. (152.4 × 200.7 cm.)
Sold 29.10.86 in New York for $385,000 (£267,362)
Record auction price for a work by the artist

JOHN RODDAM SPENCER-STANHOPE
British 1829–1908
Orpheus and Eurydice on the Banks of the River Styx
Oil on panel
$39\frac{3}{8} \times 55\frac{1}{8}$ in. (100 × 140 cm.)
Sold 25.2.87 in New York for $121,000 (£78,982)
Record auction price for a work by the artist

WILLIAM ADOPHE
BOUGUEREAU
French 1825–1905
Jeune Bergère
Signed and dated 1868
Oil on canvas
41¾ × 31 in.
(106 × 71.8 cm.)
Sold 29.10.86 in New York
for $126,500 (£89,590)

CARL SPITZWEG
German 1808–85
Der Philosoph (Der Leser im Park)
Signed with monogram
Oil on canvas
14½ × 11 in.
(37 × 28 cm.)
Sold 28.11.86 in
London for £121,000
($173,151)
Record auction price
for a work by the artist

VILHELM HAMMERSHØI
Danish 1864–1916
From the Old Christiansborg, Winter
Signed with initials
1909
Oil on canvas
48 × 66 in. (122 × 170 cm.)
Sold 26.3.87 in London for £121,000 ($192,632)
Record auction price for a work by the artist

The Bernasconi Collection of Italian 19th-century pictures exceeded all estimates in fetching £3,488,375, with only one lot out of 260 unsold. Competition for most of the items was extremely fierce, with many making five times the estimates. Most of the major collectors and dealers from northern Italy and the Ticino were present for the dispersal of the most important group of pictures of this type for many years.

Mosè Bianchi was the star of the day, with 114 lots by him realizing £2,280,410. It was tantamount to the artist's studio sale, as the brothers Juan and Felix Bernasconi, creators of the collection at the turn of the century, had been his close friends and cleared his atelier on his death. Since that time most of the Bernasconi Collection had lain untouched in the attics of a house in Switzerland, with the result that many pictures were in almost pristine condition. The highest individual price of the sale was £93,500 for the Milan street scene illustrated here.

MOSÈ BIANCHI
Italian 1840–1904
A Street Scene, Milan (recto); *Study of a Woman* (verso)
Signed
Oil on panel
16¾ × 12 in. (42.5 × 31 cm.)
Sold 27.3.87 in London for £93,500 ($149,507)
From the Bernasconi Collection
Record auction price for a work by the artist

CONSTANTINOS BOLANACHI
Greek 1839–1907
Shipwrecked Sailors on a Raft with Shipping beyond
Signed
Oil on canvas
25 × 51¼ in. (63.5 × 130.2 cm.)
Sold 26.6.87 in London for £110,000 ($176,000)
Record auction price for a work by the artist

JACQUES ÉMILE BLANCHE
French 1861–1942
Vaslav Nijinsky in 'Danse Orientale'
Signed
1910
Oil on canvas
86½ × 47¼ in. (219.7 × 120 cm.)
Sold 28.11.86 in London for £110,000 ($157,410)

UL CÉSAR HELLEU
ench 1859–1927
isy, *Princess of Pless in the Artist's Studio*
gned and stamped with the atelier mark
07
l on canvas
$\frac{1}{2} \times 28\frac{3}{4}$ in. (118 × 73 cm.)
d 26.6.87 in London for £374,000 ($598,400)
cord auction price for a work by the artist

ARTHUR FITZWILLIAM TAIT
American 1819–1905
Duck Shooting
Oil on canvas
38 × 50 in. (96.5 × 127 cm.)
Sold 27.1.87 in New York for $418,000 (£269,677)
Record auction price for a work by the artist

MARTIN JOHNSON HEADE
American 1819–1904
Hummingbirds at their
Nest
Oil on canvas laid down
on board
12³⁄₄ × 11 in.
(32.4 × 27.9 cm.)
Sold 5.12.86 in New
York for $176,000
(£121,379)

MARY STEVENSON
CASSATT
American 1844–1926
Margot in a Dark Red
Costume Seated on a
Round-backed Chair
Signed
Pastel on buff paper
25½ × 21¼ in.
(64.8 × 54 cm.)
Sold 29.5.87 in New
York for $660,000
(£388,235)

FREDERICK CARL
FRIESEKE
American 1874–1939
The Open Window
Signed
Oil on canvas
51½ × 40 in.
(130.9 × 102.9 cm.)
Sold 29.5.87 in New
York for $825,000
(£485,294)
Record auction price
for a work by the artist

JOHN HENRY TWACHTMAN
American 1853–1902
Last Touch of Sun
Signed
24¾ × 30 in. (62.9 × 76.2 cm.)
Sold 5.12.86 in New York for $605,000 (£417,241)
Record auction price for a work by the artist

ROBERT HENRI
American 1865–1929
At Joinville
Signed and dated '49 Bv. Montparnasse, Oct. 96' and inscribed with title and 'No. 6' on the stretcher
Oil on canvas
Sold 29.5.87 in New York for $462,000 (£271,764)
Record auction price for a work by the artist

FREDERICK CHILDE HASSAM
American 1859–1935
The Big Parade
Signed and dated 1917; signed with monogram 'CH' and dated again on the reverse
Oil on panel
8 × 9 in. (20.4 × 22.7 cm.)
Sold 29.5.87 in New York for $319,000 (£187,647)

JULIAN ALDEN WEIR
American 1852–1919
Nassau, Bahamas
Signed
Oil on canvas
$32\frac{1}{4} \times 36\frac{1}{4}$ in. (81.5 × 92 cm.)
Sold 29.5.87 in New York for $440,000 (£258,823)
Record auction price for a work by the artist

JOSEPH STELLA
American 1877–1946
Tree of My Life
Signed
1919
Oil on canvas
83½ × 75½ in.
(212.1 × 191.8 cm.)
Sold 5.12.86 in New
York for $2,200,000
(£1,517,241)
Record auction price
for a work by the artist

GEORGIA O'KEEFFE
American 1887–1986
Bell-Cross-Ranchos Church, New Mexico
Inscribed 'Georgia O'Keeffe' and dated 1930 by
Alfred Stieglitz on an old label attached to the
backing
Oil on canvas
30 × 16 in. (76.4 × 40.6 cm.)
Sold 5.12.86 in New York for $418,000 (£288,275)

JAMES WALLIS
British, active 1814–60
Hawkesbury and Blue Mountains, from Windsor
Signed, dated 1815 and inscribed 'with Camera Lucida'
Watercolour over pencil, pen and ink
9¼ × 14¼ in.
(23.5 × 36.2 cm.)
Sold 28.5.87 in London at South Kensington for £28,600 ($46,132)
This picture demonstrates the earliest positive recorded use of *camera lucida* in Australia

JACQUES ETIENNE VICTOR ARAGO
French 1790–1855
Une Vue du Port de Sidney, Prise de l'Observatrice (Croquis d'après Nature)
Dated 13 December 1819
Watercolour
11⅜ × 18 in.
(28.9 × 45.7 cm.)
Sold 28.5.87 in London at South Kensington for £27,500 ($44,358)

EUGENE JOHANN JOSEPH VON
GUERARD
German 1811–1901
Tower Hill
Signed and inscribed
'Joh. Eugene De Guerard
From Vienna in Austria,
Melbourne 1855'
Watercolour
$15\frac{1}{2} \times 26\frac{1}{4}$ in.
(39.4 × 66.7 cm.)
Sold 7.10.86 in Australia for
A$150,000 (£65,789)

THOMAS CLARK
British 1820–76
Muntham Homestead
c. 1860
Oil on canvas
$22\frac{1}{2} \times 34$ in. (57 × 87 cm.)
Sold 7.10.86 in Australia for
A$150,000 (£65,789)

THOMAS JACQUES SOMERSCALES
British 1842–1927
Valparaiso
Signed and dated 1910
24 × 36 in. (60.9 × 91.4 cm.)
Sold 28.5.87 in London at South Kensington
for £19,800 ($31,938)

JOHN SKINNER PROUT
British 1806–76
Willoughby Falls
c. 1842
Oil on canvas
36 × 28¾ in. (91.5 × 73 cm.)
Sold 7.10.86 in Australia for A$180,000
(£78,947)

Modern Pictures
and Sculpture

EDGAR DEGAS
French 1834–1912
Jeune Danseuse nue
Marked, stamped and numbered on the base
Bronze with brown patina
Conceived *c*.1878–9; cast after 1919
28½ in. (72.5 cm.) high, including base
Sold 30.3.87 in London for £605,000 ($969,815)
Record auction price for a sculpture by the artist

EDOUARD MANET
French 1832–83
La rue Mosnier aux Paveurs
Signed
Oil on canvas
Painted in Paris, 1878
25¾ × 32¼ in. (65.4 × 81.5 cm.)
Sold 1.12.86 in London for £7,700,000 ($10,987,900)
Formerly in the Courtauld Collection, London
Record auction price for an Impressionist picture

The rue de Berne
(formerly rue Mosnier), 1986

The view in Manet's painting *La rue Mosnier aux Paveurs* is that from the first-floor studio which Manet occupied from 1872 to early July 1878 at 4 rue St. Petersbourg (today rue de Leningrad) looking down rue Mosnier (today rue de Berne). The photograph above shows the same view from the same window. Emile Zola described the rue Mosnier in his novel *Nana*, published in 1880: '…a quiet new street in the *Quartier de l'Europe*, no shop fronts, but fine houses with narrow little apartments inhabited by ladies. It was five o'clock; along the deserted sidewalks, in the aristocratic peace of the tall white houses, stockbrokers' and merchants' coupés stood by, while men walked quickly, raising their eyes to the windows where women in *peignoirs* seemed to wait.'

   Manet painted two other pictures (in the Paul Mellon collection, Upperville, Virginia, and in a private collection, Switzerland) and also made several drawings from the window of his rue St. Petersbourg studio. It is likely that the Courtauld painting was the earliest of the three pictures.

The Sale of van Gogh's Sunflowers

JAMES ROUNDELL

The sale of van Gogh's *Sunflowers* on 30 March 1987 for the world record price of £24,750,000 was the event which dominated the 1986–7 auction season. When Christie's first announced the sale in January it immediately became the focus of experts, collectors and the media from all over the world. The interest built up steadily during the programme of pre-sale exhibitions in Tokyo, New York, Zurich and London. Reporters, photographers and television cameras from many different countries gave widespread coverage to what one paper called 'The Flight of the Sunflowers'. Press albums and filing cabinets at Christie's are still bulging with the reports and coverage of the sale. The auction was even carried live on television. By a quirk of fate 30 March turned out to be the anniversary of van Gogh's birth (he would have been 134), which added a further touch of poignancy to the auction at which his art was acknowledged as perhaps the most valuable in the world. Van Gogh could barely sell a single canvas in his own lifetime although he remained firmly convinced that his true worth would be appreciated in the future. The sales of *Sunflowers* on 30 March and *Le Pont de Trinquetaille* on 29 June were the triumphant vindications of that belief.

As Professor Ronald Pickvance observed in his *Van Gogh in Arles* exhibition catalogue, 'Sunflowers and van Gogh are irrevocably linked through the sunflowers of Arles'. The seven *Sunflower* pictures Vincent painted during his fourteen-month stay in Arles 1888–9 are one of the pinnacles of his art and very possibly the best known works of art in the world today. There were five large *Sunflower* pictures. The Chester Beatty version is one of three which depict fourteen (or more accurately fifteen) sunflowers in a large earthenware pot set against a pale yellow/green background. The other two large paintings show twelve sunflowers in the same pot against a blue/green background. Vincent came to see the two different compositions as pendants; he made one of each (those in the National Gallery, London, and the Neue Pinakothek, Munich) at the end of August 1888. It was not until late January 1889 that he took up the theme again, painting three more pictures (those in the Rijksmuseum Vincent van Gogh, Amsterdam, the Museum of Art, Philadelphia, and the Chester Beatty collection) based on the two earlier August 1888 examples. It would seem that the Chester Beatty picture was probably the last in the series, but that Vincent envisaged an even larger series which illness or circumstances forced him to abandon.

The auction catalogue attempts to present for the first time in published form a detailed examination of the *Sunflowers* pictures and their creation. Christie's are grateful to a number of experts who gave us the benefit of their knowledge, most particularly Ronald Pickvance, Dr Roland Dorn and Walter Feilchenfeldt. However, time did not allow every stone to be turned or loose end to be tied. In the following article Professor Pickvance presents some information which corrects the early provenance for the picture given in the sale catalogue. It is a fascinating document which further demonstrates how much vital information about the early history of van Gogh's pictures remains to be discovered.

VINCENT VAN GOGH
Dutch 1853–90
Sunflowers
Oil on extended
canvas
Painted end of
January 1889
$39\frac{1}{2} \times 30\frac{1}{4}$ in.
(100.5×76.5 cm.)
extended
$36\frac{3}{8} \times 28\frac{3}{4}$ in.
(92×73 cm.)
originally
Sold 30.3.87 in
London for
£24,750,000
($39,921,750)
Record auction price
for any work of art

Van Gogh's Sunflowers

RONALD PICKVANCE

The catalogue prepared by James Roundell for the sale on 30 March 1987 of the Chester Beatty *Sunflowers* by van Gogh was very well documented and contained revealing new material, especially from the Kunsthalle Mannheim, provided by Dr Roland Dorn. Most important was the installation photograph of the *Internationale Kunst-Ausstellung* at Mannheim in 1907. This is the earliest known surviving photograph of this version of the *Sunflowers*. Also of great interest was the letter of November 1909 from the Paris art dealer E. Druet, offering the picture for sale to Mannheim and quoting stock number 4113: this number and the title *Tournesols* exist still on a Druet label on the back of the stretcher.

These are verifiable and confirmatory documents. More open to question is the suggestion by Dr Dorn, set out in the sale catalogue, that the early provenance and exhibition history of the Chester Beatty painting have been confused in the literature on van Gogh with those of another *Sunflowers*, now in the Philadelphia Museum of Art. Lest this transposition becomes universally accepted, it is better to try to clarify the true position here. And since there are fifteen sunflowers in the picture, the argument can be presented in a bouquet of fifteen points.

1.   There is no evidence to suggest that the painting was bought by Comte Antoine de La Rouchefoucauld (1862–1960) from Mrs Johanna van Gogh-Bonger in the early 1890s.

2.   Nor is there any sure evidence that it was this version of van Gogh's *Sunflowers* – rather than one of the other six – that was exhibited at the Galerie le Barc de Boutteville, Paris, in April 1892 in a small retrospective of sixteen paintings arranged by Emile Bernard.

3.   As yet, there is no firm evidence of the picture's owners between 1890 and 1901; nor that it was exhibited either in France or Holland during those years.

4.   The picture's first securely recorded owner, outside the artist's family, was the artist Claude-Emile Schuffenecker (1851–1934), who lent it to the large show of van Gogh's work at the Galerie Bernheim-Jeune, Paris, in March 1901.

5.   The catalogue of the Bernheim-Jeune exhibition contained the following:

5. *Tournesols sur fond vert très pâle*	6. *Tournesols sur fond jaune*
Appartient à M.E. Schuffenecker	*Appartient à M. le Comte A. de La Rochefoucauld*

Taken literally, 'sur fond jaune' describes the Chester Beatty picture better (though not accurately) than it describes the Philadelphia version. (Paradoxically, 'sur fond vert très pâle' also better describes the Chester Beatty picture.)

6.   It has therefore been proposed by Dorn that, contrary to what has hitherto been published and accepted, the Chester Beatty picture then belonged to La Rochefoucauld and the Philadelphia picture to Schuffenecker.

7.   However, evidence can now be presented to show that it *was* the Philadelphia picture that was owned by La Rouchefoucauld in 1901. Its misleading title – certainly the flowers are not on a yellow ground – must have been the organizer's (Julien Leclercq) error. And that misleading title has been perpetuated. The painting remained in La Rochefoucauld's collection until 1928 when it was acquired by the Paris art dealer, Paul Rosenberg. On 21 July 1928, Rosenberg sold it to the Philadelphia collector, Carroll S. Tyson. The bill of sale gave the title as *Soleils sur fond jaune*, and added, 'Collection Comte Antoine de La Rochefoucauld, Paris'. An old label on the elaborate frame also carries the same title. And when the painting entered the Philadelphia Museum of Art in 1963 as part of the Mrs C.S. Tyson bequest, it was still called *'Soleils sur fond jaune'*.

VINCENT VAN GOGH
Dutch 1853–90
Twelve Sunflowers in a Vase
$36\frac{3}{8} \times 28\frac{5}{8}$ in.
(92×72.5 cm.)
(Philadelphia Museum of
Art, Mr & Mrs Carroll S.
Tyson Collection)

8.   Schuffenecker, therefore, was the owner of the Chester Beatty picture in 1901. His name is written in blue chalk across the upper part of the stretcher. Partly obscuring it are two exhibition labels, the lower one of which, from the Paris-based firm of shippers Pottier, reads 'Exposition de Bruxelles van Gogh 154(?) M. Schuffenecker'.

9.   As James Roundell has concluded (p. 28), 'this Brussels exhibition must be *Peintres-Impressionistes* at La Libre Esthétique, 25th February to 29th March 1904. No. 173 in the exhibition was *Tournesols*, which, up to now, has never been positively connected to any particular one of the sunflower series.' However, the catalogue does not give Schuffenecker's name as lender. The picture was marked for sale – actually at 5,000 francs – as an annotated copy of the catalogue now in the Rijksmuseum Vincent van Gogh shows.

10.   It was therefore the Philadelphia picture, still owned by Comte Antoine de La Rochefoucauld, and *not* the Chester Beatty picture, as the Dorn hypothesis proposes, that was exhibited as *Soleils* in the Salon des Indépendants of 1905.

11.   As Dorn notes, the Chester Beatty picture next appeared in Mannheim in 1907. There survives on the frame part of a shipping label which reads 'EXPOSITION DE MANNHEIM'. In the catalogue, it was simply called *Sonnenblumen* (with no complication of background colour). The lender was now Amédée Schuffenecker, younger brother of Emile. Amédée had taken over Emile's collection in 1903, and operated more as a dealer than a collector.

12.   As the sale catalogue goes on to record, it was another dealer, E. Druet, who next owned the picture. Druet included it as *Tournesols* in a one-man show he held in his gallery in January 1908. He showed it again in another van Gogh exhibition he organized in November 1909, the month he offered it for sale to Mannheim.

13.   By November 1910, however, the picture was acquired, presumably from Druet, by the Berlin collector Paul von Mendelssohn-Bartholdy, who that month lent it to Roger Fry's Post-Impressionist exhibition at the Grafton Gallery, London. This is confirmed by a Chenue shipping label on the stretcher. Druet probably acted as Mendelssohn-Bartholdy's agent in sending the picture to London, as his name appears on the Chenue label, where the picture is titled *Soleils*.

14.   Evidently, Paul von Mendelssohn-Bartholdy never lent the *Sunflowers* to other exhibitions. And it seems most likely that he kept the picture until the early 1930s. By 1934, it was acquired by Paul Rosenberg, who six years earlier had acquired La Rochefoucauld's *Sunflowers*. In 1934, Rosenberg sold the picture to Edith Chester Beatty (later Lady Beatty).

15.   In February 1935, the picture occupied a position of honour in an exhibition organized by Paul Rosenberg in his Paris gallery, entitled *Tableaux du XIXe siécle dans un décor ancien*. The installation photograph from the Fonds Rosenberg in the Musée d'Orsay is published here for the first time. Another Pottier shipping label on the stretcher, dated 29 3 35, possibly refers to the despatch of the picture from Paris to Edith Beatty in London after the exhibition. Apart from two periods of loan to the National Gallery, London, 1955-9 and 1983-7, the picture was not exhibited again until it was seen in Christie's pre-sale exhibitions in New York, Tokyo, Zurich and London.

The following provenance and exhibition history, revises those given in the 30 March 1987 sale catalogue.

PROVENANCE
Theo van Gogh, the artist's brother (1857–91), received as part of the consignment sent to Paris from Arles 2 May 1889
Johanna van Gogh-Bonger, Theo's widow (1862–1925)
Claude-Emile Schuffenecker (1851–1934), Paris, by 1901
Amédée Schuffenecker, Meudon, by 1903
Galerie Druet, Paris, 1908–10 (No. 4113, their label on the stretcher)
Paul von Mendelssohn-Bartholdy, Berlin, by 1910, probably bought from Galerie Druet, until the early 1930s
Galerie Paul Rosenberg, Paris, from whom bought by Edith Beatty in 1934
Sir Alfred (1875–1968) and Lady (Edith) Beatty, London
Chester Beatty (1907–1983), London, and thence to his widow Helen (1911–86)

Installation, *Tableaux du XIXe siécle dans un décor ancien*,
Galerie Paul Rosenberg, Paris, February 1935

Room 29, *Die Internationale Kunst-Ausstellung*,
Mannheim, 1907
(Städtische Kunsthalle, Mannheim, archives)

EXHIBITED

Paris, Galerie Bernheim-Jeune, *Vincent van Gogh*, March 1901, No. 5 (as *Tournesols sur fond vert très pâle*, lent by E. Schuffenecker)

Brussels, La Libre Esthétique, *Peintres Impressionistes*, February – March 1904, No. 173 (as *Tournesols*), with the Pottier shipping label on the stretcher

Mannheim, *Internationale Kunst-Ausstellung*, May – October 1907, No. 366c (as *Sonnenblumen*, lent by A. Schuffenecker), with a shipping label on the stretcher

Paris, Galerie Druet, *Vincent van Gogh*, January 1908, No. 35 (as *Tournesols*, lent by Galerie Druet)

Paris, Galerie Druet, *Cinquante Tableaux de Vincent van Gogh*, November 1909, No. 12 (as *Tournesols*, lent by E. Druet)

London, Grafton Galleries, *Manet and the Post-Impressionists*, November 1910 – January 1911, No. 72 (as *Les Soleils*, lent by Mendelssohn-Bartholdy), with the Chenue shipping label on the stretcher

Paris, Galerie Paul Rosenberg, *Tableaux du XIXe siécle dans un décor ancien*, February 1935

London, National Gallery, on loan in 1955–9 and again 1983–7

The author is extremely grateful to Anne d'Harnoncourt, Director of the Philadelphia Museum of Art, for access to her museum's archives, which corroborate the provenance and title of *Soleils sur fond jaune*; also to Anne Roquebert, Librarian of the Musée d'Orsay, Paris, for access to the Fonds Rosenberg; and to the late Alexandre Rosenberg for permission to reproduce the installation photograph of the February 1935 exhibition.

VINCENT VAN GOGH
Dutch 1853–90
Le Pont de Trinquetaille
Oil on canvas
$28\frac{3}{4} \times 36\frac{3}{4}$ in. (73 × 92 cm.)
Painted in Arles 7–13 October 1888
Sold 29.6.87 in London for £12,650,000 ($20,240,000)
From the Kramarsky Collection

Contemporary photograph
of the bridge at
Trinquetaille

The Trinquetaille bridge was an iron road-bridge crossing the Rhône at Arles, connecting the town with its suburb Trinquetaille, across the river. Van Gogh had already depicted it from further upstream in a painting and a pen drawing in July 1888. He returned to it in October for this altogether more radical and dynamic picture. In a letter of 13 October 1888 Vincent describes the scene and his picture of it to his brother Theo: 'The Trinquetaille bridge with all these steps is a canvas done on a grey morning, the stones, the asphalt, the pavements are grey; the sky a pale blue; the figures coloured; and there is a sickly tree with yellow foliage.' In the photograph of the view taken c. 1980 one can see how accurately van Gogh depicted the scene whilst imbuing it with his own distinctive artistic genius. The 19th-century iron bridge was destroyed in the Second World War and has been replaced by a new concrete bridge. Otherwise the scene is remarkably unchanged. The 'sickly tree' has prospered remarkably in the intervening 100 years.

Le Pont de Trinquetaille was one of five paintings van Gogh completed in one of the most extraordinary, feverishly active weeks of his life, between 7 and 13 October 1888. It has attracted the admiration of many van Gogh scholars. Jan Hulsker remarked, 'The Trinquetaille bridge represents in my view a high point in Vincent's *oeuvre* by reason of the colour and the daring yet balanced composition.' It is a picture of stark contrasts and vivid modernity. Ronald Pickvance remarks, 'The relatively close-up view of the approaches to the bridge produced arbitrary croppings. Spatially disparate diagonals compete for attention but are counteracted by the strategic placing of the figures, especially the woman seen from behind climbing the steps.' Van Gogh described his achievements in Arles in pushing forward the development of modern art: 'I believe that a new school of *colourists* will take root in the South, as I see more and more that those in the North rely on their ability with the brush, and so-called ''picturesque'', rather than on the desire to express something by colour itself... Here under a stronger sun, I have found...the simplicity, the fading of the colours, the gravity of great sunlight effects.'

HENRI DE TOULOUSE-LAUTREC
French 1864–1901
Au Moulin de la Galette
Signed
Peinture à l'essence on board
Painted in 1891
$26^{3}/_{4} \times 20^{1}/_{2}$ in.
(68 × 52.5 cm.)
Sold 1.12.86 in London for
£1,760,000 ($2,511,520)
The Moulin de Galette,
situated at 79 rue Lepic,
was the first of the great
Montmartre dance-halls.
P. Huisman and M.G.
Dortu described it in their
book *Lautrec by Lautrec*
(English edition, London
1964, p. 77): 'Around 1830
the millers had transformed
their mill into a dance hall
with a floor of beaten earth.
As they continued to bake
excellent little cakes known
as *galettes*, a name was easily
found for the new hall.'

HENRI FANTIN-LATOUR
French 1836–1904
Roses blanches, Chrysanthèmes dans une Vase; Pêches et Raisins sur une Table à la Nappe blanche
Signed and dated 1876
Oil on canvas
24 × 28¾ in. (61 × 73 cm.)
Sold 29.6.87 in London for £1,430,000 ($2,288,000)
Record auction price for a work by the artist

BERTHE MORISOT
French 1841–95
Le Leçon de Couture
Stamped signature
Oil on canvas
Painted in 1884
23¼ × 28 in. (59.1 × 71.1 cm.)
Sold 19.11.86 in New York for $638,000 (£443,055)
From the estates of Jack and Adele Frost
Record auction price for a work by the artist

SEIKI KURODA
Japanese 1866–1924
Sous les Arbres
Signed and dated 1898
Oil on canvas
30 × 37 in. (75 × 94 cm.)
Sold 29.6.87 in London for
£1,760,000 ($2,816,000)
Record auction price for a
work by the artist
The picture depicts a girl
picking the fruit of a
silverberry tree

Seiki Kuroda was a celebrated Japanese artist working in the Western or Impressionist style (*Yoga*) at the end of the last century. In Japan he is known as the 'father of modern painting'. He first visited Paris in 1884 to study law. Two years later he met the French artist Raphaël Collin (1850–1916) and asked to join his studio (Academie Colarossi) to receive art lessons. In 1891 and 1893 he won prizes for the works he exhibited at the Salon in Paris. On the latter occasion he was recommended for an award by Collin and Puvis de Chavannes.

Kuroda returned to Tokyo in 1893 and together with other western-style Japanese artists created a sensation there. The subject, expression, bright colours and free brushwork of his pictures were new to Japan. His work was termed *Pleinairisme*. In 1894 he began his own studio in Tokyo and two years later became the first professor of western-style painting at the Tokyo Art School. In the same year he formed an artistic group called *Hakuba-Kai* (White Horse Group), which saw itself as the progressive force in Japanese art and pioneered the introduction of Impressionism in Japan. The group organized thirteen annual exhibitions until disbanded in 1911. When Kuroda died in 1924 his will stipulated that money should be provided for the promotion of western-style art in Japan. An Institute for Art, now known as the Tokyo National Research Institute for Cultural Properties was established with the aid of his bequest.

PIERRE AUGUSTE RENOIR
French 1841–1919
Baigneuse
Signed with initials
Oil on canvas
Painted in Guernsey,
*c.*1892–3
21 × 15 in. (53.5 × 38 cm.)
Sold 1.12.86 in London for
£1,045,000 ($1,491,215)
From the collection of the
late Hans Schröder

Opposite:
PIERRE AUGUSTE RENOIR
French 1841–1919
Femme à l'Éventail
Signed
Oil on canvas
Painted in 1906
25¾ × 21⅜ in.
(65.5 × 54.2 cm.)
Sold 12.5.87 in New York
for $2,310,000 (£1,358,823)

MAXIMILIEN LUCE
French 1858–1941
Le Verger de Pissarro à Eragny
Signed and dated 95
Oil on canvas
31½ × 39 in. (81 × 100 cm.)
Sold 29.6.87 in London for £385,000 ($616,000)
From the collection of the late Mrs Claude Leigh
Record auction price for a work by the artist

HENRI EDMOND CROSS
French 1856–1910
Le Lac du Bois de Boulogne
Signed
Oil on canvas
Painted *c.*1899
25¾ × 32 in. (65 × 81 cm.)
Sold 29.6.87 in London for £374,000 ($598,400)
Record auction price for a work by the artist

ANDRÉ DERAIN
French 1880–1954
Collioure: Le Port de Pêche
Signed
Oil on canvas
Painted 1905
32 × 39 in. (81.5 × 100 cm.)
Sold 30.3.86 in London for
£2,200,000 ($3,526,600)
Record auction price for a
work by the artist

'Fauvism is as widely thought of as Matisse's invention as Cubism was at one time seen as Picasso's alone; but just as it was Braque who produced the first true Cubist painting, so Derain's work was more surely Fauvist before Matisse's.' (J. Elderfield, *The 'Wild Beasts', Fauvism and its Affinities*, New York, 1976, p. 34)

Fauvism had its first flowering in the work of Matisse and Derain at Collioure in the summer months of 1905. Following the *Indépendants* exhibition in the spring of that year Matisse and his family travelled south to Collioure, where Derain joined him in June. Derain painted more than 30 pictures, and made numerous sketches and drawings during his stay at Collioure. The present painting, produced at the height of the summer, displays the qualities John Rewald observed, 'whenever the eye roams over the sparkling canvases that Derain painted at Collioure… it discovers happy invention, solid structure and, beneath the powerful expression, a rare sensitivity.'

On his return to Paris, Derain exhibited nine pictures at the 1905 Salon d'Automne. It seems likely that the present picture was No. 439 *Port de Pêche, Paysage*. It was at this historic exhibition that the term *Fauves* was coined by the critic Louis Vauxcelles. Upon entering the *cage centrale* which was dominated by the works of Matisse and Derain he immediately perceived their contrast with Albert Marque's italianate sculpture and exclaimed 'Donatello parmi les Fauves!'

MAURICE DE VLAMINCK
French 1876–1958
La Périssoire à Chatou
Signed
Oil on canvas
Painted *c.* 1906
19¼ × 25⅝ in. (49 × 65.1 cm.)
Sold 1.12.86 in London for £484,000 ($690,668)
Record auction price for a work by the artist

GEORGES ROUAULT
French 1871–1958
Le Salon (au Théatre)
Signed and dated 1906
Gouache and pastel on
paper laid down on cradled
panel
Sold 12.5.87 in New York
for $825,000 (£507,380)
Record auction price for a
work by the artist
In the 1905 Salon
d'Automne, Rouault's
expressive new theme of
clowns and prostitutes
caused as many howls of
horror and derision as the
wild colours of the *Fauves*
exhibiting for the first time.
But for the critic of *Le
Temps*, Rouault had 'the
making of a real master'.

KEES VAN DONGEN
Dutch/French 1877–1968
L'Espagnole
Signed
Oil on canvas
Painted *c.* 1905–6
51½ × 38¼ in.
(131 × 97 cm.)
Sold 1.12.86 in London for
£396,000 ($565,092)
From the collection of the
late Hans Schröder

HENRI MATISSE
French 1869–1954
Nu couché I (Aurore)
Signed, numbered and stamped on the base
Bronze with brown patina
Executed in 1907, edition of 10
18¾ in. (47.6 cm.) long
Sold 19.11.86 in New York for $1,430,000 (£993,055)
Record auction price for a sculpture by the artist
'No sculpture by Matisse is more admirably designed to interest the eye and satisfy the sense of rhythmic *contrapposto* when seen from different points of view. *The Reclining Nude* of 1907 is one of Matisse's masterpieces.' (Alfred Barr, Jun., *Matisse, His Art and His Public*, New York, 1951, p. 94)

PAUL SIGNAC
French 1863–1935
Antibes, le Nuage rose
Signed and dated 1916
Oil on canvas
$28\frac{3}{4} \times 36\frac{1}{4}$ in. (73 × 92 cm.)
Sold 30.3.87 in London for £572,000 ($915,200)

MAX LIEBERMANN
German 1847–1935
Blumenbeet im Garten des Künstlers am Wannsee
Signed and dated 1923
Oil on canvas
22 × 29½ in. (56 × 75 cm.)
Sold 1.12.86 in London for £176,000 ($251,152)
Record auction price for a work by the artist

Opposite:
MAX SLEVOGT
German 1868–1932
Garten in Godrammstein mit verwachsenem Baum und Weiher
Signed and dated 1910
Oil on canvas
39 × 32 in. (100 × 81 cm.)
Sold 30.3.87 in London for £198,000 ($316,800)

EGON SCHIELE
Austrian 1890–1918
Vor Gottvater knieender Jüngling
Signed with initials
Oil, gold and copper paint
on canvas
Painted 1908
$31\frac{1}{4} \times 23\frac{3}{8}$ in.
(79.5 × 59.5 cm.)
Sold 29.6.87 in London for
£550,000 ($880,000)
The rigid composition and
the severely symmetrical
ornamentation of this
picture come from the
Viennese poster painting of
the early 20th century. This
seminal work in Schiele's
oeuvre was also stimulated by
Gustav Klimt's *Jurisprudence*.
Schiele had met Klimt in
1907 and his work showed
the latter's influence until
1912, but most particularly
in this picture.

PAUL KLEE
Swiss 1879–1940
Scene unter Mädchen
Signed, inscribed with title and dated 1923
Watercolour and oil transfer on thick
paper
$15\frac{3}{8} \times 9\frac{1}{2}$ in. (39 × 24 cm.)
Sold 2.12.86 in London for £187,000
($266,849)
Record auction price for a watercolour by
the artist

FRANZ MARC
German 1880–1916
Die drei Pferde
Signed and inscribed with title
Oil on paper laid down by the artist on painted board
Painted in 1913
23⅝ × 29½ in. (60 × 75 cm.)
Sold 19.11.86 in New York for $825,000 (£572,916)
Record auction price for a work by the artist

OTTO MUELLER
German 1874–1930
Drei Akte in Landschaft
Signed with initials
Leimfarbe on burlap
Painted *c.*1918–22
47 × 37⅜ in.
(119.5 × 88.5 cm.)
Sold 30.3.87 in London for
£220,000 ($352,000)
From the collection of the
St. Louis Art Museum
Record auction price for a
work by the artist
Otto Mueller was 36 years
old when he joined *Die
Brücke* in Berlin in 1910. He
found most in common with
the *Brücke* artists Kirchner
and Heckel and their
summer paintings depicting
nudes on the beach or in the
countryside. His own style
remained in harmony with
this aspect of *Brücke* art
rather than with the
expressive depiction of
dynamic city life.

AMEDEO MODIGLIANI
Italian 1884–1920
Fillette au Tablier noir
Signed
Oil on canvas
Painted in 1918
36¼ × 23¾ in. (92.5 × 60.5 cm.)
Sold 30.3.87 in London for
£2,640,000 ($4,231,920)
Record auction price for a work by the
artist

CONSTANTIN BRANCUSI
Romanian 1876–1957
The Muse
Plaster
Executed in 1912
18 in. (45.7 cm.) high
Sold 19.11.86 in New York
for $880,000 (£611,111)
From the collection of Ted
Ashley

Far left:
ALBERTO GIACOMETTI
Swiss 1901–66
Grande femme debout III
Signed, numbered and inscribed
on the base
Bronze with dark brown patina
Cast in 1960, edition of six
92½ in. (235 cm.) high
Sold 12.5.87 in New York for $2,530,000
(£1,516,735)

Left centre:
ALBERTO GIACOMETTI
Swiss 1901–66
Grande femme debout II
Signed, numbered and inscribed
on the base
Bronze with dark brown patina
Cast in 1960, edition of six
107⅞ in. (274 cm.) high
Sold 12.5.87 in New York for $3,630,000
(£1,925,000)

These sculptures are three of a total of
seven figures inspired in 1959 by the
prospect of creating a monumental group
for the plaza of the Chase Manhatten
Bank in New York City. As well as a
fourth *Grande femme debout*, Giacometti
envisaged a large head and two walking
men. Although he abandoned the
commission, all seven elements were
eventually realized as individual
monumental works and were the last
large sculptures he created before his
death in 1966.

Left:
ALBERTO GIACOMETTI
Swiss 1901–66
Grande femme debout I
Signed, numbered and stamped
on the base
Bronze with dark brown patina
Cast in 1960, edition of six
105⅛ in. (267 cm.) high
Sold 12.5.87 in New York for $3,080,000
(£1,925,000)
Record auction price for a 20th-century
sculpture

GIORGIO MORANDI
Italian 1890–1964
Natura morta
Signed and dated 9-29
Oil on canvas
24 × 25¼ in. (61 × 64.5 cm.)
Sold 12.5.87 in New York for $770,000 (£452,941)
Record auction price for a work by the artist

FERNAND LÉGER
French 1881–1955
Les Trois Personnages
Signed and dated 20
Oil on canvas
$25\frac{5}{8} \times 36\frac{5}{8}$ in. (65 × 93 cm.)
Sold 1.12.86 in London for £1,100,000 ($1,569,700)
Record auction price for a work by the artist

Opposite:
PIET MONDRIAN
Dutch 1872–1944
Tableau No. 1
Signed with initials and dated 21–25
Oil on canvas, in the artist's pale-blue
painted frame
$30\frac{1}{2} \times 26\frac{1}{2}$ in. (77.5 × 67.2 cm.)
Sold 30.3.87 in London for £1,320,000
($2,112,000)

HENRI MATISSE
French 1869–1954
Nu Rose
Signed and dated 36
Oil on canvas
24⅛ × 15⅛ in. (61 × 38.2 cm.)
Sold 29.6.87 in London for £1,045,000
($1,672,000)
From the collection of the Hebrew Home
of Greater Washington
The model depicted in this picture is
almost certainly the blonde Russian Lydia
Delectorskaya, who was Matisse's
principal model from 1935. Her distinctive
features are prominent in many of his
pictures of this period. She became
Matisse's secretary and atelier organizer
and remained with him till his death in
1954. She gave a number of Matisse
paintings to the Hermitage Museum in
1971.

PIERRE BONNARD
French 1867–1947
La Nappe blanche
Signed
Oil on canvas
Painted in 1924
46 × 35 in.
(116.8 × 89 cm.)
Sold 19.11.86 in New
York for $990,000
(£687,506)
Record auction price for
a work by the artist

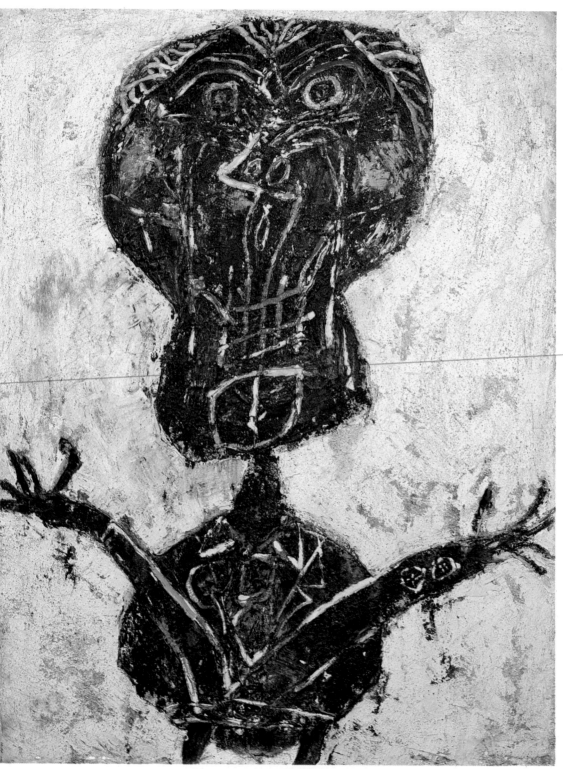

JEAN DUBUFFET
French 1901–85
Bertelé Bouquet fleuri, Portrait de Parade
Inscribed with title
Oil and sand on canvas
Painted July–August 1947
45½ × 35 in. (115.5 × 89 cm.)
Sold 12.5.87 in New York for
$1,320,000 (£791,340)
Record auction price for a
work by the artist

MARC CHAGALL
Russian/French 1882–1985
Le Peintre à la Colombe
Signed
Oil on canvas
Painted in 1978
45½ × 31¾ in.
(115.5 × 80.5 cm.)
Sold 29.6.87 in London for
£682,000 ($1,091,200)

WASSILY KANDINSKY
Russian 1866–1944
Für Gropius
Signed with monogram and dated 22
Watercolour and pen and ink on paper
12¾ × 18⅞ in. (32.5 × 47.8 cm.)
Sold 30.6.87 in London for £220,000 ($352,000)

HENRY MOORE, O.M., C.H.
British 1898–1986
Mother and Child against Open Wall
Bronze with brown patina
Conceived 1956–7; cast shortly afterwards in an edition of 12
9 in. (23 cm.) high
Sold 2.12.86 in London for £192,500 ($274,698)
From the collection of the late Mrs A.E. Goldberg

FRANCIS BACON
British b.1909
Study for Portrait II
1953
Oil on canvas
60⅛ × 46 in.
(152.7 × 116.9 cm.)
Sold 5.5.87 in New York
for $1,760,000
(£1,052,003)
Record auction price for
a work by the artist

MARK ROTHKO
American 1903–70
Yellow, White, Blue over Yellow on Gray
Signed and dated 1954 on the reverse
Oil on canvas
$94\frac{5}{8} \times 59\frac{3}{4}$ in.
(240.3 × 151.8 cm.)
Sold 5.5.87 in New York for
$924,000 (£552,302)

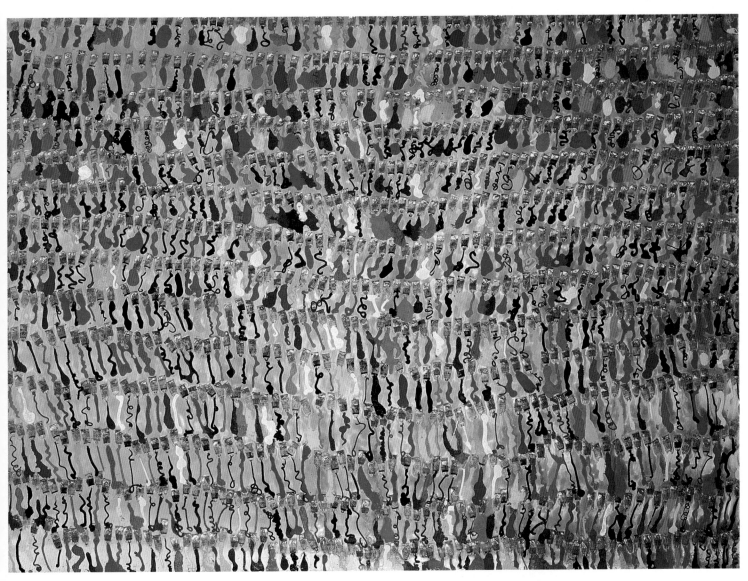

Opposite:
KAREL APPEL
Dutch b.1921
Le Grand Chef Cobra
Signed and dated 50
Oil on canvas
39¼ × 35⅜ in. (99.7 × 89.8 cm.)
Sold 3.7.87 in London for £198,000 ($316,800)
Record auction price for a work by the artist

ARMAN (ARMAND FERNANDEZ)
Spanish b.1928
Grande Polychromie
Coloured paint tubes in polyester
59 × 78¾ in. (149.8 × 200 cm.)
Sold 3.7.87 in London for £77,000 ($123,200)
Record auction price for a work by the artist

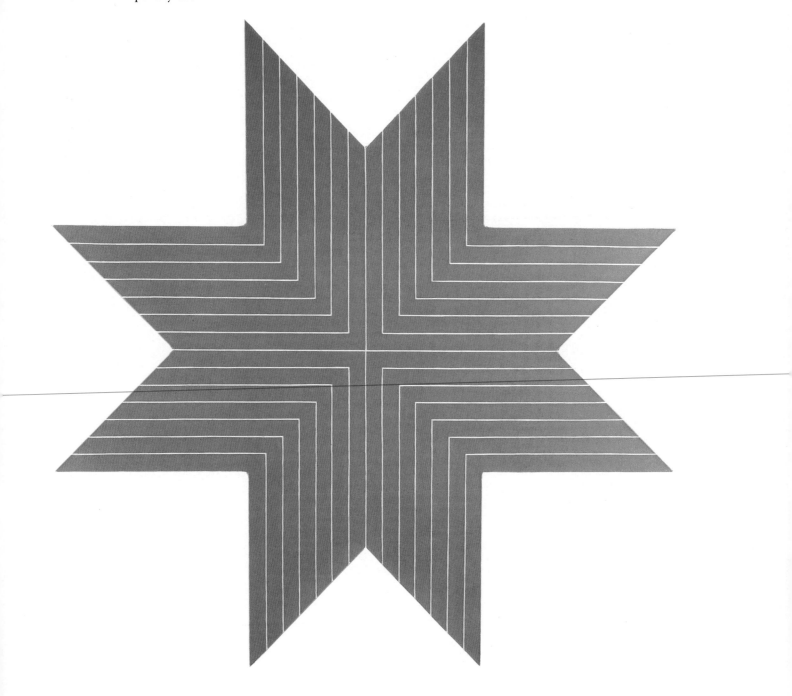

FRANK STELLA
American b.1935
Port Tampa City
Red lead paint on canvas
102 × 102 in. (259 × 259 cm.)
Sold 5.5.87 in New York for $418,000 (£248,083)

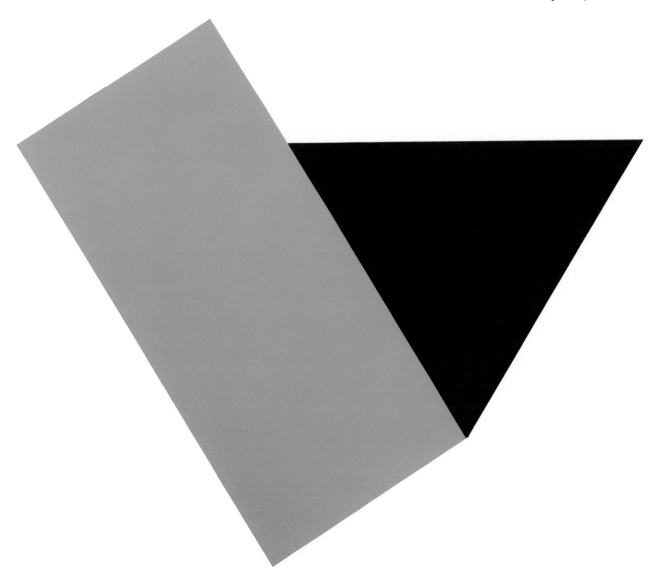

ELLSWORTH KELLY
American b.1923
Green Black
Signed with initials and dated 74 on the reverse
Two panels, oil on canvas
78$\frac{1}{2}$ × 93$\frac{1}{4}$ in. (201.3 × 237 cm.)
Sold 5.5.87 in New York for $312,000 (£186,492)
From the collection of the Gilman Paper Company
Record auction price for a work by the artist

ROY LICHTENSTEIN
American b.1923
Blang
Signed, inscribed 'panel 3 of 5' and dated 62 on the reverse
Oil and magna on canvas
68 × 80 in. (172.7 × 203.2 cm.)
Sold 12.12.86 in New York for $792,000 (£546,206)
From the collection of Ted Ashley
Record auction price for a work by the artist

ANDY WARHOL
American 1930–87
White Car Crash 19 Times
Synthetic polymer silkscreened on canvas
145 × 83¼ in. (368.3 × 211.5 cm.)
Sold 5.5.87 in New York for $660,000
(£394,501)
Record auction price for a work by the artist

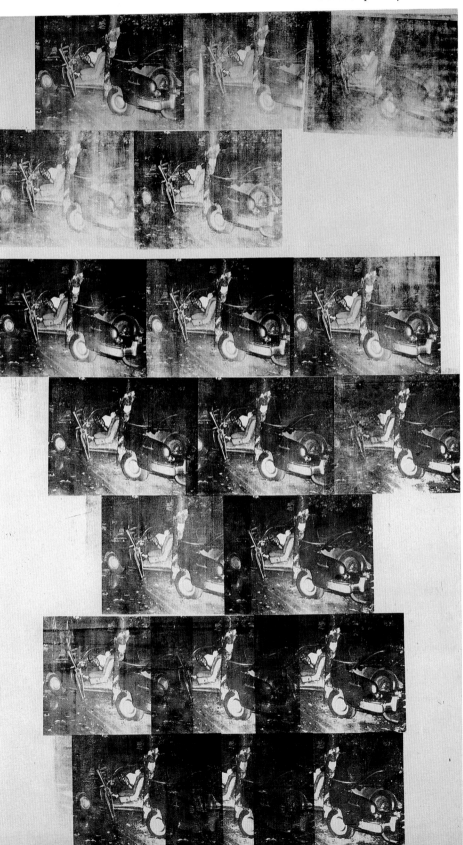

HANS HOFMANN
American 1880–1966
Jardin d'Amour
Signed and dated 59
Oil on canvas
60 × 72¼ in. (152.4 × 183.5 cm.)
Sold 5.5.87 in New York for $715,000 (£427,376)
Record auction price for a work by the artist

SAM FRANCIS
American b.1923
Summer No. 1
Oil on canvas
95½ × 71¾ in.
(242.5 × 182.3 cm.)
Sold 12.11.86 in New York
for $825,000 (£568,965)
Record auction price for a
work by the artist

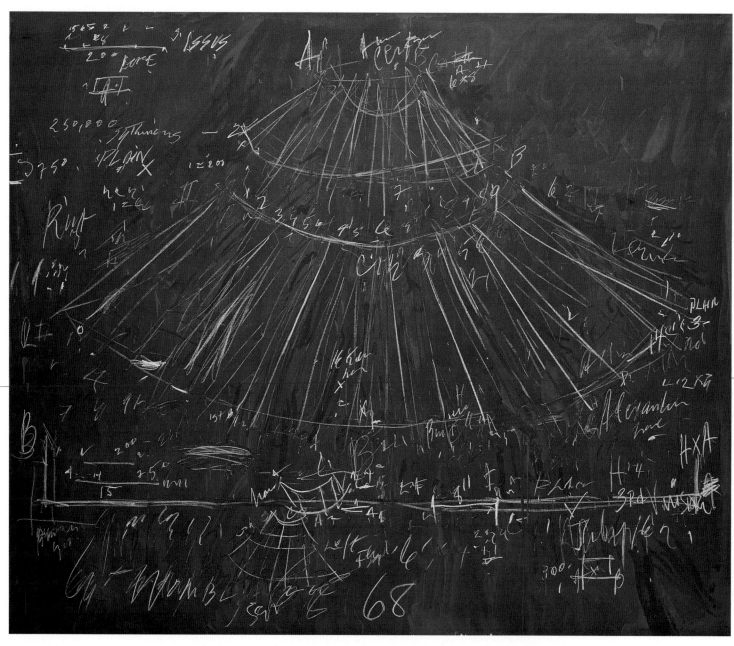

CY TWOMBLY
American b.1929
Untitled
Signed and dated 68
Oil and white crayon on canvas
68 × 81¾ in. (172.8 × 207.7 cm.)
Sold 5.5.87 in New York for $462,000 (£271,000)
Record auction price for a work by the artist

SERGE POLIAKOFF
Russian 1906–69
Jaune et noir sur fond rouge foncé
Signed
Oil on canvas
51¾ × 38¼ in.
(131.5 × 97.5 cm.)
Sold 3.7.87 in London
for £99,000 ($158,400)
Record auction price for
a work by the artist

JOHN SINGER SARGENT, R.A.
British 1856–1925
Unloading Boats
Signed, dated and dedicated to 'Miss Essie Wertheim with best wishes John Singer Sargent Jan 1904'
Watercolour
$9\frac{7}{8} \times 13\frac{7}{8}$ in. (20 × 35.4 cm.)
Sold 13.11.86 in London for £55,000 ($78,045)

SIR GEORGE CLAUSEN, R.A.
British 1852–1912
Sons of the Soil
Signed and dated 1901
Oil on canvas
27¼ × 30¼ in. (69 × 77 cm.)
Sold 13.11.86 in London for £60,500 ($85,850)
Record auction price for a work by the artist

SPENCER FREDERICK GORE
British 1878–1914
From a Window in Hampstead
With stamped signature
Oil on canvas
15 × 12 in. (38.1 × 30.5 cm.)
Sold 5.3.87 in London for £30,800 ($47,987)

WALTER RICHARD SICKERT, A.R.A.
British 1860–1942
The Lion Comique
Signed
Oil on canvas
$19\frac{3}{4} \times 11\frac{3}{4}$ in. (50 × 30 cm.)
Sold 13.11.86 in London for £71,500 ($101,459)

SIR WILLIAM NEWENHAM ORPEN,
R.A., R.H.A.
British 1878–1931
Young Ireland
Signed and dated 1907
Oil on canvas
35 × 25 in. (89 × 63.5 cm.)
Sold 13.11.86 in London at
South Kensington for £37,400
($53,071)

SIR WILLIAM NEWENHAM ORPEN, R.A., R.H.A.
British 1878–1931
The Blue Hat
Signed
Oil on canvas
37 × 34¼ in. (94 × 87 cm.)
Sold 13.11.86 in London for £126,500 ($179,504)
Record auction price for a work by the artist

VANESSA BELL
British 1879–1961
Portrait of Lytton Strachey reading
Oil on panel
36 × 24 in. (91.5 × 61 cm.)
Sold 12.6.87 in London for £88,000
($145,640)
Record auction price for a work by
the artist

DAME LAURA KNIGHT, R.A.
British 1877–1970
Evening on the Beach
Signed
Watercolour and gouache
25 × 21¼ in. (63.5 × 54 cm.)
Sold 5.3.87 in London for £20,900 ($32,563)

DAVID BOMBERG
British 1890–1957
San-Miguel, Toledo, Afternoon
Signed and dated 'Bomberg 29', inscribed on the reverse 'No. 4 San-Miguel Toledo
Afternoon'
Oil on canvas
28 × 28 in. (71.1 × 71.1 cm.)
Sold 12.6.87 in London for £71,500 ($118,333)
Record auction price for a work by the artist

SIR STANLEY SPENCER, R.A.
British 1891–1959
The Coming of the Wise Men
1940
Oil on canvas
36 × 24 in. (91.5 × 61 cm.)
Sold 12.6.87 in London for £82,500
($136,538)
Record auction price for a work by
the artist

JACK BUTLER YEATS
British 1871–1957
Shouting
1950
Signed
Oil on canvas
40 × 60 in. (102 × 152.5 cm.)
Sold 2.12.86 in London for £77,000 ($109,879)
Record auction price for a work by the artist

PETER LANYON
British 1918–64
Straw Lady
Signed and dated 'Lanyon 1/5/6/62'
Gouache on paper
46½ × 41¾ in. (118 × 106 cm.)
Sold 5.3.87 in London for £13,200 ($20,566)
Record auction price for a work by the artist

ROBERT GEMMELL HUTCHISON, R.S.A., R.S.W., R.O.I.
British 1855–1936
Dreams
Signed
Oil on canvas
28 × 44½ in. (71.2 × 113 cm.)
Sold 18.9.86 in Glasgow for £19,800 ($29,146)
Record auction price for a work by the artist

FRANCIS CAMPBELL BOILEAU
CADELL, R.S.A., R.S.W.
British 1883–1937
The Black Hat
c. 1921
Signed
Oil on canvas
24 × 20 in. (61 × 50.8 cm.)
Sold 28.4.87 in Edinburgh
for £35,200 ($57,975)
Record auction price for a
work by the artist

JOHN MACLAUGHLAN MILNE
British 1886–1957
A Busy Paris Street Scene with Numerous Figures
Signed and dated 1922
Oil on canvas
Sold 28.4.87 in Edinburgh for £22,000 ($36,234)
Record auction price for a work by the artist

SAMUEL JOHN PEPLOE, R.S.A.
British 1871–1935
Afternoon, Paris Plage, Le Touquet
Inscribed
Oil on panel
$9\frac{1}{2} \times 7\frac{1}{2}$ in. (24.1 × 19.1 cm.)
Sold 28.4.87 in Edinburgh for £21,450 ($35,329)

GEORGE LESLIE HUNTER
British 1877–1931
Anemones in a Blue and White Vase
Signed
Oil on board
16 × 14 in. (40.6 × 35.6 cm.)
Sold 28.4.87 in Edinburgh for £17,600 ($28,988)
Record auction price for a work by the artist

MATTA
Chilean b.1911
L'Interrompu
Oil on canvas
81½ × 159½ in. (207 × 405 cm.)
Sold 19.5.87 in New York for $209,000 (£125,075)
Record auction price for a work by the artist

Opposite:
DIEGO RIVERA
Mexican 1886–1957
Muchacha con Girasoles
Signed and dated 1941
Oil on masonite
36¼ × 29¼ in. (92.5 × 74.5 cm.)
Sold 19.5.87 in New York for $495,000 (£296,230)
Record auction price for a Latin American
painting

WIFREDO LAM
Cuban b.1902
La Mañana Verde
Oil on paper mounted on canvas
$73\frac{1}{2} \times 48\frac{3}{4}$ in. (186.5 × 124 cm.)
Sold 19.5.87 in New York for
$418,000 (£250,150)
Record auction price for a work
by the artist

Drawings, Watercolours and Prints

XAVIERO DELLA GATTA
Italian 18th–19th century
View of Naples from Portici
Signed 'Xav^s. Gatta p. 17(83?)'
Bodycolour
20¾ × 30¼ in. (52.6 × 76.9 cm.)
Sold 9.12.86 in London for £19,800 ($28,116)

BALDASSARE PERUZZI
Italian 1481–1536
*Design for an Altar with a
pedimented Tabernacle supported
on paired Corinthian Statues of
Saint Lucy, Saint Agnes, Saint
Ansanus and Saint Stephen in
Niches between these*
Inscribed and with
measurements
black chalk, pen and brown
ink, brown wash over
perspectival indications with
the stylus
17¾ × 14¾ in.
(45.2 × 37.6 cm.)
Sold 6.7.87 in London for
£154,000 ($247,940)

Opposite:
GIOVANNI ANTONIO DA
PORDENONE
Italian 1483–1576
The Death of Saint Peter Martyr
Red chalk, with scraped
highlights to the dagger and
to the face of the Saint
9⅝ × 8¼ in.
(24.5 × 20.7 cm.)
Sold 6.7.87 in London for
£550,000 ($885,500)

PAOLO CALIARI, IL VERONESE
Italian 1528–88
The Martyrdom of Saint Justina
Pen and brush and grey ink, grey washes heightened
with white (partly oxidized), squared in black chalk, on
grey-blue paper, inscribed arched top
18½ × 9½ in. (47 × 24.1 cm.)
Sold 6.7.87 in London for £605,000 ($974,050)
Record auction price for a drawing by the artist
Modello for the high altarpiece in the Church of Santa
Giustina, Padua, of 1575

FEDERICO BAROCCI
Italian 1526–1612
The Madonna del Popolo
Black and white chalk, the figures
of Christ and the Virgin with red
chalk, pen and brown ink, brown
and grey wash heightened with
white (partly oxidized), lightly
squared in black and red chalk
over perspectival indications with
the stylus, on light brown paper,
$21\frac{1}{2} \times 15$ in. (54.9 × 38.2 cm.)
Sold 6.7.87 in London for
£1,760,000 ($2,833,600)
Record auction price for a
drawing by the artist
A study for the altarpiece for the
Church of Santa Maria della
Pieve at Arezzo, now in the
Uffizi. This was finished in 1576

REMBRANDT HARMENSZ. VAN RIJN
Dutch 1606–69
The Ramparts near the Bulwark beside the St. Anthoniespoort
Inscribed
Pen and brown ink, brown wash with scraped highlights on light brown preparation, ink framing lines
$5\frac{1}{2} \times 7\frac{1}{8}$ in. (14.2 × 18.1 cm.)
Sold 6.7.87 in London for £1,375,000 ($2,213,750)
Record auction price for a drawing by the artist
The drawing dates from around 1649–50

LUCAS VAN UDEN
Flemish 1595–1672
A Road skirting a Wood with a Woman and Cattle, a Church beyond: Evening
Inscribed 'x.v̄iv̄' in ink
Black chalk, pen and grey-brown ink and watercolour, ink framing lines
$7\frac{1}{4} \times 11\frac{1}{4}$ in. (18.7 × 28.9 cm.)
Sold 1.12.86 in Amsterdam for D.fl.87,000 (£27,187)
Formerly in the collection of William Forbes, 7th Bt. of Pitsligo

SIR PETER PAUL RUBENS
Flemish 1577–1640
Anatomical Study: A Nude Striding to the Right, his Hands behind his Back
Black chalk, pen and brown ink
11¼ × 7¼ in. (28.8 × 18.8 cm.)
Sold 6.7.87 in London for £198,000 ($318,780)

Part of a group of eleven drawings which Rubens probably intended to be engraved as illustrations for a projected book on anatomy. Eight of this previously unpublished collection were known only through copies by an unknown studio assistant in the Statens Museum for Kunst, Copenhagen, and four were engraved by Pontius after Rubens's death. The eleven drawings sold for a total of £1,204,500 ($1,939,245)

SIR PETER PAUL RUBENS
Flemish 1577–1640
Anatomical Studies: Nudes in Combat
Pen and brown ink
11 × 7½ in. (27.9 × 18.9 cm.)
Sold 6.7.87 in London for £286,000
($460,460)

FRANCESCO GUARDI
Italian 1712–93
The Grand Canal with the Ca' Pesaro (recto); *The Grand Canal by Santa Stae* (verso)
Black chalk, pen and brown ink, brown wash, watermark CPV
17¼ × 23½ in. (44 × 59.3 cm.)
Sold 6.7.87 in London for £429,000 ($690,690)
Record auction price for a drawing by the artist

ANTONIO CANAL, IL CANALETTO
Italian 1697–1768
The Interior of a Church, with Figures at Prayer
Pen and brown ink, grey wash
12³⁄₄ × 18 in. (32.4 × 45.7 cm.)
Sold 6.7.87 in London for £121,000 ($194,810)
The drawing suggests a knowledge not only of the Pantheon but also of the London churches of Wren and Gibb

JACQUES ANDRÉ PORTAIL
French 1695–1759
*A Music Party: a Flautist
and two Ladies holding a
Songbook, a Gentleman
behind*
Red and black chalk,
watermark small
posthorn(?)
$12\frac{3}{4} \times 9\frac{5}{8}$ in.
(32.2 × 24.5 cm.)
Sold 9.12.86 in
London for £93,500
($132,770)

JEAN AUGUSTE DOMINIQUE INGRES
French 1780–1867
The Gatteaux Family
Signed and dated 'Ingres à son/Excellent ami/Gatteaux 1850'
Pencil and engraving, the figures of Nicolas Marie Gatteaux, Madame Nicolas Marie Gatteaux and Edouard Gatteaux engraved
separately and mounted by Ingres with an additional sheet on which he drew the figure of Madame Edouard Brame (centre right),
the background, the figure of Mademoiselle Anfrye (extreme left) and most of the costume of Edouard Gatteaux entirely drawn or
reworked by the artist
$17\frac{3}{8} \times 24$ in. (44.1 × 60.7 cm.)
Sold 6.7.87 in London for £143,000 ($230,230)

The Studio Sale that Christie's Never Held

ROBERT CUMMING

On 1 April 1987, amid a blaze of fireworks which lit up the Thames at Millbank, Her Majesty the Queen opened the new Clore Gallery for the Turner Collection at the Tate. The event would undoubtedly have pleased Turner, for light and colour are one of the glories of his art and the Thames was the waterway around which he spent his boyhood, and in sight of which he died at 119 Cheyne Walk in 1851. He would also have applauded the generosity of the Clore Foundation and Mrs Vivien Duffield who supported and financed the building of the gallery, for Turner himself sought to set up a charitable foundation with his own considerable fortune. But the establishment of a permanent gallery for his collection at Millbank would certainly have surprised him, for not only did the Tate Gallery not exist at the time of his death in 1851 – but the idea of such a permanent memorial was as far as could be from Turner's mind.

Turner died a rich man and in possession of a large number of his own works, which he kept in his gallery in Queen Anne Street. The disposition of his fortune and these works exercised his mind considerably during his last years and were referred to in a number of wills and codicils. His exact intentions have often been misunderstood (and on some occasions misrepresented), yet as I have shown in a recent article (*Turner Studies* Volume 6, No. 2, pp. 3–8) a careful analysis of the documents shows that his wishes were in fact quite clear.

The first surprise is that Turner did not unconditionally leave all his works to the nation – neither the finished and unfinished oil paintings which formerly were housed by the National Gallery and Tate, nor the 19,000 watercolours and drawings which were housed in the British Museum. Turner's own wishes were for the large part of them to be sold. He wanted to be remembered of course, but not through a permanent gallery. His own desired memorial was to be a Charitable Institution – to be called Turner's Gift – which would benefit those artists less fortunate than himself, whom he described as 'decayed male English artists'. His financial fortune which was in Government Securities was left specifically to benefit the Institution, as were many of his pictures. The National Gallery was left some works, notably *Dido Building Carthage* and *Sun Rising through Vapour*, on the condition that they hang for ever between Claude's *Seaport* and *Mill* (a condition still adhered to). His finished oil paintings were also left to the National Gallery to be 'kept, deposited or preserved in a room or rooms' (although significantly there was no stipulation that the National Gallery should exhibit them). If the National Gallery failed to accept these finished oil paintings they were to be sold together with all his other works, the unfinished oils, the watercolours and the sketches for the benefit of his Charity. The sale of the works was to be, 'for the most money that can be had or obtained for the same by Public Auction or Private Sale...'

Why then did Turner's Charitable Institution fail to come into existence (and why did Christie's not have an opportunity to hold one of the most remarkable of the studio sales for which they were justly famous in the 19th century)?

When the will was read, Turner's relations, who were not included among the substantial beneficiaries, were not pleased. The result was predictable. They went to court, saying first that Turner was insane (and therefore the will was invalid) and when that argument failed they claimed that the will was faulty in Law, contravening the Charitable Uses Act of 1761. The exact legal argument is unimportant, but it had sufficient merit to worry the executors. They

had two options open to them. They could fight the court case, but this was the age of notorious delays of the Chancery courts, and like Dickens's famous fictional case of *Jarndyce v. Jarndyce* they might have seen the whole estate swallowed up by lawyers' fees and costs. Their second option was to settle the case out of court, and this they did.

The settlement which was ratified by Vice-Chancellor Kindersley on 19 March 1856 awarded Turner's financial fortune to the relations, and, 'all the Pictures, Drawings and Sketches by the Testator's hands, without any distinction of finished or unfinished' to the Trustees of the National Gallery. Thus the Turner Bequest, which was divided between the National Gallery, the Tate Gallery, and the British Museum and is now reunited in the Clore Gallery, came into existence. Turner's Charitable Institution, the one thing by which he wished to be remembered, disappeared without trace.

It is by no means certain that Turner's will was invalid. He took good legal advice, and authoritative lawyers have said subsequently that the executors could have fought the case and won, although in winning they might still have lost substantially in costs.

Turner's charitable interests had developed before he conceived his own Institution, for in 1814 he became a founder member of the Artists' General Benevolent Institution, a charity which still exists, giving much needed support to impoverished artists, and which Christie's is proud to support. In time Turner became Treasurer of the AGBI, but this brought him into conflict with the Committee, since he wished to hoard funds and the Committee wished to spend them. He therefore resigned in 1830 and a year later, in June 1831, he wrote his will establishing his Charitable Institution.

There is no doubt that the effect of the executors' decision was to rewrite Turner's will. He did not leave all his work to the nation, but the court settlement made it seem as though he did. Thus it is to the executors and the Clore Foundation, rather than Turner himself, that those future generations of Turner enthusiasts, who will rejoice that so much of his work is kept together and displayed in one gallery, will have reason to be grateful. One of the executors was Ruskin, and it may be that he saw the opportunity to keep the work together and considered it ultimately a more important priority than fighting to maintain Turner's own wishes. This is pure speculation on my part, but Ruskin's admiration for Turner's work had never diminished, and in January 1847 he had written to *The Times*, arguing for the didactic and collective display of works of art. He was specifically arguing for the National Gallery to display and collect early Italian works for even if such works were, 'of little value individually, their collective teaching is irrefragable authority, and if we wish to have a Buonarotti and Titian of our own we shall with more wisdom learn of those from whom Buonarotti and Titian learned'. Did Ruskin, then, realize, how much future generations would learn if all of Turner's work was kept together, and so seize the opportunity created by the court case to override Turner's own wishes for much of it to be dispersed?

The number of works by Turner that pass through the saleroom is relatively small, given his prodigious output, and the story of the will demonstrates that nearly all of them are works which must have passed into the hands of collectors during Turner's own lifetime. This season Christie's have sold three Turner watercolours. Two are highly finished works of the type which appealed to contemporary collectors. *Norham Castle* was in all probability exhibited at the Royal Academy in 1798. It was well received by the critics, and in due course was purchased by the Thwaites family. *Arundel Castle and Town* has a particularly interesting provenance for it is one of the works which were commissioned by Charles Heath for his publishing venture entitled *Picturesque Views in England and Wales*. Turner was commissioned to paint a large number of watercolours, from which 120 were to be selected for line engraving. *Arundel Castle and Town*, executed in the early 1830s, was one of the paintings so chosen. It is an exquisite work showing Turner at the height of his powers, but even so it did not save Heath's publishing venture from financial disaster. Heath sold the watercolours to collectors after they had been engraved, but the prints did not sell well, and eventually in 1839 the remaining copper plates and print stock were put up for auction by Messrs. Southgate & Co. Turner, however, had not lost interest in the venture; as the sale was about to begin he intervened and bought the plates and the stock of prints for the reserve price of £3,000, taking them back to Queen Anne Street where they were found mouldering away after his death. Although Turner's action caused considerable annoyance to the potential collectors at the auction, if not the auctioneer, it was a characteristic gesture. His motive was not financial in any sense, but to prevent the plates being used again, which would have allowed poor quality prints to be made when the plates became excessively worn. The engravings were eventually sold at Christie's in 1874 and the copper plates destroyed to preserve the market value of the prints (see E. Shane's *Turner's Picturesque Views in England and Wales 1825–1838*, 1980, pp. 10–15). *Arundel Castle and Town* itself passed through Christie's in 1866 and was sold to Agnew for 240 guineas. On 24 March 1987 it realized £176,000.

The third watercolour sold by Christie's, *An Alpine Valley, probably the Val d'Aosta*, is quite different in character,

JOSEPH MALLORD WILLIAM
TURNER, R.A.
British 1775–1851
*An Alpine Valley, probably the
Val d'Aosta*
Watercolour
$9\frac{1}{2} \times 13\frac{3}{8}$ in.
(24.1 × 34.1 cm.)
Sold 24.3.87 in London for
£99,000 ($158,895)
Sold by order of the
executors of the late
Mrs Wilfrid Janson
Previously sold at Christie's
23.5.1891 for 95 gns.
Probably dating from
Turner's 1836 tour of
Switzerland

evidently a sketch and with no pretence to the finish of the other two.

Works such as this were for Turner's own use – aides memoire or preliminary workings for projected finished paintings – and would not have been exhibited in Turner's lifetime, or collected except in the most unusual circumstances. Many of the drawings and watercolours in Turner's studio at his death were therefore of this type. That some 'escaped' from his studio immediately after his death and before the National Gallery took possession of them seems undeniable, though understandable, given the quantity of them and the delays and uncertainty of the will. Whether this is a watercolour which 'escaped' after Turner's death and, if so, how and when it did so, is unknown. Nevertheless it is yet another example of the works by Turner which have visited Christie's more than once, having been sold by us at auction in 1891 for 95 guineas. This time round it sold for £99,000.

THOMAS ROBINS, SEN.
British 1715–70
The Grounds of Honington Hall showing the Ornamental Water designed by Sanderson Miller
Pencil, pen and brown ink and bodycolour on vellum
$13\frac{1}{4} \times 19\frac{3}{8}$ in. (33.6 × 49.4 cm.)
Sold 14.7.87 in London for £49,500 ($79,200)
By order of the trustees of Townsend Hall, (Warwickshire)
One of two views of Honington Hall, Warwickshire, commissioned from the artist by Joseph Townsend in August 1759. The gardens at Honington are almost contemporary with those at Stourhead

EDWARD LEAR
British 1812–88
Philae
Inscribed as title and with colour notes, dated 'Feby 1.6.P.M. 1854', and numbered 174
Pencil, pen and brown ink and watercolour
13⅛ × 19⅜ in. (33.2 × 49.3 cm.)
Sold 24.3.87 in London for £20,900 ($33,712)
Of all the temples and scenery observed by Lear as he travelled down the Nile in January and February
1854, on his second visit to Egypt, Philae impressed him the most

Left:
EDWARD DAYES
British 1763–1804
Durham Cathedral from the Weir below Elvet Bridge c.1795
Signed
Pencil and watercolour
9¾ × 15½ in. (25.2 × 39.3 cm.)
Sold 24.3.87 in London for £16,500 ($26,483)

FREDERICK CATHERWOOD
British 1799–1854
A Panorama of Baalbec (detail)
Numbered 1-7
Pencil and watercolour, on seven sheets
$10\frac{7}{8} \times 14\frac{3}{4}$ in. (27.8 × 37.5 cm.)
Sold 14.7.87 in London for £26,400
($42,240)

Catherwood was born in East London in 1799, and, having been apprenticed to an architect, enrolled at the Royal Academy in 1820. By the end of 1821 he was in Rome and thereafter led an itinerant life in Sicily, Greece, Egypt and Syria. After a brief trip to England (1825–8), he returned to Egypt to work for the pioneer Egyptologist, Robert Hay. Intermittently from this date until 1834 he worked for Hay, and made trips as far as Palestine, Lebanon, Syria and Tunisia. Returning to England in 1835, Catherwood embarked on panorama painting, and used the experience he had gained to set up a permanent panorama in New York in 1838. Next, he returned to archaeology, and made two important expeditions to Mexico and Guatemala in 1839–40 and 1841–2, where he produced the first accurate drawings of Mayan inscriptions and buildings ever recorded. From these drawings he produced a series of engravings in two books, published in 1841 and 1843; they are a fitting memorial to Catherwood the artist-archaeologist. After a further career as a railway engineer in South America (1845–9), Panama (1849–50) and California (1850–2), Catherwood drowned in the Atlantic in 1854. Architect, archaeologist, panoramist, engineer and businessman, Catherwood led an amazingly versatile career, and his importance has often been overlooked because of the rarity of his drawings. The collection sold on 14 July provided a fascinating insight into the career of one of the 19th century's more neglected artists.

MYLES BIRKET FOSTER
British 1825–99
The Ferry
Signed with monogram
Watercolour heightened
with bodycolour
$17\frac{1}{2} \times 35\frac{5}{8}$ in.
(44.5 × 90 cm.)
Sold 28.10.86 in London for
£23,100 ($32,548)

HELEN ALLINGHAM
British 1848–1926
Old Kentish Manor House
Signed, and with the artist's
label
Watercolour
$14\frac{5}{8} \times 21\frac{3}{4}$ in.
(36.9 × 58 cm.)
Sold 28.10.86 in London for
£11,550 ($16,274)

AMADEO, COUNT PREZIOSI
Italian d.1882
*A View from the Terrace of a House
in Galata, with a Turk and a
Servant, looking towards the Mouth
of the Golden Horn and the
Bosphorous*
Signed and dated 1855
Pencil and watercolour
heightened with white
Oval, 17 × 20½ in.
(43 × 52 cm.)
Sold 25.6.87 in London for
£17,600 ($28,160)

ADRIAN LUDWIG RICHTER
German 1803–1884
A Harvest Thanksgiving
Signed with initials
Pencil and watercolour
heightened with white and
gum arabic
7½ × 11½ in. (19 × 29 cm.)
Sold 27.11.86 in London for
£38,500 ($54,747)

FRIEDRICH OVERBECK
German 1789–1869
Gerusalemme Liberata
Inscribed on the mount with lines from *Tasso*
14 × 20 in. (28 × 52.7 cm.)
Sold 27.11.86 in London for £68,200 ($96,980)
A drawing for one of the ceiling frescos in the
Tasso Room in the Cassino Massimo, Rome

LUIGI LOIR
French 1845–1916
Figures on a Street in a French Coastal Town
Signed
Gouache and watercolour over traces of black chalk and pencil, with
pen and brown and black ink
18⅝ × 12⅛ in. (47.4 × 30.9 cm.)
Sold 29.10.86 in New York for $26,400 (£18,697)
Record auction price for a watercolour by the artist

ERNST LUDWIG KIRCHNER
German 1880–1938
Russisches Tänzerpaar
(Schiefler 89)
Lithograph printed in black,
blue, pink and lime-yellow,
1909, a superb impression
of this early, extremely rare
print
L.12¾ × 15¼ in.
(32.7 × 38.5 cm.)
Sold 2.7.87 in London for
£165,000 ($264,000)
Record auction price for a
German Expressionist print

The *Russiches Tänzerpaar* depicts Olga Preobrajensky and Georges Kiatsck, dancers of the St. Petersburg Court Theatre who Kirchner had seen perform on their visit to Dresden in September 1909. The print displays the freedom and spontaneity of line and colour so typical of the early lithographic works of *Die Brücke* artists who first came together in the summer of 1905. The artist's personal involvement in the actual mechanical processes of printmaking led to the development of new techniques in fixing images, ink and colour to the block, plate or stone. In this case the same stone was used for the printing of each of the colours, which were fixed to the stone using a variety and mixture of acids, turpentines, waters and inks never before employed. The editions of such early prints are unknown but impressions tend to be extremely rare due to their experimental nature, the cost of producing a large edition and the lack of a wide and appreciative audience. That audience has now grown and the desire to obtain such a rare, lively and colourful print by one of the leading *Brücke* artists no doubt contributed to the establishment of a new auction record.

ERNST LUDWIG KIRCHNER
German 1880–1938
Halbakt
(Schiefler 130)
Lithograph, 1909, a fine
impression of this early,
extremely rare print, signed in
pencil, inscribed 'Handdruck'
L.10 × 5¾ in. (25.6 × 14.9 cm.)
Sold 2.7.87 in London for
£24,200 ($38,720)

ERNST LUDWIG KIRCHNER
German 1880–1938
Promenade vor dem Cafe
(Schiefler 266)
Lithograph printed in black and pink, 1914, second state (of three), a very fine impression of this extremely rare print,
inscribed 'Versuchsdruck' L.20¼ × 23½ in. (51.5 × 59.6 cm.) Sold 4.12.86 in London for £55,000 ($78,320)

The *Promenade vor dem Cafe* is typical of the *Strassenszene* works executed by Kirchner in Berlin between 1913 and 1915.
The lyrical line of 1909, used to such great effect in the *Russisches Tänzerpaar* and which gives the *Halbakt* a uniquely
uninhibited sensuality, has been abandoned in favour of an energetic interplay of vertical and diagonal strokes and
lines. Only seven impressions of this print are recorded, but each has a unique quality due to the way the artist altered
the application of the pink colour in each example.

ERICH HECKEL
German 1883–1970
Fränzi Liegend
(Dube 188b2II)
Woodcut printed in black and red, 1910, a fine and well printed impression, signed, titled and dated in pencil,
inscribed 'Hand Druck'
L.9 × 16½ in. (22.9 × 42 cm.)
Sold 18.11.86 in New York for $132,000 (£93,551)
Record auction price for a print by the artist

Franzi and her older sister Marzella, daughters of an artist's widow, were the principal models for the *Brücke* artists
in 1910-11. The depiction of such a youthful model (Franzi was only twelve years old when this print was executed)
is typical of *Die Brücke's* penchant for adopting a new approach to a traditional subject, in this case the reclining nude.
Further innovations can be seen in the use of an irregular format, the broad planes of colour and the vigorous cutting
of the block, all of which combine to create what has been considered to be one of the most beautiful of all woodcuts
produced by a *Brücke* artist.

ERICH HECKEL
German 1883–1970
Männerbildnis
(Dube 318IIA)
Woodcut printed in
black, olive-green, brown
and blue, 1919, the rare
second state (of three), a
superb impression,
signed and dated in
pencil, inscribed
'Eigendruck Probe'
L.18¼ × 12¾ in.
(46.3 × 32.7 cm.)
Sold 2.7.87 in London
for £57,200 ($91,520)

EMIL NOLDE
German 1867–1956
Prophet
(Schiefler, Mosel 110)
Woodcut, 1912, a superb, rich
impression, signed in pencil, from
the edition of about 20
12½ × 9 in. (31.6 × 22.6 cm.)
Sold 2.7.87 in London for
£33,000 ($52,800)

ROLF NESCH
German 1893–1975
Negerrevue
Etching with drypoint and aquatint
printed in black, orange-red and deep
mustard-yellow, 1930, a very fine, rich
impression, signed and titled in pencil,
inscribed 'Selbst druck'
P. 13 × 17½ in. (33.2 × 44.6 cm.)
Sold 2.7.87 in London for £19,800
($31,680)

JEAN DUBUFFET
French b. 1901
Nez Carotte
Lithograph printed in
colours, 1962, signed, titled
and dated in pencil,
numbered 44/50
S. 23⅝ × 14⅞ in.
(60 × 38 cm.)
Sold 11.5.87 in New York
for $49,500 (£29,588)
Record auction price for a
print by the artist

OTTO DIX
German 1891–1969
Kupplerin
(Karsch 69 II)
Lithograph printed in red,
yellow and blue, 1923,
signed and dated in pencil,
numbered 5/65, published
by Karl Nierendorf, Berlin
L. 19 × 14½ in.
(48.2 × 36.7 cm.)
Sold 2.7.87 in London for
£22,000 ($35,200)
Record auction price for a
print by the artist

EDOUARD MANET
French 1832–83
L'Exécution de Maximilian
(Delteil 79)
Lithograph, *c.*1867-8, on Chine appliqué, from
the first, contemporary printing before all letters
and apparently one of three or four such
impressions, a fine, rich impression with excellent
contrasts
L.13⅛ × 17⅛ in. (33.4 × 43.5 cm.)
Sold 18.11.86 in New York for $55,000 (£38,194)
Record auction price for a print by the artist

PAUL CÉZANNE
French 1839–1906
Les Baigneurs (Grande Planche)
(Druick 1; Johnson 23)
Lithograph printed in colours,
*c.*1898, Druick's second state (of
three), Johnson's first state (of
two), with the inscription in the
stone below, from the edition of at
least 100 in this state, a good
impression
L.16½ × 20¾ in.
(41.9 × 52.8 cm.)
Sold 4.12.86 in London for
£19,800 ($28,196)

PABLO PICASSO
Spanish/French 1881–1974
La Femme au Tambourin
(Bloch 310)
Etching with aquatint,
1938, a very good
impression with strong
contrasts, signed in pencil,
numbered 29/30
P.26¼ × 20¼ in.
(66.6 × 51.3 cm.)
Sold 18.11.86 in New York
for $137,500 (£97,449)

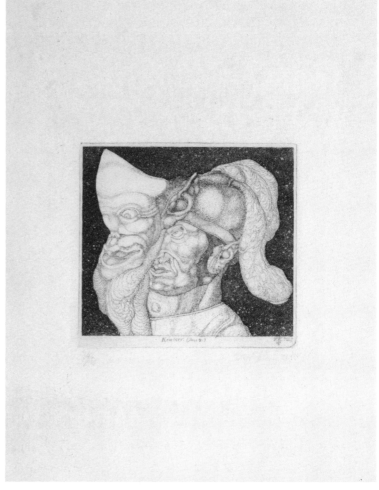

MAX ERNST
German 1891–1976
Pays sage I
(Spies/Leppien 10)
Drypoint, 1923, a fine, delicate impression of this very rare,
early print, signed in pencil, numbered 'no. 6', from the
edition of about 10
P.6¾ × 5¼ in. (17.3 × 13 cm.)
Sold 2.7.87 in London for £35,200 ($56,320)
Record auction price for a print by the artist

PAUL KLEE
Swiss 1879–1940
Der Komiker
(Kornfeld 10 IIb)
Etching, 1904, second (final) state, signed and dated in pencil,
numbered 34/50, inscribed with the work number 14
P.6 × 6¾ in. (15.4 × 17.2 cm.)
Sold 18.11.86 in New York for $35,200 (£24,947)

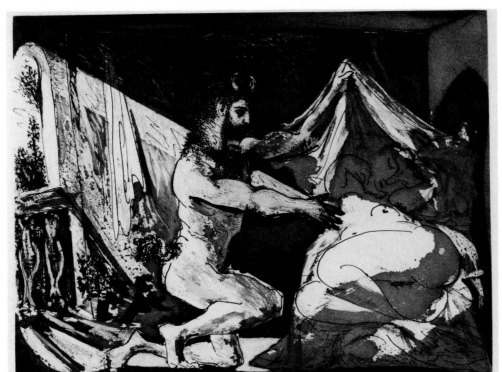

PABLO PICASSO
Spanish/French 1881–1974
Faune dévoilant une Femme, Plate 27 from
The Vollard Suite
(Bloch 230)
Aquatint, 1936, signed in pencil, from the
edition of 250
P.12½ × 16½ in. (31.7 × 41.8 cm.)
Sold 2.7.87 in London for £26,400
($42,240)

HENRI MATISSE
French 1869–1954
Odalisque à la Culotte de Satin rouge
(Dutuit-Matisse 456)
Lithograph, 1925, a fine impression,
signed, inscribed 'epr. d'artiste' and
numbered 8/10 in pencil, dedicated
'à H. Purrmann Souvenir de Nice Nov.
1926' also in pencil
L.7½ × 10¾ in. (19.1 × 27.2 cm.)
Sold 2.7.87 in London for £38,500
($61,600)

JACQUES VILLON
French 1875–1963
Portrait de jeune Femme
(Ginestet & Pouillon E282)
Drypoint, 1913, signed in
pencil, numbered 7, from
the edition of about 30
P.21¾ × 16¼ in.
(55.1 × 41.4 cm.)
Sold 2.7.87 in London for
£33,000 ($52,800)

MARC CHAGALL
French 1887–1985
Daphnis et Chloë
(Mourlot 308–49)
Lithographs printed in colours, 1961, the set of 42 unsigned plates, signed in black ink on the justification, copy
82 of 250, published by Editions Verve, Paris
Overall S.17½ × 13¾ in. (44.6 × 34.7 cm.)
Sold 11.5.87 in New York for $264,000 (£187,102)

GEORGES ROUAULT
French 1871–1958
Christ en Croix
(Chapon & Rouault 286)
Aquatint printed in
colours, 1936, a very
fine, rich impression of
an extremely rare trial
proof, inscribed and
signed 'Bon à tirer GR' in
pen and ink, with
extensive pen and ink
instructions to the printer
P.25¾ × 19½ in.
(65.7 × 59.4 cm.)
Sold 2.7.87 in London
for £33,000 ($52,800)
Record auction price for
a print by the artist

BARNETT NEWMAN
American 1905–70
18 Cantos
Lithographs printed in colours, 1963–4, the set of 19 plates,
signed, titled and dated, all numbered 16/18, published by
ULAE, West Islip
Overall S.25 × 19¼ in. (63.5 × 49 cm.)
Sold 13.5.87 in New York at Christie's East for $148,500
(£105,245)
Record auction price for a set of prints by the artist

DAVID HOCKNEY
British b.1937
The Weather Series
(Scottish Arts Council Exhibition 136–41)
Lithographs printed in colours, 1973, the set of six plates,
signed, titled and dated, all numbered 53/98, published by
Gemini GEL, Los Angeles
L.40 × 31 in. (101.5 × 78.5 cm.)
Sold 13.5.87 in New York at Christie's East for $66,000
(£46,776)
Record auction price for a set of prints by the artist

JASPER JOHNS
American b.1930
Flags I
Screenprint in colours, 1973, signed, dated and inscribed 'I', numbered 45/65
S.27½ × 35 in. (69.8 × 88.9 cm.)
Sold 13.5.87 in New York at Christie's East for $71,500 (£50,674)

ALBRECHT DÜRER
German 1471–1528
The Nativity
(Bartsch 2)
Engraving, 1504, a fine, clear Meder b
impression, with very good contrasts
S.7⅜ × 4¾ in. (18.6 × 12.1 cm.)
Sold 20.11.86 in New York for $68,200 (£47,979)

ALBRECHT DÜRER
German 1471–1528
Erasmus of Rotterdam
(Bartsch 107)
Engraving, a fine Meder a impression with very
good contrasts
S.10 × 7½ in. (25.2 × 19.2 cm.)
Sold 1.7.87 in London for £18,700 ($29,920)

LUCAS VAN LEYDEN
Dutch 1494–1538
The Virgin and Child with two Angels
(Bartsch 84)
Engraving, a fine, sharp impression
P.5¾ × 4 in. (14.7 × 10.1 cm.)
Sold 1.7.87 in London for £11,000 ($17,600)

THE MONOGRAMMIST M
Italian, 16th century
Death surprising a nude Woman looking at herself in a Mirror
(Bartsch 1)
Engraving, a fine impression of this rare print
P.14 × 10 in. (35.8 × 25.4 cm.)
Sold 1.7.87 in London for £6,600 ($10,560)

GIOVANNI BATTISTA PIRANESI
Italian 1720–78
Carceri: Fifteen plates
(Hind 1, 3–16)
Etchings, from the set of 16, from the second edition, third issue, fine, strong impressions
Averaging P.16½ × 21½ in. (41.5 × 54.5 cm.)
Sold 1.7.87 in London for £30,800 ($49,280)

ANTONIO CANAL, IL CANALETTO and MICHELE MARIESCHI
Italian 1697–1768 and 1696–1743
Vedute altre prese da i Luoghi altre Ideate da Antonio Canal and *Magnificentiores selectioresques Urbis Venetiarum Prospectus*
(Bromberg 1–11, 13–16, 18–33 and Mauroner 2–22)
Etchings, the first series complete with title and 30 plates on 18 sheets, the second series complete with title and 21 plates, fine impressions, bound together in 18th-century vellum boards
Overall S.17 1/4 × 24 3/4 in. (43.5 × 62.5 cm.)
Sold 1.7.87 in London for £93,500 ($149,600)
The property of the Newdegate Settlement
Purchased by Sir Roger Newdigate in Venice in 1775 for £120

GEORGE CATLIN
American 1794–1872
Catlin's North American Indian portfolio, Hunting Scenes and Amusements of the Rocky Mountains and Prairies of America from Drawings and Notes of the Author
Lithographs with hand-colouring and gum arabic, the set of 25 plates published by Catlin, London, 1844
Overall S.17¼ × 23⅜ in. (43.8 × 59.3 cm.)
Sold 17.9.86 in New York for $38,500 (£25,666)

STUART DAVIS
American 1894–1964
Detail Study for 'Cliche'
Lithograph printed in colours, 1957, signed in
pencil, numbered 24/40
L.12½ × 15 in. (31.7 × 38.1 cm.)
Sold 17.9.86 in New York for $9,350 (£6,383)

After JOHANN ZOFFANY, R.A.
British 1733–1810
James Sayer by R. Houston
(Chaloner Smith 109)
Mezzotint, first state (of two), a fine, rich impression, published by
R. Sayer, London, 1772
P.19¾ × 5¼ in. (50.2 x13.2 cm.)
Sold 19.5.87 in London for £1,540 ($2,574)

Books and
Manuscripts

Selection of illustrated French almanacs formerly in the library
of Sir David Salomons (1851–1925)
Sold 3.12.86 in London for a total of £389,106 ($553,698)
By order of the L.A. Mayer Memorial Foundation

Carroll and Tenniel as Illustrators of the 'Alice' Books

KATE HEDWORTH

This season we had the unusual good fortune of being able to offer two groups of extremely rare original illustrations to Lewis Carroll's 'Alice' stories – illustrations which shed new light not only on the author's own vision of his characters, but also on the development of the finished illustrations by the artist, John Tenniel.

Alice's Adventures in Wonderland and *Through the Looking-glass and What Alice Found There* are the most famous and best loved of modern works of literature for children. From their first publication in 1866 and 1872 respectively, when each was an immediate success, their popularity has never waned. However, although the printed works are familiar enough and an enormous scholarly industry has grown up on the subject of Carroll and his creations, some aspects of the production and especially the illustration of these books had remained obscure. On 3 December 1986, a group of nine original pen and ink drawings by Lewis Carroll illustrating scenes from *Alice's Adventures in Wonderland* was sold for £187,000 – a world record for a series of illustrations for a children's book sold at auction. The illustrations, each somewhat smaller than a postcard, were carefully executed copies of some of Tenniel's best-known designs, including the White Rabbit, the Mock Turtle and the Mad Hatter's Tea Party. Part of the value of these drawings lay in the great scarcity of any autograph material in Carroll's hand relating to *Alice's Adventures in Wonderland*. The autograph manuscripts of both this text and that of *Through the Looking-glass* are two of the great lost literary manuscripts; they are presumed to have been inadvertently destroyed just after Carroll's death, when many of his seemingly uninteresting papers were burnt. The only material by Carroll for *Alice's Adventures in Wonderland* which is known to have survived are the autograph manuscript of *Alice's Adventures Under Ground* (the first version of *Alice's Adventures in Wonderland* and only about half its length, which Carroll wrote out and presented to Alice Liddell, the original Alice, in 1864, and which is now in the British Library) and a few trial sketches for the 'Under Ground' manuscript at Christ Church, Oxford. Nothing in Carroll's hand connected with the story had ever come onto the market.

The 'Under Ground' manuscript was illustrated by Carroll himself, but the quality of the finished drawings is, at best, very uneven and the most accomplished are clearly copies. The sketches at Christ Church confirm that Carroll was a very competent copyist but an unskilled original artist. When Carroll decided to expand and publish his 'Under Ground' story as *Alice's Adventures in Wonderland*, he recognized his own artistic limitations and so he commissioned John Tenniel to produce the illustrations.

The group of drawings by Carroll, which were unsigned, were, until a few years ago, thought to be the work of Tenniel himself. They had been mounted in an album which bore a label on the upper cover stating: 'Tenniel's Drawings for Alice', and it is possible that Carroll, who seems to have been extremely shy and self-effacing in relation to Alice, never indicated to her that the drawings were his own, rather than Tenniel's work, when he presented them to her,

LEWIS CARROLL
Through the Looking-glass, and What Alice Found There
First edition, extra-illustrated with original drawings, proofs and
working sketches by John Tenniel
1872
Sold 24.6.87 in London for £148,500 ($237,600)
The illustration reproduced here of *Queen Alice and the Frog at the
door* is one of 35 working sketches by John Tenniel, drawn in
pencil on tracing paper

LEWIS CARROLL
The Mad Hatter's Tea Party, one of nine original pen and brown
ink drawings illustrating scenes from *Alice's Adventures in
Wonderland*
*c.*1865
Sold 3.12.86 in London for £187,000 ($266,101)
Record auction price for a manuscript relating to children's
literature

possibly as a gift for her thirteenth birthday just before the publication of the story. The drawings passed from Alice Liddell to her son and eventually, in 1961, were acquired by Harriet
Borland, a noted American collector; they again changed hands when she disposed of her library
in 1979. For more than a century Alice and her family, booksellers, librarians and collectors
accepted the drawings as Tenniel's work, including an authentication by the Victoria and Albert
Museum in 1961. It was only when in 1979 they were shown to Justin Schiller, the specialist
dealer in rare children's books, who was working on a *catalogue raisonné* of Tenniel's drawings
for the 'Alice' books, that they were identified as being by Carroll. The most obvious piece
of evidence were the captions on seven of the drawings, each in Carroll's distinctive cursive
or roman scripts. Further, when the drawings were compared with Carroll's illustrations in
the 'Under Ground' manuscript it was quite clear that they were in the same hand, using the
same sepia ink and the same nib. The Christ Church drawings also revealed many similarities
including some of Carroll's work as a copyist which is quite as accomplished as these drawings.
The illustrations were not lavish reproductions, however, as, perhaps unwittingly, Carroll's
own concept of his characters crept into the pictures. In the Mad Hatter's Tea Party, for instance, Carroll's Cheshire Cat has a much less sinister grin than Tenniel's, and most tellingly,
the face of Alice herself is not at all like Tenniel's Alice, but bears a marked resemblance to
Carroll's illustrations of Alice in the 'Under Ground' manuscript with the same distinctively
pointed features.

Carroll, who was a hypercritical taskmaster, is recorded as stating that he found only one
of Tenniel's illustrations to his stories an absolute success and that was a scene from *Through
the Looking-glass* of Humpty Dumpty offering Alice his hand. In fact, Tenniel's all too successful
interpretation of his text must have piqued Carroll into trying to prove that he himself could
draw as skilfully.

On 24 June 1987, a collection of Tenniel's original preparatory pencil drawings for *Through
the Looking-glass* realized £148,500. Three finished preliminary drawings signed with Tenniel's
monogram, thirty-five working sketches on tracing paper and two signed proofs were all bound
into a fine copy of the first edition of *Through the Looking-glass*. This sumptuous volume was
further extra-illustrated with the only extant letter from Lewis Carroll to the Dalziel brothers,
who engraved the 'Alice' illustrations; a rare printed leaflet by Carroll, 'An Easter Greeting
to Every Child who Loves Alice' with an autograph inscription; a pencil portrait of Lewis Carroll
by Emily Gertrude Thomson; and a pencil portrait of Tenniel by Bernard Partridge. The whole
collection had been assembled and bound together by Harold Hartley, the most important collector of mid-19th-century British book illustrations in the early part of this century, to form
a highly important collection of Tenniel's working drawings. Similar collections demonstrating
Tenniel's working processes in the 'Alice' illustrations are in only three public institutions in
America, and this group remains probably the only collection of its kind in private hands.

Although the collaboration of Tenniel and Carroll on *Alice's Adventures in Wonderland* had produced a most successful marriage of Carroll's interpretation, the task exhausted Tenniel's pa-
tience with this 'impossible' and 'conceited old Don', and it was only with the greatest difficulty
that Carroll persuaded Tenniel to undertake the illustrations to *Through the Looking-glass*. Carroll was well aware that first-rate illustrations were necessary to the success of his
work – descriptions of characters are often minimal and the reader depends heavily on the illustrations for information – and despite the differences between author and artist, Tenniel's
illustrations were remarkably well-attuned to Carroll's curious imagination. However, Ten-

niel evidently enjoyed working with Carroll on this second 'Alice' volume as little as he had on the first. He later wrote to Carroll, a touch sarcastically, when refusing to undertake a third commission, 'It is a curious fact that with Through the Looking-glass the faculty for making drawings for book illustrations departed from me, and notwithstanding all sorts of tempting inducements, I have done nothing in that direction since.'

Apart from Tenniel's recognized artistic qualities, he was also very much a professional artist, practised in the tight discipline of the commercial world of producing regular weekly contributions to *Punch*. His style of line drawing was, further, particularly well suited to the printing techniques of wood-engraving. The engravers for both the *Alice* books were the highly respected Dalziel brothers, the leading exponents of this most demanding and delicate of crafts, with whom Tenniel enjoyed an excellent working relationship. Tenniel's magazine work was produced at high speed and he described his working process as follows: 'I get my subject on Wednesday night; I think it out carefully on Thursday, and make my rough sketch. On Friday morning I begin, and I stick to it all day, with my nose well down on the block. By means of tracing paper – on which I make such alterations of composition and action I may consider necessary I transfer my design to wood and draw on that....' Tenniel would execute his finished design with an extremely hard pencil on the end of a block of boxwood, which the Dalziels would then painstakingly engrave, cutting away the tiny areas of blank wood between Tenniel's pencil strokes until the design was left in relief. A hard-wearing electrotype plate was then cast from the block for production. We have no reason to doubt that Tenniel's technique for creating *Alice* illustrations was any different from his magazine work except that without the pressure of a deadline he was able to take his time (as he clearly did, to Carroll's grief). Tenniel, therefore, was able to work at his designs, alter and improve them until he achieved just the effect he was seeking. These *Looking-glass* drawings sold by Christie's clearly demonstrated this, for the sketches on tracing paper gave extraordinarily clear evidence of Tenniel's working practice of making compositional corrections to his original ideas in order to achieve more effective illustrations to the text. In fact, each drawing and sketch contained a wealth of information on Tenniel's creative process, showing how he resolved one, or often many more ideas, including basic problems of composition, such as the presence or absence of a figure, or finer details such as Tweedledum and Tweedledee's clothes (they have large waistcoats in the sketch), Queen Alice's hooped 'chesspiece' skirt, or the clock and Alice smiling at each other as she climbs into the looking-glass room, which were incorporated or, as in these examples, abandoned in the finished scheme. Even the corrected proofs were interesting sources of information on Tenniel's technique as a professional artist, each one covered in the shorthand by which he communicated with the Dalziel brothers, a combination of colour-coding, markings and disjointed instructions: 'Light on hair. Arms. Lighter, Legs', etc.

Tenniel's illustrations for *Through the Looking-glass*, as this remarkable collection of drawings and sketches showed, were the painstaking work of a highly professional artist. His careful preparations and reworkings led to the enormously successful finished illustrations, which are as memorable and beloved as Carroll's text. After all: 'what is the use of a book', thought Alice, 'without pictures or conversation?'

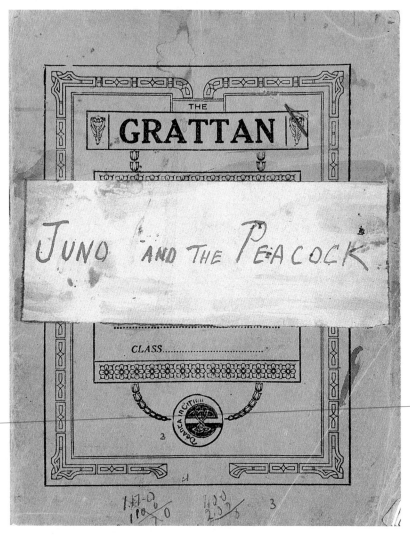

SEAN O'CASEY
Autograph manuscript of *Juno and the Paycock*, first draft
1923
Sold 3.12.86 in London for £63,800 ($89,512)

T.E. LAWRENCE
Seven Pillars of Wisdom
The first privately printed edition
1926
Sold 13.5.87 in London for £16,500 ($26,400)

Admiral Horatio Nelson's will including three codicils
making bequests to Emma Hamilton
Dated 5 March 1801
Sold 24.6.87 in London for £24,200 ($38,720)
Nelson drew up the will of 5 March 1801 just
before setting sail on the Baltic Campaign, which
was to culminate in the Battle of Copenhagen on
1 April. He had separated permanently from his
wife, Fanny, two months earlier, and wrote his
letter of dismissal to her from the *St George* on
4 March. In his will he deals quite abruptly with
any claims she may have on him '...where the
interest of that twenty thousand pounds to be paid
to Lady Nelson during her natural life and I
having in my life time made her a present of four
thousand pounds. I think I have done very
handsomely towards her.'

Albert Einstein
Old Grove Rd.
Nassau Point
Peconic, Long Island

August 2nd, 1939

F. D. Roosevelt
President of the United States,
White House
Washington, D.C.

Sir:

    Recent work in nuclear physics made it probable that uranium may be turned into a new and important source of energy. New experiments performed by E.Fermi and L.Szilard, which have been communicated to me in manuscript, make it now appear likely that it will be possible to set up a chain reaction in a large mass of uranium and thereby to liberate considerable quantities of energy. Less certain, but to be kept in mind, is the possibility of making use of such chain reactions for the construction of extremely powerful bombs. Such bombs may be too heavy for transportation by air plane, but not too heavy for being carried by boat, and a single bomb exploded in a port might very well destroy the port together with the surrounding territory.

    This being the situation, you may find it desirable that some contact be established between the Administration and the group of physicists who are working in this country on the subject of chain reactions. One possible way of achieving this would be for you to entrust a person who has your

ALBERT EINSTEIN
Typed letter, signed, to President Franklin D. Roosevelt, dated 2 August 1939, concerning the discovery of nuclear fission and advising the urgent development of the atomic bomb
$1\frac{1}{2}$ pages
$10\frac{7}{8} \times 8\frac{1}{2}$ in. (27.7 × 21.6 cm.)
Sold 19.12.86 in New York for $220,000 (£151,724)
Record auction price for a 20th-century letter

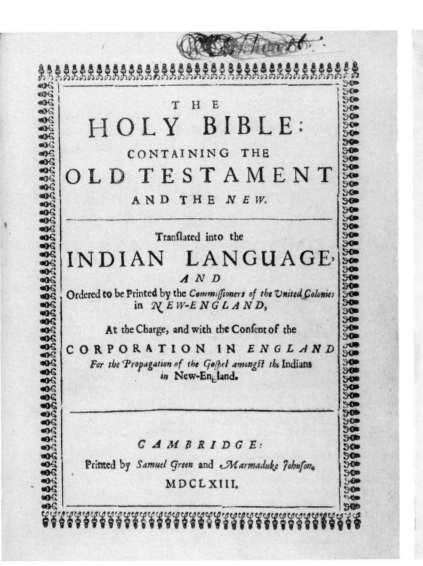

The Holy Bible
First edition of John Eliot's Indian Bible, the first Bible to be printed in America, and one of probably 20 copies sent to the Corporation in England, morocco-bound for presentation
Cambridge (Massachusetts), 1663
Sold 19.12.86 in New York for $220,000 (£151,724)

OBED MACY
The History of Nantucket; Being a Compendious Account of the First Settlement of the Island by the English, together with the Rise and Progress of the Whale Fishery, the copy belonging to Herman Melville, author of *Moby Dick* (published 1853)
First edition
Hilliard, Boston, 1835
Sold 19.12.86 in New York for $10,450 (£7,349)

TWO TREATISES OF Government:
In the former,
The *false Principles*, and *Foundation*
OF
Sir *ROBERT FILMER,*
And his FOLLOWERS,
ARE
Detected and Overthrown.
The latter is an
ESSAY
CONCERNING THE
True Original, Extent, and End
OF
Civil Government.

LONDON,
Printed for *Awnsham Churchill,* at the *Black
Swan* in *Ave-Mary-Lane,* by *Amen-
Corner,* 1690.

Above left:
PETER ILICH TCHAIKOVSKY
Autograph manuscript of 12 bars of
the song *Rondel*, the last of the *Six
Melodies*, opus 65
Words by Paul Collin
Notated in black ink on three
systems, each of three staves, 1 page
$10\frac{1}{2} \times 16\frac{7}{8}$ in. (27 × 43.2 cm.)
Sold 3.12.86 in London for £5,500
($7,827)

Left:
FRANZ LISZT
Autograph manuscript *Das deutsche
Vaterland* for chorus and orchestra; an
unrecorded orchestration of this song
*c.*1841
Brown ink on four different sorts of
ruled staff paper, 39 pages
$10\frac{3}{4} \times 13$ in. (26 × 34.8 cm.) and
$11\frac{1}{4} \times 14\frac{3}{4}$ in. (28.5 x 37.5 cm.)
Sold 19.12.86 in New York for
$8,250 (£5,802)

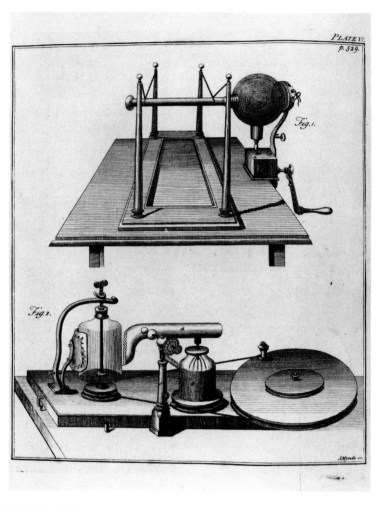

JOSEPH PRIESTLEY
The History and Present State of Electricity, with Original Experiments
First edition, with eight engraved plates
1767
Sold 12.12.86 in London for £1,430 ($2,031)
From the library of Matthew Boulton (see article on p.203)

Opposite above right:
JOHN LOCKE
Two Treatises of Government
First edition
1690
Sold 12.12.86 in London for £6,600
($9,372)

ESTHER INGLIS
Calligraphic manuscript *Le livre de l'Ecclesiaste ensemble les
Lamentations de Ieremie, de la main d'Esther Anglois françoise*
Dedicated to Archibald Campbell, 7th Earl of Argyll
Edinburgh, 1602
6¾ × 5 in. (17 × 13 cm.)
Sold 12.12.86 in London for £18,700 ($26,554)
Esther Inglis (1571–1624) is regarded as one of the
outstanding calligraphers and miniaturists of the late 16th and
early 17th centuries

Book of Hours in Latin
Made for François I, King of France
Illuminated manuscript on vellum, 18
large miniatures
1532–40
8 × 5⅜ in. (20 × 13.5 cm)
Sold 24.6.87 in London for £198,000
($316,800)

WILLIAM CAVENDISH, DUKE OF NEWCASTLE
A General System of Horsemanship
Two volumes
Antwerp, 1658
Sold 8.4.87 in London for £2,860 ($4,605)

ROBERT FULTON
Torpedo War, and Submarine Explosions
First edition
New York, 1810
Sold 13.5.87 in London for £2,420 ($4,008)

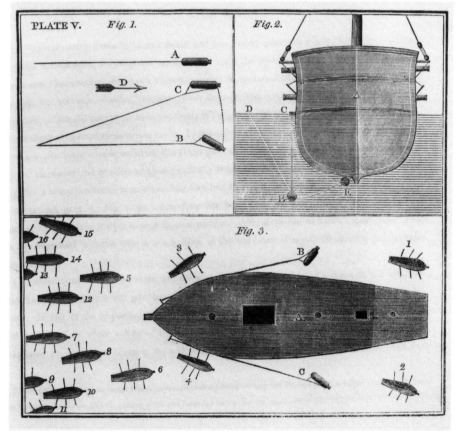

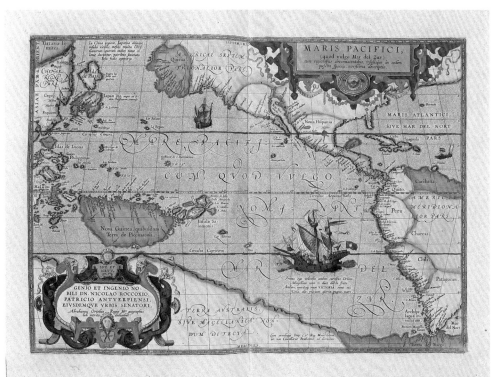

ABRAHAM ORTELIUS
Theatrum Orbis Terrarum
147 coloured maps
Antwerp, 1595
Sold 15.10.86 in London for £27,500
($39,105)

THOMAS MALTON
A Picturesque Tour through the Cities of
London and Westminster Illustrated
Two volumes in one, 100 aquatint
plates, partly printed in colour and
finished by hand
1792–1801
Sold 15.10.86 in London for £17,600
($25,028)

JOHN GOULD
The Mammals of Australia
Three volumes, 182 hand-
coloured lithographed plates by
H.C. Richter and Gould
1845–63
Sold 15.10.86 in London for
£52,800 ($75,082)

JOSEPH LYCETT
*Views in Australia, or New South
Wales & van Diemen's Land
Delineated*
24 hand-coloured aquatint views
1824
Sold 15.10.86 in London for
£24,200 ($34,413)

JOHN GOULD
The Birds of Australia
Eight volumes including Supplement, 681 hand-coloured
lithographed plates by John and Elizabeth Gould and H.C.
Richter
1848–69
Sold 15.10.86 in London for £126,500 ($179,883)
Record auction price for a book by the author

PRIDEAUX JOHN SELBY
Plates to Selby's Illustrations of British Ornithology
First edition
Four volumes, 218 hand-coloured engraved plates
1819–34
Sold 15.10.86 in London for £27,500 ($39,105)

Furniture

One of a pair of Regency mahogany benches
38 in. (96.5 cm.) high; 34 in. (87.5 cm.) wide;
21 in. (53 cm.) deep
Sold 22.9.86 at Callaly Castle in Northumberland
for £59,400 ($86,843)

Great Tew Park

NICHOLAS GOODISON

Country house sales never fail to attract crowds. So it was with Great Tew Park, Oxfordshire, where Christie's sold many of the contents – furniture, oil paintings, watercolours, prints, ceramics, silver, silver plate, textiles, carpets and books – on 27/29 May 1987. Despite heavy rain on the first viewing day, people came in their hundreds, risked leaving their cars in the increasingly muddy field which served as the car park, and quickly exhausted the supply of catalogues.

No doubt people come to such previews hoping to spot a bargain: but they come too, I suspect, out of curiosity. The chance to look at a great house which has not been accessible before – and Great Tew had been accessible only to very few – and to see everything at close quarters, indeed to touch things, to sit on chairs, to hold pieces of silverware, to open books, to marvel at 19th-century 'night stools', is irresistible. At the same time there is a sadness that after generations in the ownership of the same family the contents of a house, both showpieces and things of utility, have to be sold. For that we have to thank the originality of Sir William Harcourt's Finance Act of 1894, which first introduced estate duty and, by causing the sale of the contents of so many houses, has been of immeasurable benefit to private and public collections abroad.

Great Tew was bought by Matthew Robinson Boulton (1770–1842) in 1815. He was the son of Matthew Boulton (1728–1809), best known to historians as the developer of James Watt's steam engine and therefore as a key figure in the Industrial Revolution. Matthew Boulton would have been a great figure in Britain's industrial history even without his crucial entrepreneurial role in the manufacture and sale of Watt's steam engine. He greatly enlarged the button, buckle and 'toy' business which he inherited from his father. He became a substantial manufacturer of silver and silver plate. He founded the Birmingham Assay Office. He was the best known manufacturer of decorative ormolu ornaments of his day. He revolutionized the minting of coins, founding the Soho mint and providing technical advice and machinery to other mints both in England and abroad. The machinery which he supplied to the new Royal Mint in 1805 was not replaced until 1882. He also at various times made japanned goods, clocks, mechanical paintings, lamps and copying machines. His factory at Soho near Birmingham, opened in 1762, was one of the wonders of the industrial world, and attracted visitors from all over Europe. His friend Josiah Wedgwood called him, 'the most complete manufacturer in England in metal'. He was besides a keen natural philosopher and a founder member of the Lunar Society, a group of remarkable scientists and philosophers which met regularly to discuss scientific and philosophical matters at his house in Soho. The Society included Erasmus Darwin, Joseph Priestley, James Watt, Josiah Wedgwood, John Whitehurst, William Small, James Keir, and William Withering. During his long and very active business life he came to know a large number of influential people both through the marketing of his many products and through his lobbying activities leading to the establishment of patent rights on the steam engine, of the Assay Office and of the Mint. In late 18th-century industrial and social history he is a toweringly important figure.

The Library, Great
Tew Park
Designed by Thomas
Fulljames of
Gloucester for
M.R. Boulton in the
early 1830s and
furnished by George
Morant a decade
later. Some of
Morant's work was
carried out for
M.P.W. Boulton, who
succeeded his father at
Tew in 1842.

J.S.C. SCHAAK
Portrait of Matthew Boulton, aged 42
Signed and dated 1770
29 × 24 in. (73.5 × 61 cm.)
Sold 27.5.87 at Great Tew Park in Oxfordshire for £20,900 ($33,900)

Black basalt library bust of Venus
By Wedgwood & Bentley
*c.*1775
17¼ in. (44 cm.) high
Sold 27.5.87 at Great Tew Park in Oxfordshire for £2,860 ($4,639)

Not surprisingly, most of the objects in the sale at Great Tew dated from the 19th century. To historians of 19th-century furniture the most intriguing things were a large number of pieces of furniture supplied to M.R. Boulton, shortly after his purchase of the estate, by the London furniture-maker George Bullock, who began his career in Liverpoool and Birmingham before setting up in Tenterden Street, near Hanover Square, in 1815. The young Boulton presumably met him in Birmingham and appears from surviving letters to have been on familiar terms with him. Bullock's 42-page bill, dated 1817, for the supply of furniture, curtains and upholstery, together with the surviving correspondence between the two men, enabled the identification of a large number of pieces. Veneered with oak, and inlaid with holly, the furniture is of great interest for two reasons. First, it confirms Clive Wainwright's comment that at this stage in his career Bullock made a particular virtue of using native British woods. Second, in its design and in its use of decorative inlay based mainly on local flowers and foliage rather than on the more familiar classical motifs of the day, the furniture is revolutionary. It would not have been surprising if we had been told that it was made twenty or thirty years later. Although lacking the elegance and the quality of the best 18th-century furniture, Bullock's *avant-garde* pieces fetched high prices at the sale. Other furniture, supplied by G.J. Morant in similar style in the 1840s, especially for the new Gothic library, also proved popular.

To my mind the other notable feature of the sale of M.R. Boulton's things was the large group of pieces of Sheffield plate. Objects of plate stamped with the mark of Matthew Boulton & Co. are not very rare. But here was a series of fine pieces, made in about 1810–15, delivered straight from the factory, as it were, to Boulton's inherited home at Soho and all engraved with the family crest. One tray was also engraved with the family coat of arms.

But to me, and I suspect to others, the great figure of Matthew Boulton himself was never far away. Although the objects associated with him were vastly outnumbered, they were of the greatest interest. The uncompromising pair of 'klismos' chairs and the large ormolu-mounted cupboard (tentatively attributed by Christie's to Bullock, partly on the strength of the four English ormolu laurel wreath mounts; the four central mounts surely French and not from the Soho Manufactory, as hinted in the catalogue) may not have been ordered by Boulton, but were probably installed in Soho House before he died: and the tradition that the members of the Lunar Society sat on the ebonized and gilt chairs at the table sold in the adjacent lot is an intriguing one. But how about the pieces of Wedgwood and Bentley – for example, the black basalt bust of Venus or the portrait plaque of Louis XIV, both dating from *c.*1775–80 and presumably bought direct from his friend Wedgwood? And, consider the charming Derby two-handled cup dating from about 1800; or G.B. Piranesi's print, published in 1766, of the building of Blackfriars Bridge; or the four copies of the print, published by W. Sharp in 1801, after Sir William Beechey's well-known portrait of Boulton himself; or the portrait of Boulton at the age of 42 by J.S.C. Schaak, not a distinguished picture but showing him typically in fine clothes and powdered hair, holding a book, as if caught contemplating a matter of practical scientific interest before going off to receive some fine people at Soho or to persuade Mr Christie to hold the first sale of ormolu ornaments in London. Surely these were all treasured by Boulton himself at Soho?

There were two outstanding pieces of silverware in the sale. These were a dish-warmer by Boulton and Fothergill, 1778, similar to one which survives in the Birmingham Assay Office and based on a drawing in the Boulton and Fothergill pattern books, and a rare tea-urn also by Boulton and Fothergill, 1775. This tea-urn, both in the classicism of its design and in the quality of its decoration, is one of the finest pieces of Boulton and Fothergill silver to have been

Regency ormolu-mounted mahogany cabinet
Attributed to George Bullock
96¼ in. (244.5 cm.) high; 57 in. (145 cm.)
wide; 20 in. (51 cm.) deep
Sold 27.5.87 at Great Tew Park in
Oxfordshire for £110,000 ($178,420)

Pair of Regency mahogany
'klismos' chairs
Both stamped 'H'
20³/₄ in. (52.5 cm.) wide
Sold 27.5.87 at Great Tew
Park in Oxfordshire for
£37,400 ($60,663)

One of a pair of Regency oak
and holly window-seats
By George Bullock
23¹/₄ in. (59 cm.) high;
37 in. (94 cm.) wide; 18 in.
(46 cm.) deep
Sold 27.5.87 at Great Tew
Park in Oxfordshire for
£52,800 ($85,642)
Made for the Library at Great
Tew and invoiced in 1817 as
follows: '2 Oak Window-Seats
inlaid french stuf'd & covered
with Green twilled Calico
welted with yellow Velvet
£23 2s.'

sold for many years. On one side of the urn is mounted an oval medallion of Hygieia (not Minerva, as stated in the catalogue), modelled after a design by Tassie, suggesting perhaps a connection between tea and health which would please all tea importers. On the other side are engraved the arms of Boulton, quartering Lowth, Robinson and Babington, denoting Boulton's lineage and marriage, beneath the family crest. This surely is an outstanding object from the domestic possessions of an outstanding man.

At other sales in December 1986 Christie's sold a large number of books and architectural drawings and watercolours taken from Great Tew. The books included several from Matthew Boulton's library, demonstrating the wide range of his interests. Of particular interest was a bound collection of 69 pen, ink and wash maps and plans of copper and tin mines to which Boulton and Watt supplied steam engines from 1778. Among the architectural drawings were important series of drawings by Samuel Wyatt, James Wyatt and others of Soho House, and of drawings for the Soho Mint, the St. Petersburg Mint and the Royal Mint.

Christie's also offered for sale on 9 December 1986 a charming portrait dated 1773 of Matthew Robinson Boulton at the age of three, by Jean Etienne Liotard. This pastel drawing, done on paper and fixed to a copper plate, which is engraved on the back: 'M.R. Boulton. Painted at Soho in 1773 and at time allowed to be a strong likeness', must have been commissioned by Boulton on Liotard's second visit to England.

Finally, the most renowned treasure from Great Tew, Matthew Boulton's 'sidereal' clock (see p. 16). I gave an account of the manufacture of this clock and of the ormolu case in my book *Ormolu: The Work of Matthew Boulton* (1974) and shall be describing it in greater detail shortly in a separate article. Suffice it to say here that following its completion in 1772 Boulton tried to sell it at Christie and Ansell's. It failed to reach the reserve. He subsequently sent it to the Empress Catherine the Great in St. Petersburg. The Russians were not impressed. How could a clock which did not strike the hours or play any tunes cost 2,500 roubles? It returned unsold in 1778. It is satisfying that Christie's, having failed to find a buyer in 1772, have now negotiated the transfer of this remarkable monument of English 18th-century neo-classical decoration and philosophical curiosity to the State in lieu of estate duty. We are lucky that neither Catherine the Great nor her courtiers were interested.

The prices fetched at the Great Tew sale were greatly affected, I suspect, by the romantic connection with Matthew Boulton, even though most of the objects were not connected with him at all. The prices were too high in some cases for the public collections which were interested. The silver and silver plate escaped. At least, however, the 'sidereal' clock is safely back in Birmingham, as are the most important of the architectural drawings and books, the portraits of Matthew Boulton by Schaak, of M.R. Boulton as a boy by Liotard and of M.R. Boulton by Lawrence/Shee. The Birmingham Museum also acquired furniture, including the ormolu-mounted cupboard and the chairs and table from Soho traditionally said to have been used by the Lunar Society. Many of these purchases were aided by the National Heritage Memorial Fund and by the National Art Collections Fund.

I hope that it will not be long before the authorities in Birmingham restore Soho House and establish it as a fitting memorial to one of their most distinguished citizens. I look forward to seeing these various objects from Great Tew restored to it.

Regency oak and parcel-gilt sofa
Attributed to George Bullock
37¾ in. (98 cm.) high; 61½ in. (156 cm.) wide; 31 in. (79 cm.) deep
Sold 25.6.87 in London for £66,000 ($105,600)

One of a pair of Regency pollard oak side cabinets
Attributed to George Bullock
39 in. (99 cm.) high; 53½ in. (136 cm.) wide; 23 in. (58 cm.) deep
Sold 25.6.87 in London for £242,000 ($387,200)

Two from a set of 18
Regency oak and parcel-gilt
dining-chairs
Attributed to George
Bullock
34¾ in. (88 cm.) high;
19 in. (48 cm.) wide
Sold 25.6.87 in London for
£88,000 ($140,800)

Regency oak footstool
Attributed to George
Bullock
7½ in. (19 cm.) high;
13½ in. (34 cm.) square
Sold 25.6.87 in London for
£13,750 ($22,000)

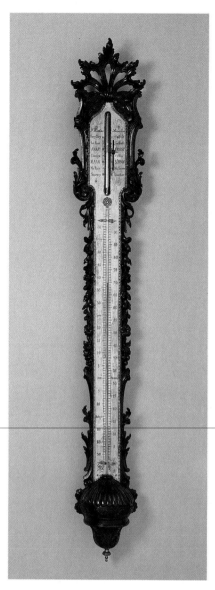

George III giltmetal
automaton toilet-mirror
By James Cox
20 in. (51 cm.) high;
11½ in. (29 cm.) wide;
7¼ in. (18.5 cm.) deep
Sold 20.11.86 in
London for £63,800
($89,831)

George II mahogany stick
barometer
By F. Watkins, London
40½ in. (103 cm.) high
Sold 25.6.87 in London for
£24,200 ($38,720)

This unusual toilet-mirror seems to correspond exactly with the
description of one included in James Cox's Lottery, which was held
in 1775 to dispose of 'the Several Exquisite and Magnificent Pieces
of Mechanism and Jewellery' from his museum in Spring Gardens,
Charing Cross. The description reads: 'Piece The Fifth A Musical
Chime, with mechanical movements...It is contained within a richly
ornamented pedestal, which stands on feet of jeweller's work; on
every side, within frames of jewellery, are figures, animals, and
other pleasing objects in progressive motion: the pedestal supports
an elegant toilet dressing glass, and on the back of the glass is a
concave magnifying mirror; the glass turns on a swivel, so that
either side may be used at pleasure, and is calculated to adorn the
commode of the greatest personage.'

Pair of Regency ormolu
wine-coolers
After a design by
J.J. Boileau
Both inscribed 'BOUGHT AT
EARL NELSON'S SALE, JULY 1895'
11½ in. (29 cm.) high;
11¾ in. (30 cm.) wide
Sold 22.10.86 at
Sheringham Hall in Norfolk
for £37,400 ($53,520)

Regency scarlet and gilt
japanned papier mâché tray
20¼ in. (72 cm.) wide
Sold 20.11.86 in London for
£6,380 ($8,984)

Pair of Regency simulated bronze and parcel-gilt bergères
After a design by George Smith
35$\frac{1}{2}$ in. (90 cm.) high; 24 in. (61 cm.) wide
Sold 20.11.86 in London for £57,200 ($80,538)

Two from a set of eight George I walnut dining-chairs
40½ in. (103 cm.) high; 23½ in. (60 cm.) wide
Sold 20.11.86 in London for £104,500 ($147,345)

George I walnut and beechwood settee
64 in. (163 cm.) wide
Sold 20.11.86 in London for £41,800 ($58,855)

George I cream-
lacquered secretaire-
cabinet
86½ in. (220 cm.) high;
43¾ in. (111 cm.) wide;
22 in. (56 cm.) deep
Sold 25.6.87 in London
for £264,000 ($422,200)

One of a pair of George III
giltwood mirrors
By Thomas Chippendale
Senior or Junior
77½ × 46½ in.
(197 × 118 cm.)
Sold 25.6.87 in London for
£242,000 ($387,200)

Regency giltwood settee
By Gillow's of London
32½ in. (82.5 cm.) high; 78 in. (98 cm.) wide; 31 in. (79 cm.) deep
Sold 22.10.86 at Sheringham Hall in Norfolk for £77,000 ($110,187)

One of a pair of George III painted and parcel-gilt side tables
32 in. (81.5 cm.) high; 60½ in. (153.5 cm.) wide; 23 in. (58.5 cm.) deep
Sold 9.4.87 in London for £71,500 ($115,258)

George II ormolu-mounted mahogany and parcel-gilt kneehole desk
Attributed to John Boson
31¾ in. (80.5 cm.) high; 55¾ in. (141.5 cm.) wide; 23¾ in. (60.5 cm.) deep
Sold 25.6.87 in London for £148,500 ($237,600)

One of a pair of early George III mahogany serpentine commodes
In the style of Thomas Chippendale
34¼ in. (87 cm.) high; 51¼ in. (130 cm.) wide; 24½ in. (62 cm.) deep
Sold 25.6.87 in London for £121,000 ($193,600)

Fine George II parcel-gilt
mahogany and olive-wood
bureau bookcase
In the manner of William
Kent
*c.*1735
85¼ in. (191 cm.) high;
40½ in. (103 cm.) wide;
23½ in. (60 cm.) deep
Sold 19.6.87 in New York
for $154,400 (£96,500)

Queen Anne walnut bureau-cabinet
92 in. (234 cm.) high; 39 in. (99 cm.) wide
Sold 9.4.87 in London for £93,500
($150,722)

One of a pair of George III giltwood side tables
Designed by Robert Adam; made by Sefferin Alken; each with a 'Mosaic' scagliola top made by Bartoli and Richter
35¾ in. (90.7 cm.) high; 65½ in. (166.5 cm.) wide; 29¾ in. (75.5 cm.) deep
Sold 20.11.86 in London for £286,000 ($457,600)

This pair of 'Mosaic' scagliola-top side tables was made for the 6th Earl of Coventry for the Great Room of Coventry House, Piccadilly, in 1768, for a total of £212. 6s. 11d. The documentation for the tables is particularly rich and gives some indication of the changes and deliberations that were made before the final design was executed. The full-scale and partly coloured drawing for one of the tops illustrated opposite (now in the Sir John Soane Museum) shows that there was some doubt about colouring in the original designs; the drawing is inscribed, 'Mr Adam has not time to fix the Colours of the Border but thinks that need not stop the Estimate from being made. When that is fixt if the drawing is return'd to Mr Adam he will settle the other Parts of the Colouring.' When compared with the actual top it is clear that considerable modifications were indeed made in colouring, and also in design, the general effect being much simpler than the unusually richly ornamented French-style stretcher depicted in the drawing.

Regency ormolu-mounted rosewood writing-table
In the manner of John McLean
29 in. (73.5 cm.) high; 42¼ in. (107.5 cm.) wide; 27 in. (68.5 cm.) deep
Sold 20.11.86 in London for £39,600 ($55,757)

Regency mahogany Carlton House desk
61½ in. (161 cm.) wide
Sold 25.6.87 in London for £132,000 ($211,200)

George III mahogany breakfront bookcase
114 in. (290 cm.) high; 132½ in. (335 cm.) wide; 25½ in. (65 cm.) deep
Sold 9.4.87 in London for £165,000 ($265,980)

Queen Anne green-lacquered
cabinet
98½ in. (250 cm.) high; 43¼ in.
(110 cm.) wide
Sold 27.9.86 at Villa Nora in
Bologna for L.310,500,000
(£144,419)

Far left:
Needlework picture worked in petit point on ivory satin
English, mid-17th century
15 × 19 in. (38 × 48 cm.)
Sold 21.5.87 in London for £9,350 ($15,634)

Left centre:
Needlework mirror worked in coloured silks on ivory silk
English, mid-17th century
25 × 28 in. (63.5 × 71 cm.)
Sold 21.5.87 in London for £3,740 ($6,254)

Left:
Needlework picture
English, 17th century
15 × 21 in. (38 × 53.5 cm.)
Sold 21.5.87 in London for £6,600 ($11,036)

Far left:
Oak joint stool
Early 17th century
18 in. (46 cm.) wide
Sold 21.5.87 in London for £4,400 ($7,357)

Left centre:
Oak court cupboard
Early 17th century
27½ in. (69.5 cm.) wide
Sold 21.5.87 in London for £6,600 ($11,036)

Henry VII oak chalice-casket
Early 16th century; the internal metal work and lock 17th–18th century
12 in. (30.5 cm.) high; 16½ in. (42 cm.) wide; 7½ in. (19 cm.) deep
Sold 21.5.87 in London for £26,400 ($44,141)

Left:
Oak joint stool
Early 17th century
18 in. (46 cm.) wide
Sold 21.5.87 in London for £1,540 ($2,575)

All from the collection of the late Mary Bellis

One of a pair of malachite Empire vases
42¼ in. (107.5 cm.) high
Sold 27.9.86 at Villa Nora in Bologna for
L.322,000,000 (£149,767)

Red porphyry urn
18th century
35 in. (89 cm.) high
Sold 10.7.87 in London for £29,700 ($47,520)
From the collection at Marbury Hall

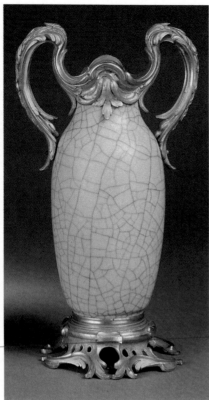

Far left:
One of a pair of Louis XVI ormolu-mounted Sèvres pot-pourri vases
8½ in. (22 cm.) high
Sold 17.6.87 in London for £17,600 ($28,160)

Left:
One of a pair of Louis XV ormolu and Chinese crackled grey celadon vases
12¼ in. (31.4 cm.) high
Sold 17.6.87 in London for £35,200 ($56,320)

Louis XV ormolu encrier
Stamped 'Osmond'
14 in. (36 cm.) wide
Sold 17.6.87 in London
for £30,800 ($49,280)

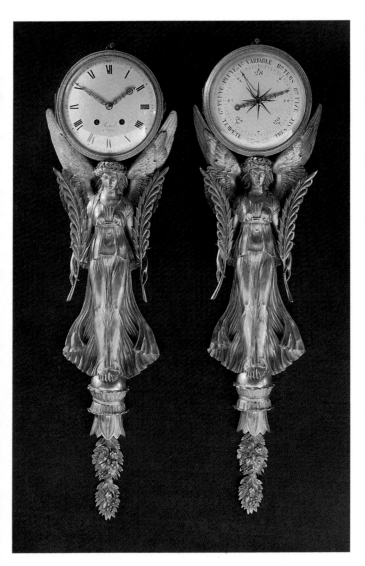

Empire ormolu cartel clock and matching barometer
The clock with dial signed 'Revel à Paris'
37½ in. (95 cm.) high; 10½ in. (27 cm.) wide
Sold 18.6.87 in London for £55,000 ($88,000)

Louis XV ormolu-mounted Boulle mantel clock
26½ in. (67.5 cm.) high; 16¼ in. (42 cm.) wide at base
Sold 17.6.87 in London for £61,600 ($98,560)
Traditionally believed to be a gift from Louis XVI to Frederick I of Prussia

The Thomire Firegrate

MARTIN CHAPMAN

The Victoria and Albert Museum has been fortunate in buying the magnificent gilt bronze firegrate by the great *bronzier* Pierre-Philippe Thomire, which was one of the major lots in the sale of important French furniture on 17 June 1987. With its dwindling funds the museum is rarely able to compete for important objects at auction, but with the generous assistance of both the National Heritage Memorial Fund and the National Art Collections Fund (Eugene Cremetti Fund) the firegrate was secured for a national collection and it will be the centrepiece of French 18th-century gilt bronzes already assembled at South Kensington.

The significance of this firegrate lies not only in its spectacular craftsmanship, but also in its rarity, both as an example of Thomire's pre-Revolutionary work and as an example of English patronage of the luxury products of France. Throughout the 18th century *milords anglais* were a lucrative source of revenue for the Parisian traders. Several discerning English collectors and connoisseurs, notably the Prince of Wales, the 5th Duke of Bedford and William Beckford, commissioned expensive objects and furnishings from Paris in the last quarter of the century. This firegrate is one such commission, either given directly to Thomire, or more probably made through the agency of a *marchand mercier*, the French dealers who traded in luxury objects.

Pierre-Philippe Thomire (1751–1843) was already a prominent craftsman in the art of making gilt bronze in the final decade of the *ancien régime*. He vied with the greatest craftsmen for important commissions and is known to have worked extensively for the Crown and the Sèvres porcelain manufactory, whom he provided with gilt bronze mounts. Despite his eminence surprisingly little is known of what he produced during the early years of his highly successful career, though his subsequent work in the Empire period is fully charted. Only a few objects from the period 1776–89 can be securely attributed to Thomire, and this grate, signed twice by him and dated 1788, is an important document which broadens our knowledge of his *oeuvre*.

The substantial size of the firegrate allows us an opportunity to make a proper appraisal of Thomire's craftsmanship. The execution and handling of the ornaments and the rich gilding are outstanding. Thomire had been trained as a sculptor and was able to produce both the simply decorative and the more difficult figure work. His mastery of casting is evident and he had a special reputation for the quality of his gilding, in particular the subtle interplay of finish between the grainy matt backgrounds and the brilliant areas of burnishing. The skilful use of these techniques is amply demonstrated on this firegrate and confirms Thomire's reputation as one of the few true masters of the medium of gilt bronze.

The unusual design of the firegrate is due to the combination of a virtuoso display of French craftsmanship with the singularly English form of a basket grate. These English grates were designed for burning coal, they were characterized by a semicircular opening for the basket and were usually made of practical polished steel. As this firegrate is made of expensive gilt bronze it can only have been intended as an ornamental piece , for the precious gilding (which is still largely intact) would have been damaged had it ever been used.

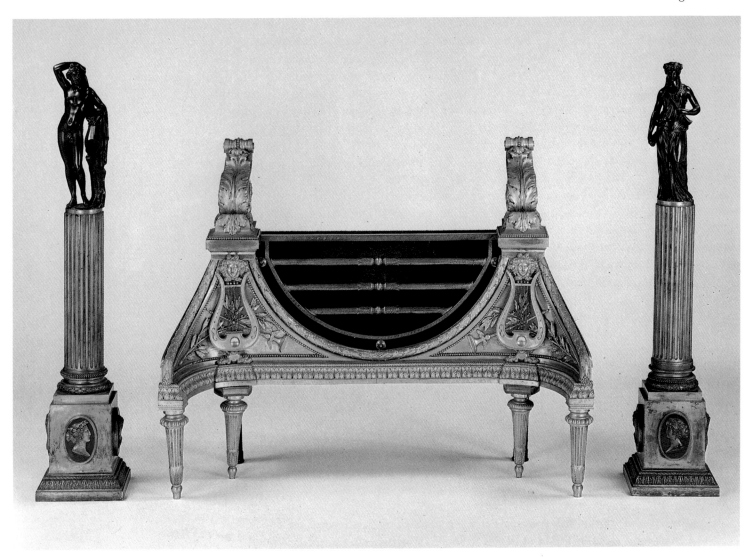

Firegrate and pair of columns
Signed 'Thomire à Paris'
Dated 1788
The grate 33¼ in. (84.5 cm.) high; 43 in. (109.5 cm.) wide; 19 in. (48.5 cm.) deep; the columns 41½ in. (105 cm.) high
Sold 17.6.87 in London for £154,000 ($246,400)
Now in the Victoria and Albert Museum

The known history of the grate does not convincingly explain its original commission. Until recently it stood in the music-room at Powderham Castle in Devon. This room was completed for the 3rd Viscount Courtenay to the designs of the architect James Wyatt between 1794 and 1796. The prominent attributes of music on the grate, the lyres and trumpets, and the figures of the god Apollo and of the Muse of music, Euterpe, are especially appropriate themes for such a room. However, the massive chimneypiece provided for the Powderham music-room by Westmacott does not accommodate this firegrate, together with its columns, in any felicitous arrangement. And the lapse of time between the manufacture of the grate in 1788 and the construction of the music-room six to eight years later does not encourage the notion that it was originally made for the room. Courtenay was only twenty years old in 1788, and unless he was exceptionally precocious, it is unlikely that he would order this sophisticated object at such a tender age. However, the influence of his friend, the great connoisseur William Beckford (1759–1844), might provide a clue to the commission – the magnificence and consummate craftsmanship of the firegrate are just what we should expect of Beckford's dazzling taste. He was in Paris in 1788, the year of its manufacture, which was also the year that Courtenay inherited. It is tempting to suggest that there might be a connection between these events.

An alternative explanation for the original commission is suggested by a series of drawings that are conserved in the museum's Print Room. The drawings are from the workshop of the eminent London cabinet-maker John Linnell (1729–96), and are collectively known as the 'Linnell Album'. They include two designs relating to the Thomire firegrate, which were recognized by Mr Hugh Roberts of Christie's. The drawing shown here illustrates two alternative projects, one of which is substantially similar to the completed grate. In the Christie's catalogue of 17 June 1987, Mr Roberts pointed out that this drawing is French, from its inscription 'Echelle de quatre Pieds d'Angleterre' and from its draughtsmanship, and thus it may have come from Thomire's workshop. Linnell is known to have had contacts with the Parisian *marchand mercier* Dominique Daguerre (see H. Hayward and P. Kirkham *William and John Linnell*, 1980, p. 68), who had a thriving trade with England, and this was possibly how the grate came to be commissioned. The second drawing is a sketch showing a project for arranging the firegrate and the columns in a small chimneypiece where the grate is squeezed into the opening and the two free-standing columns are displayed either in front of or recessed into the jambs. This drawing is by C.H. Tatham (I am grateful to Michael Snodin for this information), Linnell's nephew and compiler of the 'Album', who was working with his uncle at this time.

These drawings were published in *Furniture History*, vol. v, 1969, where Mrs Hayward, the author of the piece, suggests that some of the drawings for firegrates are projects for Uxbridge House, Burlington Gardens. This house was sumptuously refurbished for Lord Uxbridge in the period 1785–90 to the designs of the architect John Vardy, with furnishings supplied by Linnell. The 'Great Music-Room' was the most elaborate interior in the house, which was ready for furnishing in 1788. Here Linnell provided an organ and it is possible that he also proposed the Thomire firegrate, with its appropriate attributes of music, for the large chimneypiece carved by Westmacott. This chimneypiece, now in the Bank of England, is rich with allusions to music, in an elaborate frieze depicting Apollo and the Muses.

Several of Linnell's designs for grates in the 'Album' are undoubtedly projects for the chimneypiece in the music-room at Uxbridge House. They demonstrate that he was trying to conceive a more formal and architectural type of grate by including integral sculptural features, such as figures on columns. The early French drawing follows the principles of Linnell's new

Two alternative proposals
for the firegrate, possibly
from Thomire's workshop
French, late 18th century
Inscribed 'Echelle de quatre
Pieds d'Angleterre'
From the 'Linnell Album'
in the Victoria and Albert
Museum and reproduced by
courtesy of the Trustees

Sketch of the proposed
setting for the firegrate and
columns, by C.H. Tatham
English, late 18th century
From the 'Linnell Album'
in the Victoria and Albert
Museum and reproduced by
courtesy of the Trustees

type of grate, but Thomire's finished piece is a compromise. He adopts the conventional English form of a steel basket grate leaving the columns with their figures as separate free-standing elements. It is possible that although Linnell gave the commission for the new firegrate to Thomire, when it arrived from France it was found to be unsuitable. Linnell may have tried to solve the difficulty by using it elsewhere and the sketch by Tatham might represent an attempt to squash the grate into another, smaller chimneypiece at Uxbridge House, perhaps the one in the new drawing-room, to appease his client. Lord Uxbridge was increasingly concerned about the expense of furnishing his house and he complained in 1790 that Linnell 'is certainly making a property out of me and will never let me out of his books if he can help it' (*Survey of London*, vol. XXXII, 1963, p. 463). Uxbridge may not have accepted the grate and Linnell (or his successors) may have sold it to Courtenay for the new music-room at Powderham later.

Whatever the answers are to these questions of the history of the original commission, this grate is a key object in the study of French 18th-century gilt bronzes, both for its superlative quality of workmanship and its rare distinction as a fully authenticated example of Thomire's early work. That it documents advanced English patronage in the late 18th century and that two drawings relating to the grate already exist in the museum's collection, only further enhances the importance of the acquisition. It is undoubtedly the museum's most significant purchase in the field of French 18th-century decorative arts in recent years.

Empire ormolu-mounted
mahogany fauteuil de
bureau
31¼ in. (79 cm.) high;
21½ in. (54.5 cm.) diameter
Sold 18.6.87 in London for
£60,500 ($96,800)
From a collection of
Napoleonic memorabilia

Pair of Louis XV giltwood
bergères
By Jean-Baptiste Gourdin
Sold 17.6.87 in London for
£77,000 ($123,200)

Two of a set of six Louis XV
giltwood fauteuils
By François Reuze
38 in. (96.5 cm.) high; 28¾ in.
(73 cm.) wide
Sold 17.6.87 in London for
£154,000 ($246,400)

Louis XIV ivory table à écrire
26¼ in. (66.5 cm.) high; 17¼ in. (44 cm.) wide; 12½ in.
(32 cm.) deep;
Sold 17.6.87 in London for £49,500 ($79,200)

Louis XVI ormolu-mounted amboyna bonheur du jour
Attributed to Adam Weisweiler
c. 1785
42 in. (105 cm.) high, 28¼ in. (71.2 cm.) wide, 16¼ in.
(41.2 cm.) deep
Sold 20.5.87 in New York for $154,000 (£91,613)
From the estate of Henry P. McIlhenny

Louis XIV walnut, marquetry and ivory-inlaid cabinet-on-stand
68½ in. (174 cm.) high; 49 in. (124 cm.) wide; 18¼ in. (46.5 cm.) deep
Sold 18.6.87 in London for £37,400 ($59,840)

Louis XVI porcelain and ormolu-mounted bois satiné commode
By Godefroy Dester
35¼ in. (89.5 cm.) high; 41 in. (104 cm.) wide; 20½ in. (52 cm.) deep
Sold 17.6.87 in London for £550,000 ($880,000)

The Knole Bureau

HUGH ROBERTS

This exceptional piece of furniture came for sale from Knole where it had lain unremarked in an attic for many years. The phenomenal interest it aroused was no doubt mainly due to its jewel-like, glittering appearance, but for furniture historians the fascination lay in the absence of any certainty as to its country – or place – of origin. All that is known is that it was probably purchased by Lord Whitworth on his embassy to Paris in 1802–3. Before that there is a complete lack of documentation. The only other comparable piece of furniture seems to be a nearly identical bureau now in a French private collection. This too lacks any provenance, though it has in the past been dated *c.*1680 and attributed to the Gobelins workshop of Domenico Cucci the Italian artist imported for Louis XIV's *Manufacture Royale*. Our catalogue for the Knole bureau suggested that a later date (*c.*1720) and a German origin were likely to be more realistic: the flamboyant use of shell, brass, pewter and copper allied to extravagant Chinoiserie decorations all seem to point to Germany – Dresden, Berlin or Munich being the principal contenders. Though all three cities boasted courts rich enough to have provided the means to commission a piece of this extravagance, no directly comparable piece seems to have survived, so we shall have to await the discovery of some previously unread inventory or other related document to provide the key to the mystery of the exact origin of this remarkable desk.

Mother-of-pearl and polychrome Boulle marquetry bureau
*c.*1720
49$\frac{1}{4}$ in. (125 cm.) high;
35$\frac{1}{4}$ in. (89.5 cm.) wide;
20$\frac{1}{4}$ in. (52.5 cm.) deep
Sold 17.6.87 in London for £1,210,000
($1,936,000)
Sold by order of the trustees of the Knole Estate

Louis xv kingwood and tulipwood commode
By Jacques Dubois
36 in. (91.5 cm.) high; 57 in. (145 cm.) wide; 24½ in. (62 cm.) deep
Sold 17.6.87 in London for £176,000 ($281,600)

Louis XVI tulipwood and parquetry commode
By Guillaume Beneman
35 in. (89 cm.) high; 51¾ in. (132 cm.) wide; 22¾ in. (58 cm.) deep
Sold 17.6.87 in London for £374,000 ($598,400)

Louis XIV Boulle bureau plat
31½ in. (80 cm.) high; 72 in.(183 cm.) wide; 33½ in. (85 cm.) deep
Sold 17.6.87 in London for £154,000 ($246,400)

Pair of Louis XIV Boulle pedestals
One stamped 'E. LEVASSEUR' and also inscribed under the top 'Danchot 1784'
49 in. (124.5 cm.) high; 19¼ in. (49 cm.) wide; 14 in. (35.5 cm.) deep
Sold 17.6.87 in London for £115,500 ($184,800)

Louis XVI parquetry table à écrire
Stamped 'L. BOUDIN'
29¼ in. (74 cm.) high; 18¾ in. (47.5 cm.) wide; 13 in. (33 cm.) deep
Sold 17.6.87 in London for £49,500 ($79,200)

Louis XVI tulipwood and end-cut marquetry table à écrire
Stamped 'L. BOUDIN JME'
27 in. (68.5 cm.) high; 25¼ in. (64 cm.) wide; 16¼ in. (41 cm.) deep
Sold 17.6.87 in London for £46,200 ($73,920)

Louis XVI tulipwood and parquetry bureau à cylindre
46 in. (117 cm.) high; 38 in. (96.5 cm.) wide; 22¼ in. (56.5 cm.) deep
Sold 17.6.87 in London for £121,000 ($193,600)

Louis XVI parquetry commode à encoignures
Stamped 'RVLC'
40½ in. (103 cm.) high; 73½ in. (187 cm.) wide; 22½ in. (57 cm.) deep
Sold 17.6.87 in London for £126,500 ($202,400)

One of a pair of Louis XV/XVI ormolu-mounted tulipwood, amaranth and parquetry commodes
*c.*1775
Each stamped 'M.G. CRAMER JME'
57¾ in. (144.4 cm.) wide
Sold 5.11.86 in New York for $187,000 (£131,969)
From the estate of Ethel Shields Garrett
Previously sold at Christie's 18.5.1922 for £3,465

Left and opposite:
The Edwards-Harrison family Chippendale carved mahogany high chest of drawers, dressing-table and pair of side chairs
By Thomas Tufft, Philadelphia
1775–6
The chest 96 in. (244 cm.) high; 44 in. (112 cm.) wide; 22½ in. (57 cm.) deep
The dressing-table 30 in. (76 cm.) high; 33½ in. (85 cm.) wide; 19½ in. (49.5 cm.) deep
The chairs 38 in. (96.5 cm.) high
Sold 28.5.87 in New York for $1,760,000 (£1,035,294)
The importance of this group is not only in its completeness and fine design, but also in its documentation, which identifies both the original owner and the maker. The high chest, dressing-table, and pair of chairs are described in an account book kept by Richard Edwards at Lumberton, New Jersey, who entered purchases both for his general store at Lumberton and for his own household. The group was sent for sale by a descendant of Edwards.

The Colonel Isaac Gardiner Reed
presentation banjo clock
By Aaron Willard, Jun., Boston
1812–16
29³⁄₄ in. (75.5 cm.) high
Sold 18.10.86 in New York for
$121,000 (£85,092)
Record auction price for an
American banjo clock

Silver teapot
By Peter Van Dyck, New York
c.1720–35
7¾ in. (19.5 cm.) high
Sold 18.10.86 in New York for $93,500 (£65,753)
Record auction price for an American silver teapot

Silk needlework picture
By Mary Flower, Philadelphia
Mounted on cedar panel bearing ink inscription 'Mary Flower her Work in the Year 1768'
18½ × 23 in. (47 × 58.4 cm.)
Sold 24.1.87 in New York for $187,000 (£120,465)
Record auction price for a piece of needlework

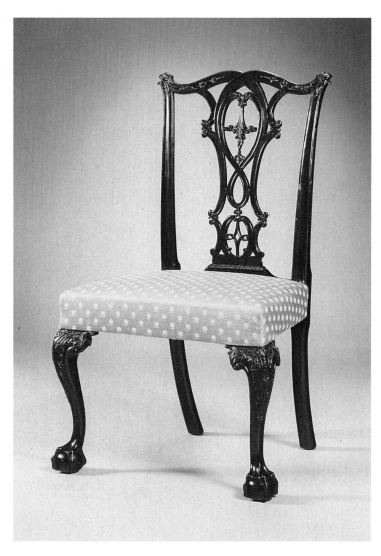

Charles Thompson Chippendale carved mahogany side chair
Philadelphia, 1765–80
38¼ in. (97 cm.) high; 23½ in. (59.7 cm.) wide
Sold 24.1.87 in New York for $341,000 (£227,333)
Record auction price for an American side chair

John Penn Chippendale carved mahogany slab-top table
Philadelphia, 1765–75
31 in. (78.7 cm.) high; 44¾ in. (110.5 cm.) wide; 24 in. (61 cm.)
deep
Sold 18.10.86 in New York for $605,000 (£422,458)
Record auction price for an American slab-top table

Double-manual
harpsichord
By Jacob Kirkman
The nameboard
inscribed 'Jacobus
Kirckman Londini
Fecit 1761'
91½ × 37 in.
(231 × 94 cm.)
Sold 26.6.87 in
London for £77,000
($123,200)
Record auction price
for a harpsichord

Right:
Viola da gamba
by Joachim Tielke
Labelled 'Joachim
Tielke/in Hamburg/An
1685', with repairer's
label 'Reparerat af Petter
Allberg/1 Uddevalle
1803'
Length of back 26 in.
(66 cm.)
Sold 11.11.86 in London
for £33,000 ($47,388)

Far right:
Italian violoncello
By Giovanni Grancino
Labelled 'Giovanni
Grancino in
Contrada/Largha di
Milano al segno/della
Corona 1703'
Length of back 30 in.
(76.1 cm.)
Sold 26.6.87 in London
for £52,800 ($84,480)

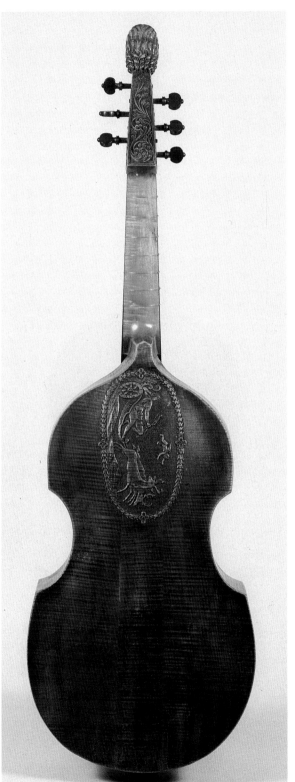

Far left:
The Falmouth
Stradivari: Italian
violin
By Antonio Stradivari
Labelled 'Antonius
Stradivarius
Cremonensis/Faciebat
Anno 1692'
Length of back 14⅜ in.
(36.3 cm.)
Sold 26.6.87 in
London for £192,500
($308,000)
Previously sold at
Christie's on 2.6.82
for £102,600
This violin was once
owned by the Earl of
Falmouth, a notable
collector, who sold it
in 1853 for £110

Left:
Italian violin
By Pietro Guarneri
Labelled 'Petrus
Guarnerius
Cremonensis
fecit/Mantuae sub tit.
Sanctae Teresiae
1707'
Length of back 14 in.
(35.5 cm.)
Sold 11.11.86 in
London for £88,000
($126,368)

The Colossus
Stradivari: Italian
violin
By Antonio Stradivari
Labelled 'Antonius
Stradiuarius
Cremonensis/Faciebat
Anno 1716'
Length of back 14⅛ in.
(35.8 cm.)
Sold 29.4.87 in London
for £440,000 ($724,680)
From the estate of
Dr Simon Carfagno
Record auction price
for a violin

Verneh
6 ft. 6 in. square
Sold 16.10.86 in London for £8,800 ($12,655)

Soumac carpet
10 ft. 10 in. × 7 ft. 9 in. (329 × 236 cm.)
Sold 16.4.87 in London for £10,450 ($16,898)

North-west Persian rug
7 ft. 6 in. × 5 ft. 10 in. (228 × 178 cm.)
Sold 11.6.87 in London for £12,100 ($20,026)

Bakshaish carpet
Dated 1273 (AD 1856)
17 ft. × 12 ft. 7 in.
(518 × 383 cm.)
Sold 9.12.86 in New York at
Christie's East for $25,300
(£17,868)

Silk Tabriz pictorial rug
6 ft. 5 in. × 4 ft. 3 in.
(196 × 130 cm.)
Sold 16.4.87 in London for
£11,550 ($18,677)

Tabriz carpet
12 ft. 4 in. × 9 ft. 3 in.
(376 × 281 cm.)
Sold 16.4.87 in London for
£22,000 ($35,574)

Empire Aubusson carpet (detail)
15 ft. 9 in. × 19 ft. 4 in. (480 × 590 cm.)
Sold 26.3.87 in London for £14,300
($22,880)

Savonnerie carpet (detail)
Mid-19th century
21 ft. 10 in. × 17 ft. 4 in.
(666 × 528 cm.)
Sold 25.6.87 in London for £60,500
($96,800)

George III octagonal needlework carpet
Designed by Robert Adam
14 ft. 9 in. (448 cm.) diameter
Sold 25.6.87 in London for £26,400 ($42,240)

Clocks and Watches

Original key (with serial number) to
walnut longcase clock by George
Graham, London, No. 655
*c.*1724–5
Clock and key sold 11.3.87 in London
for £38,500 ($61,023)

South German astronomical table clock
The relief in the manner of Hans Krels, the
movement probably by the unidentified maker MIA
c.1570
9 in. (23 cm.) diameter
Sold 12.11.86 in Geneva for Sw.fr.528,000
(£217,731)
This clock is a previously unrecorded example of a
group known as 'The Orpheus Clocks'

Opposite right:
George II mahogany month-
going longcase regulator
clock
By George Graham,
London, unnumbered
c.1750
6 ft. 1 in. (186 cm.) high
Sold 27.5.87 in London for
£35,200 ($57,095)

Opposite centre:
Charles II walnut month-
going longcase clock
By Thomas Tompion,
London
c.1680
6 ft. 4 in. (193 cm.)
Sold 15.10.86 in London for
£46,200 ($65,706)

Opposite far right:
Queen Anne ivory-japanned
longcase clock
By Daniel Quare, London
c.1710
8 ft. 1 in. (238 cm.) high
Sold 9.4.87 in London for
£220,000 ($354,640)

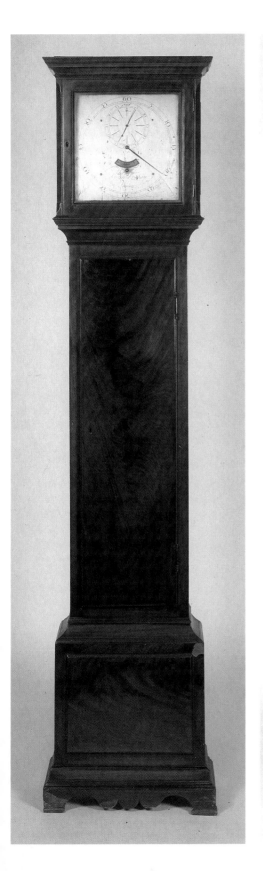

Enamelled silver grande sonnerie world time
clock
By Patek Philippe & Co., Geneva, No. 860708
Completed 1938
7½ in. (19 cm.) diameter
Sold 6.6.87 in New York for $38,500
(£23,532)
From the collection of a New England
museum

Silver quarter-striking carriage clock with
alarm
By Breguet Neveu & Co., No. 3992
2nd quarter of the 19th century
5½ in. (13.5 cm.) high
Sold 28.11.86 in London for £23,100
($32,502)

Mid-Georgian quarter-striking musical and automaton bracket
clock on turntable base
The japanning in the style of Giles Grendey
37 in. (94 cm.) high
Sold 20.11.86 in London for £55,000 ($77,440)

Charles II ebony timepiece
By Thomas Tompion, London
13 in. (33 cm.) high
Sold 11.3.87 in London for £19,800 ($31,383)
By order of the estate of Hugh Cholmondeley

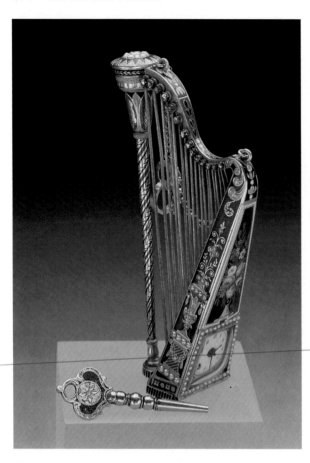

Louis XVI ormolu-
mounted Sèvres
porcelain lyre clock
By Kinable, Paris
The dial signed
'Coteau'
24 in. (61 cm.) high
Sold 6.6.87 in New
York for $93,500
(£58,000)

Above:
Genevan enamelled and gem-set gold miniature
harp with watch and musical movement
*c.*1800
Sold 17.12.86 in New York for $38,500 (£27,132)

Swiss ormolu bird-cage
clock
Early 19th century
19½ in. (50 cm.) high;
13 in. (33 cm.) square
Sold 4.12.86 in London
for £27,500 ($39,160)

Right:
Empire gold and enamel-cased *montre à tact*
with enamelled and diamond-set arms of
Lucien Bonaparte
By Breguet, No. 654
With original certificate of sale to Lucien
Bonaparte on 17 Brumaire, An. 9 (1802)
for 1440 francs
1½ in. (3.9 cm.) diameter
Sold 12.11.86 in Geneva for Sw.fr.88,000
(£36,288)

Far right:
George II gold, enamel and repoussé pair-
cased watch
The movement signed 'Ellicott, London
4819', the enamel signed 'G.M. Moser'
*c.*1755
2 in. (5 cm.) diameter
Sold 12.11.86 in Geneva for Sw.fr.60,500
(£24,973)

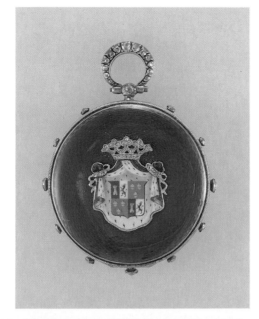

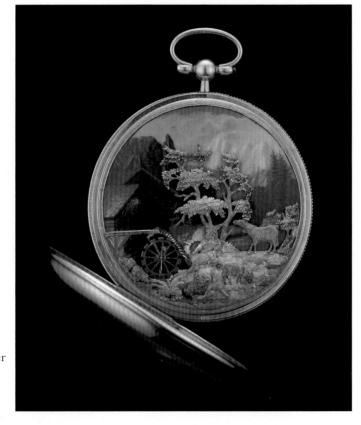

Gold double-dial musical
automaton watch
By Henry-Daniel Capt,
Geneva, No. 264
Dated 1806 on the
mainspring
2¼ in. (5.8 cm.) diameter
Sold 17.12.86 in
New York for $46,200
(£32,559)

Anglo-Swiss gold, enamel and pearl-set
duplex watch
By William Anthony, London, No. 1854
1798
2½ in. (6.4 cm.) diameter
Sold 12.11.86 in Geneva for Sw.fr.55,000
(£22,680)

Far left:
Edwardian gold
hunter-cased split-
second chronograph
with tourbillon lever
escapement
By Charles Frodsham,
London, No. 09765
1904
2 in. (5.5 cm.)
diameter
Sold 6.6.87 in New
York for $49,500
(£30,255)

Left:
Gold experimental
watch, with equation
of time, indication
of longitude at sea and
on land, and a variant
form of single pin-
pallet lever
escapement
By Greppin, Paris,
No. 1
*c.*1785-6
2 ¼ in. (5.8 cm.)
diameter
Sold 13.5.87 in
Geneva for
Sw.fr.71,500
(£29,183)

Swiss white-gold cased perpetual calendar minute-
repeating keyless lever watch
By Audemars Piguet Brassus, No. 26859
2 in. (4.8 cm.) diameter
Sold 12.11.86 in Geneva for Sw.fr.60,500
(£24,973)

Left:
Gold minute-
repeating split-second
lever chronograph
with perpetual
calendar
By Patek Philippe,
Geneva, No. 90241
2 in. (5.2 cm.)
diameter
Sold 6.6.87 in New
York for $66,000
(£40,964)

Above left:
Gentleman's split-second chronograph gold wrist-watch
By Patek Philippe, Geneva, No. 198098
Completed 1924
$1\frac{3}{4} \times 1\frac{1}{4}$ in. (4.2 × 3.4 cm.)
Sold 13.5.87 in Geneva for Sw.fr.132,000 (£53,877)

Above:
Gentleman's perpetual calendar chronograph gold wrist-watch
By Patek Philippe, Geneva, No. 867742
Completed 1950
$1\frac{1}{2}$ in. (3.5 cm.) diameter
Sold 12.11.86 in Geneva for Sw.fr.99,000 (£40,824)

Left:
Gentleman's perpetual calendar chronograph gold wrist-watch
By Patek Philippe, Geneva, No. 869486
Completed *c.*1980
$1\frac{1}{2}$ in. (3.9 cm.) diameter
Sold 13.5.87 in Geneva for Sw.fr.66,000 (£26,938)

Mahogany Helmholtz tangent galvanometer
By Elliot Brothers, London
Late 19th century
16 in. (40.6 cm.) high
Sold 5.3.87 in London at South Kensington for £770 ($1,200)
From the collection of scientific instruments and philosophical apparatus from the Wheatstone Laboratory, King's College, London

Oxydized and lacquered brass magnetometer
By Thomas Jones, London
23½ in. (59.7 cm.) long
Sold 5.3.87 in London at South Kensington for a £605 ($943)
From the collection of scientific instruments and philosophical apparatus from the Wheatstone Laboratory, King's College, London

Sir Charles Wheatstone and the Wheatstone Laboratory, King's College, London

The collection of scientific instruments from the Wheatstone Laboratory, sold on 5 March 1987 at South Kensington, was a clear reflection of the developments in science made in the 19th century, in which Sir Charles Wheatstone played an immensely important part.

Charles Wheatstone was appointed Professor of Experimental Philosophy at King's College in 1834 and remained there until his death in 1875. During this period, Wheatstone and his laboratory became justly famous. From 1860–5 James Clerk Maxwell was the Professor of Natural Philosophy at King's, and his unification of the phenomena of electricity and magnetism into one theory, together with the pioneering work of Wheatstone and his friend Michael Faraday, formed the scientific base from which the modern electrical world was to develop. Wheatstone was also a prolific inventor, being responsible for the telegraph, the stereoscope, the rheostat and the first practical electrical generator, all of which form a legacy which lives on at the core of modern systems of communications and electric motors.

In his will, Wheatstone bequeathed to King's some 1,500 books, together with scientific apparatus and £500 to be expended on laboratory equipment. The College Council established the 'Wheatstone Laboratory' in fulfilment of this bequest, and Wheatstone's collection became the foundation stone around which a physics laboratory was built that has since won four Nobel prizes.

The collection sold for a total of £19,663 ($30,635).

Brass circle of proportion of Oughtered type
Unsigned and unfinished
Early 18th century
6 in. (15.2 cm.) diameter
Sold 4.6.87 in London at South Kensington for £8,800 ($14,080)

George II glass celestial
globe
By Thomas Heath, the
engraving by John Crowley,
the terrestrial globe by
Nathaniel Hill
29 in. (73.7 cm.) high
Sold 4.6.87 in London at
South Kensington for
£40,700 ($65,120)

Jewellery

Art deco coral, emerald and diamond chimera bangle
Signed by Cartier
Sold 14.5.87 in Geneva for Sw.fr.150,000 (£61,225)

A Red Diamond in New York

EMMANUEL FRITSCH, PH.D.

On 28 April 1987, when François Curiel, Head of the Jewellery Department in New York, closed the bidding at $880,000 for a purplish-red diamond of 0.95 carats, the audience applauded and several diamond dealers gathered to congratulate him: 'We have just turned a page in the history of diamonds.'

Lot 408, described as an extremely rare unmounted circular-cut fancy purplish-red diamond, had generated a lot of pre-sale interest and was accompanied by two laboratory reports from the Gemological Institute of America and Gübelin Laboratory in Switzerland. Charles Schiffman, Head of the Swiss Laboratory, commented: 'Even in our laboratory, where outstanding members of the gemstone kingdom continually turn up, this diamond was regarded as a great rarity.'

At an unprecedented $926,000 per carat, the 'petite' stone was purchased by Theodore Horovitz, a leading Swiss stone merchant, competing with an anonymous telephone bidder, later identified as Lisa Moussaieff, the owner of London Hilton Jewellers in London. This record-breaking sale was more than seven times greater than the previously highest documented price per carat for a diamond at auction ($127,000 in May 1980). Earlier during the same sale this record had already been broken when an even smaller purple-pink diamond of 0.59 carats sold for $148,000 ($250,000 per carat) to William Goldberg, a leading New York dealer, who purchased the stone for his private collection. Both the *New York Times* and the *International Herald Tribune* reported on this historical auction the day after the sale.

The fact that such amazing prices are being paid for such relatively small stones is partly explained by their colour. In the range of colours that diamonds are known to exhibit, red (actually a deep purple-pink) is the rarest of all. It is probably safe to say that less than a dozen stones of this hue have ever been documented.

Adding to the lure of its uniqueness, this colour is also something of a mystery for scientists: although most colorations in diamonds are comparatively well understood, this one is still puzzling. For example, natural blue diamonds are well known to contain boron and conduct electricity, and most yellow colours in a diamond are related to some extent to the presence of nitrogen in the stone. Whether the red colour is similarly correlated to an impurity, and to which one, is still very unclear. Moreover, the non-destructive detection of elements such as nitrogen or oxygen in minute concentrations in a diamond (a few parts per million!) requires the use of extremely sophisticated technologies. Taking a radically different approach, scientists have been able to induce a very dark red coloration in a diamond by use of irradiation. As a consequence, this hue is thought to occur naturally primarily through a structural defect, but no conclusive proof has ever been published, and active research is still going on.

Fancy-coloured diamonds are increasingly sought after, as awareness of their rarity grows. The 28 April record sale was a spectacular demonstration of this trend and it will be interesting to observe in the near future how this important transaction affects the diamond market as a whole.

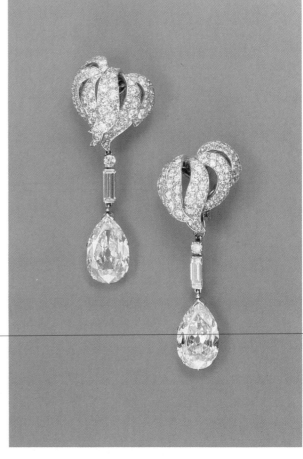

Above left:
Diamond rectangular panel
Signed by Koch
Sold 13.11.86 in Geneva for Sw.fr.71,500 (£29,607)

Above:
Pair of diamond ear-pendants, each pavé-set diamond palm frond mount suspending a pear-shaped diamond drop weighing 7.46 and 7.55 carats respectively
Signed by Cartier
Sold 13.11.86 in Geneva for Sw.fr.330,000 (£136,646)

Left:
Art deco diamond brooch set with a rectangular-cut diamond weighing 5.07 carats, enhanced by four pear-shaped diamonds weighing 2.92, 3.52, 6.42 and 6.94 carats, mounted in platinum
Signed by Cartier
Sold 28.4.87 in New York for $220,000 (£133,577)

Right:
Diamond single-stone ring, the hexagonal diamond weighing 8.39 carats
With a certificate from the Gemological Institute of America stating that the diamond is D colour, clarity VVS
Sold 14.5.87 in Geneva for Sw.fr.380,000 (£155,102)

Far right:
Unmounted pear-shaped diamond weighing 15.75 carats
With a certificate from the Gemological Institute of America stating that the diamond is E colour and internally flawless
Sold 13.11.86 in Geneva for Sw.fr.715,000 (£264,182)

Right:
Diamond ring, set with an oval-cut diamond weighing 21.21 carats
With gemological certificate number 5152858 stating that the diamond is E colour and VS
Sold 28.4.87 in New York for $638,000 (£387,371)

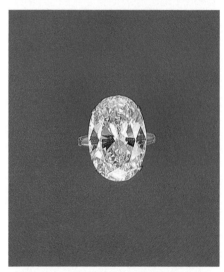

Far right:
Navette-cut fancy pink diamond weighing 3.22 carats
With a certificate from the SSEF stating that the diamond is of natural colour, clarity VVS
Sold 14.5.87 in Geneva for Sw.fr.462,000 (£188,571)

Right:
Unmounted pear-shaped diamond weighing 24.77 carats
With a certificate from the Gemological Institute of America stating that the stone is D colour and flawless, and noting that it is a rare colourless type IIB diamond
Sold 13.11.86 in Geneva for Sw.fr.1,760,000 (£728,778)

Far right:
Single-stone diamond ring, set with a pear-shaped diamond weighing 23.44 carats
With gemological certificate number 5085568 stating that the diamond is D colour and internally flawless
Sold 28.4.87 in New York for $1,100,000 (£667,881)

Above:
Diamond bracelet set with
12 graduated marquise-cut
diamonds weighing a total
of 38.88 carats
By Harry Winston
Sold 22.10.86 in New
York for $550,000
(£384,347)
The property of Caroline
Ryan Foulke

Left:
Diamond floral necklace,
the total weight of the
eight pear-shaped
diamonds in floral clusters
23.29 carats
Signed by Van Cleef &
Arpels, No. NY29073
Sold 22.10.86 in New
York for $385,000
(£269,043)
The property of Caroline
Ryan Foulke

Opposite:
Diamond necklace set with
128 diamonds weighing a
total of 168 carats
By Harry Winston
Sold 22.10.86 in New
York for $902,000
(£630,329)
The property of Caroline
Ryan Foulke

Diamond tiara in the Kokoshnik style
Signed by Cartier
Commissioned in 1928
Sold 14.5.87 in Geneva for Sw.fr.682,000 (£278,367)
This model boldly adopts the traditional Russian Kokoshnik form
and blends it with a structured geometric pattern which was peculiar
to Cartier, London, at the end of the 1920s

Opposite:
Antique emerald and diamond necklace with three
square-cut emeralds weighing 8.84, 13.03 and 6.48
carats and two pear-shaped emeralds weighing
5.74 carats and 6.96 carats
Sold 13.11.86 in Geneva for Sw.fr.825,000
(£341,615)
Previously sold at Christie's on 23 November 1960
on behalf of the Earl of Harewood for £36,000

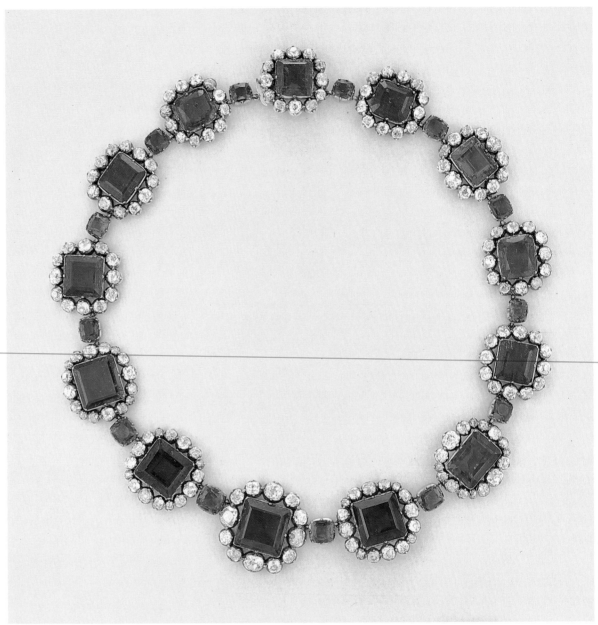

Above:
Emerald and diamond
three-stone ring,
vertically set with a
square-cut emerald of
8.13 carats between two
pear-shaped diamonds
weighing 5.81 carats
and 5.61 carats
respectively
Signed by Boucheron
Sold 14.5.87 in Geneva
for Sw.fr.320,000
(£130,613)

Antique emerald and diamond necklace
Sold 22.11.86 in New York for
$715,000 (£427,120)

Pair of art deco cabochon emerald and diamond ear-pendants, the emeralds weighing 40.04 and 42.01 carats respectively
Sold 28.4.87 in New York for $220,000 (£133,552)

Emerald and diamond clip brooch, the cushion-shaped cabochon emerald carved with an ancient Mughal lily flower and weighing 131.22 carats
Sold 14.5.87 in Geneva for Sw.fr.480,000 (£195,919)

Emerald and diamond bracelet, the fourteen emeralds weighing a total of 35.5 carats
Sold 28.4.87 in New York for $605,000 (£369,579)

Emerald and diamond ring, the square-cut emerald weighing 5.74 carats
Signed by Cartier, No. 3817515
Sold 28.4.87 in New York for $462,000 (£282,224)

Square-cut emerald single-stone ring, the emerald weighing 2.35 carats
Sold 10.12.86 in London for £39,600 ($56,232)

Emerald and diamond pendant including a large square-cut emerald weighing 22.19 carats
Sold 14.5.87 in Geneva for Sw.fr.550,000 (£224,490)

Antique emerald and diamond pendant, the emerald weighing 8.48 carats and the pear-shaped diamonds a total of 28.93 carats
Sold 24.6.87 in London for £187,000 ($299,200)

Above:
Ruby and diamond bracelet
Sold 13.11.86 in Geneva for
Sw.fr.143,000 (£59,214)

Oval cushion-shaped
ruby single-stone ring,
the ruby weighing 3.57
carats
Sold 24.6.87 in London
for £46,200 ($73,920)

Left:
Ruby and diamond clip brooch
Sold 13.11.86 in Geneva for
Sw.fr.214,500 (£88,820)

Diamond and sapphire clip brooch
and pair of ear-clips en suite
Signed by Van Cleef & Arpels
Sold 14.5.87 in Geneva for
Sw.fr.77,000 (£31,885)

Pair of diamond ear-clips
Signed by Bulgari
Sold 14.5.87 in Geneva for
Sw.fr.140,000 (£57,019)

Ruby and diamond ring,
the cushion-cut ruby
weighing 7.43 carats
With certificate number
CS22162 stating that the
ruby is of Burmese origin
Sold 28.4.87 in New York
for $506,000 (£309,103)

Three-stone ruby and diamond ring,
set with an octagonal ruby weighing
17.57 carats, flanked on each side by
a rectangular-cut diamond weighing
4.65 and 4.70 carats respectively
With certificate number CS22146
stating that the ruby is of Burmese
origin
Sold 28.4.87 in New York for
$110,000 (£67,197)

Pair of invisibly-set ruby and
diamond ear-pendants
Signed by Van Cleef & Arpels,
No. NY45196
Sold 28.4.87 in New York for
$110,000 (£67,197)

Diamond necklace
By Harry Winston
Sold 13.11.86 in Geneva for Sw.fr.825,000 (£341,615)

Sapphire and diamond
necklace
Sold 13.11.86 in
Geneva for
Sw.fr.198,000
(£81,988)

Pair of sapphire and
diamond tassel ear-
pendants
Signed by Boucheron
Sold 13.11.86 in
Geneva for
Sw.fr.33,000
(£13,665)

Sapphire and diamond
bracelet
Sold 13.11.86 in
Geneva for
Sw.fr.99,000
(£40,994)

Sapphire single-stone ring, the rectangular sapphire weighing 34.03 carats
With an expertise by Gübelin stating that the sapphire is from Burma
Sold 24.5.87 in Geneva for Sw.fr.950,000 (£387,756)

Antique cabochon sapphire and diamond choker, designed as a line of seven clusters, each set with a cabochon Kashmir sapphire weighing 72.43 carats in total; together with an extension of similar design set with a cabochon Cambodian sapphire weighing 5.33 carats
c.1880
12 in. long
Sold 22.10.86 in New York for $825,000 (£574,113)
From the estate of Mary Stanley-Clarke

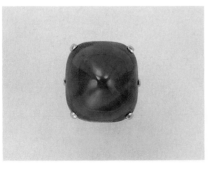

Cabochon sapphire single-stone ring, the rectangular cabochon sapphire of pyramid form and weighing 53.92 carats
With a personal affidavit from Dr Eduard Gübelin stating that the sapphire is from Kashmir
Sold 14.5.87 in Geneva for Sw.fr.1,000,000 (£408,164)

Sapphire and diamond ring set with a sugar-loaf cabochon sapphire weighing 31.21 carats
By Winston
Sold 14.5.87 in Geneva for Sw.fr.280,000 (£114,286)

Pair of black and white pearl and diamond ear-clips, the circular-cut diamond four-stone mounts set with one black and one white button pearl measuring 16.6 mm. and 17.9 mm. respectively
With an expertise by Gübelin stating that the pearls are natural
Sold 14.5.87 in Geneva for Sw.fr.100,000 (£40,816)

Natural pearl and diamond
necklace, the largest pearl
measuring 18.5 × 12.5 mm.
*c.*1913
Signed by Cartier, Paris,
Londres, New York
With gemological certificate
number 1929532 stating
that the pearls are natural
Sold 22.10.86 in New York
for $82,500 (£56,507)

The 'Pelegrina' Pearl

HANS NADELHOFFER

Princess Tatiana Youssoupoff wore it dangling from her right ear, 150 years later Princess Zenaîde wore it as a pendant on a long pearl sautoir: the pearl that outshone so many of the dazzling jewels in the Youssoupoff vaults was 'La Pelegrina'.

Where and when Princess Tatiana acquired the pearl is not certain. However, the Princess, a contemporary of Napoleon, Stendhal and Pushkin, and a true romantic whose ideals had once led her to refuse the inheritance of the eccentric Duchess of Kingston, treasured the 'Pelegrina' as no other jewel, with the possible exception of the Polar Star Diamond (the fabulous 41 carat Golconda stone, later seen in the collection of Lydia, Lady Deterding).

The pearl, remarkable for its oval shape and lustrous skin, was the finest in a collection of pearls unparallelled even in Tsarist Russia. It is interesting to note that the Régente Pearl of 337 grains, a particular favourite of Empress Eugénie, was added to the collection in 1887 follow-ing the sale of the French crown jewels. Peter Fabergé purchased it in Paris and brought it to Russia. He paid 176,000 French francs, whereas the price of 'La Pelegrina' in 1826 was rumoured to have been 200,000 roubles, a much steeper sum by comparison.

Twenty-five emerald necklaces, 255 brooches, thirteen tiaras and forty-two bracelets were allegedly found by the Bolsheviks in Youssoupoff's Moscow palace in 1925, but the 'Pelegrina' was surprisingly not amongst this staggering collection. Prince Felix had cunningly rescued the pearl and spirited it away to the West. Sadly, financial troubles plagued the prince, forcing him initially to pledge all his jewellery and eventually to sell it piece by piece. Only the 'Pelegrina' remained, from which he could not bear to be parted. In 1953 he finally sold it to the Geneva jeweller Jean Lombard, who had maintained close contact with the ancient Russian nobility.

The sale organized by Christie's Geneva proved a sensational success. The price of the pearl spiralled to Sw.fr.682,000 (£278,367), a figure which no other pearl had ever reached at auction.

Pearl and diamond pendant 'La Pelegrina', the pear-shaped
pearl of 133.16 grains
Sold 14.5.87 in Geneva for Sw.fr.682,000 (£278,367)
Record auction price for a pearl

Watercolour of Princess Tatiana Youssoupoff wearing the
Pelegrina pearl as an earring

Aquamarine and
diamond parure
comprising a necklace,
an aquamarine and
diamond lattice-work
bracelet, a pair of
aquamarine and
diamond ear-
pendants, an
aquamarine bar
brooch and an
aquamarine single-
stone ring
Signed by Cartier,
London
Sold 13.11.86 in
Geneva for
Sw.fr.82,500
(£34,162)

Right:
Art deco black onyx and
diamond bracelet watch
By Cartier
Sold 5.11.86 in London for
£8,250 ($11,691)

Right centre:
Diamond and ruby clip brooch
Signed Cartier
Sold 1.10.86 in London for
£25,300 ($36,306)

Far right:
Carved tourmaline, citrine,
turquoise, enamel and
brilliant-cut diamond flowerpot
brooch
By Cartier
Sold 24.6.87 in London for
£2,530 ($4,048)

Right:
Art deco banded agate and
coral pen with 18 carat gold
and black enamel mounts
By Cartier
Sold 29.4.87 in London for
£3,300 ($5,436)

Right:
Art deco lapis lazuli, diamond
and jade 'Stalactite' fob watch
Signed by Janesich
Sold 13.11.86 in Geneva for
Sw.fr.60,500 (£25,052)

Ruby, diamond and amethyst
clip brooch
Signed by Cartier, London
Sold 14.5.87 in Geneva for
Sw.fr.52,800 (£21,535)

Multi-gem and diamond pendant
Signed by Boucheron
Sold 14.5.87 in Geneva for
Sw.fr.22,000 (£8,987)

Cabochon sapphire, diamond and ruby fringe necklace
Signed by Bulgari
The sapphires weighing 304.00 carats total, the rubies weighing 21.00 carats total, the diamonds weighing 33.00 carats total
Sold 28.4.87 in New York for $88,000 (£53,757)

Blond horn and enamel
stomacher
Engraved Lalique
Sold 13.11.86 in Geneva for
Sw.fr.176,000 (£72,877)

Aquamarine, diamond, enamel and glass brooch
Engraved Lalique
Sold 13.11.86 in Geneva for Sw.fr.209,000 (£86,542)

Far left:
Agate cameo and gold brooch
Signed by Carlo Castellani
Sold 14.5.87 in Geneva for
Sw.fr.12,000 (£4,898)

Left:
Renaissance jewelled gold and enamel
pendant
Last quarter of the 16th century; the
ring with later Dutch control mark
1½ in. (3.8 cm.) long
Sold 24.6.87 in London for £16,500
($26,400)

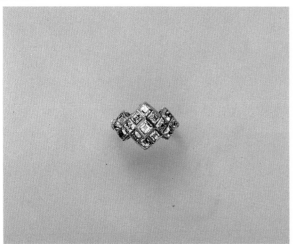

Gold and diamond ring
*c.*1680
Sold 24.6.87 in London for £29,700 ($47,520)

Antique emerald and gold brooch, the emerald
weighing 89.47 carats and engraved on the rear
with 'M' within foliate scrolls
Sold 14.5.87 in Geneva for Sw.fr.120,000
(£48,980)
By family tradition given by Napoleon III to the
daughter of the Egyptian Khedive. A more
likely source is however Princess Mathilde,
cousin of the Emperor, who was fond of
jewellery symbolic of her Christian name.

Silver

Oval two-handled monteith
By Hendrik van Heuven
Arnhem, *c.*1740
14³⁄₄ in. (37.6 cm.) long
Sold 27.3.87 in Amsterdam for D.fl.104,400 (£31,164)

The Patiño Collection

CHRISTOPHER HARTOP

Traditionally quiet, low-key affairs composed mainly of serious collectors and dealers, silver sales seldom generate the excitement of major picture sales. The Patiño sale last autumn, however, held in the modern ambiance of Christie's New York saleroom, had all the glitter and heady atmosphere of an evening Impressionist sale. For, in addition to collectors and dealers from around the world, many of the late Antenor Patiño's friends had gathered to pay tribute to a defiantly traditional collector with a much celebrated discerning eye.

Antenor Patiño's collecting career spanned six decades. First introduced to silver by his father, Simon Patiño, the Bolivian 'Tin King', surprisingly his collection was started with modern silver – a magnificent dinner service commissioned from Chaumet in 1918. Renewed interest today in the Louis XVI revival style was reflected in a total price of $144,100 for the service.

As a collector, Antenor Patiño concentrated on the period 1680–1800, and although his tastes were traditional, they were far-ranging. It was not surprising to his friends that the best pieces of rococo silver in the collection were the Meissonnier-inspired candelabra made, not in France, but in Spain by the Madrid court goldsmith, Juan de San Fauri, which sold for $88,000.

The richness of the Patiño Collection lay in silver-gilt, the taste for which he had also inherited from his father. From the massive dishes and covers commissioned by Augustus the Strong for the Dresden Green Vaults in 1718 to the superb salvers, or *tazze*, engraved with the arms of the first Duke of Devonshire, it is easy to see why silver-gilt exerted such a great fascination over Antenor Patiño. The Devonshire *tazze* were returning to Christie's – in a different location – after nearly twenty years, having first appeared on the market in the sale of objects from Chatsworth held at King Street in 1958. Then the price had been £400; now they realized $220,000.

The sale totalled an astounding $2,398,660, a record for a silver sale held anywhere in the world.

One of a pair of German
silver-gilt second-course
dishes and covers
The dishes by Gottlieb
Menzel, Augsburg,
1717–18; the covers by
Christian Winter,
Augsburg, 1729–30
The dishes 12¾ in.
(32.7 cm.) diameter; the
covers 11⅜ in.
(29 cm.) diameter
Sold 28.10.86 in New York
for $192,500 (£136,622)
From the Patiño Collection

Pair of German four-light candelabra
By Christian Heinrich Ingermann
Dresden, mid-18th century
18 in. (45.5 cm.) high
Sold 27.10.86 in New York for $121,000 (£85,877)

Pair of William and Mary silver-gilt salvers
c. 1690
11¼ in. (28.5 cm.) high
Sold 28.10.86 in New York for
$220,000 (£156,140)
From the Patiño Collection

Charles II parcel-gilt cage-work cup
London *c.* 1670
6⅛ in. (15.5 cm.) high
Sold 10.12.86 in New York for
$66,000 (£46,479)
From the collection of Mrs Elizabeth and the late Dr Edward F. Rosenberg

Pair of Queen Anne
cylindrical wine-coolers
By John Bodington
*c.*1710
9½ in. (24 cm.) high
Sold 20.5.87 in London for
£231,000 ($388,311)

Set of six Charles II shell-
shaped dishes
By Samuel Hood
1675
4¾ in. (11.9 cm.) wide
Sold 8.7.87 in London for
£35,200 ($56,320)

George II plain oval shaving bowl, jug and
soap box
By James Shruder
1744
The bowl 12¾ in. (32.5 cm.) wide; the jug
7½ in. (19.1 cm.) high
Sold 20.5.87 in London for £110,000
($184,910)

Set of three Charles II casters
The smaller casters 1682, the larger caster
1683
6in. (16.1 cm.) and 7 in. (17.8 cm.) high
Sold 8.7.87 in London for £44,000
($70,400)

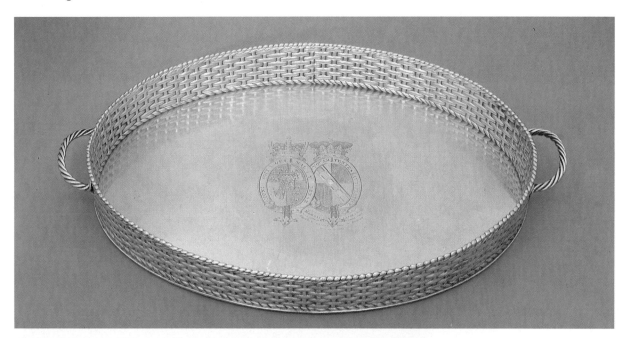

George III silver-gilt two-handled tray
By John Pitts or Joseph Preedy
Engraved with the royal arms, the Sackville coat of arms and inscribed 'Given by his most Excellent MAJESTY GEORGE the third, to his Godson, George John Frederick Sackville, Duke of Dorset. Born Novr. 15 1793'
1803
26¼ in. (66.8 cm.)
Sold 20.5.87 in London for £41,800 ($70,266)

George II circular bread basket
By Thomas Farren
1725
12¾ in. (32.5 cm.) diameter
Sold 20.5.87 in London for £66,000 ($110,946)

The Richmond race
cup
By Daniel Smith and
Robert Sharp
1764
19 in. (48.3 cm.) high
Sold 8.7.87 in London
for £66,000 ($105,600)

George II kettle, stand and
lamp
By Paul de Lamerie
London, 1751
14½ in. (37 cm.) high
Sold 27.10.86 in New York
for $220,000 (£156,473)

Two from a set of four George III silver-gilt two-handled wine-coolers, collars and liners
By Paul Storr
The bases stamped 'RUNDELL BRIDGE ET RUNDELL AURIFICES REGIS ET PRINCIPIS WALLIAE REGENTIS BRITANNIAE'
1813
11 in. (28 cm.) high
Sold 20.5.87 in London for £220,000 ($369,820)
By order of the trustees of the Knole Estate

George II épergne
By Paul de Lamerie
The waiters 1736, the centrepiece 1737, the branches and brackets with the Sterling Standard mark in use until 1739, and the feet
with the maker's mark of John S. Hunt and addition marks for 1846
14¼ in. (36.3 cm.) high; 27¼ in. (69.3 cm.) long; the oval central dish
13¾ in. (35 cm.) long; the waiters 7 in. (17.8 cm.) diameter
Sold 17.12.86 in London for £770,000 ($1,092,630)
From the collection of the Earl of Portalington and the Hon. John Dawson-Damer
Record auction price for any single piece of silver

George III two-handled tea-urn and cover
By Matthew Boulton and John Fothergill
Birmingham, 1775
18½ in. (47 cm.) high
Sold 27.5.87 at Great Tew Park in Oxfordshire for £40,700 ($66,016)

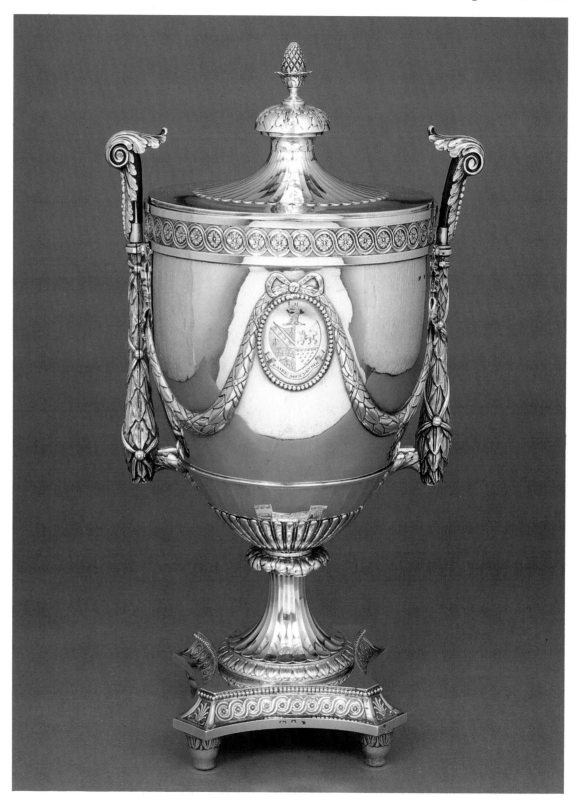

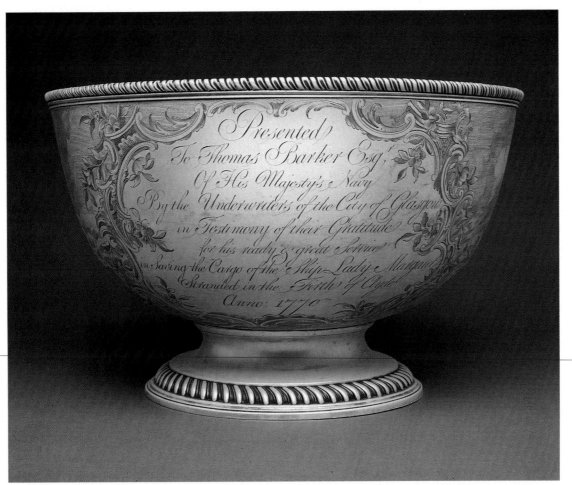

George III presentation
punch-bowl
By Daniel Smith and
Robert Sharp
London 1770
14⅛ in. (36 cm.) diameter
Sold 29.4.87 in New York
for $220,000 (£133,577)

'Last night the owners of the ship *Lady Margaret* received intelligence by an express from Huntersound, of that vessel's being stranded a little to the southward of Pencorse. In the last violent gale of wind, she was bound for James River, Virginia, with a very valuable cargo on board, and about half an hour after eleven o'clock on Tuesday night, steering close under the lee of the Little Cumraes, with the wind at west, they were unluckily overtaken with a hard gale of wind which suddenly shifting them to the northward, drove them right on shore. The master and crew did everything in their power to prevent the ship striking against the rocks, by cutting away the main and foremasts – it is thought that the cargo will be very much damaged, when the express came away, the hold of the ship was full of water.'

This dramatic contemporary account of the wreck of the *Lady Margaret* appeared in the Glasgow Journal of 18–25 January 1770. The event was also commemorated by the presentation of this punch-bowl to Thomas Barker, Esq., of His Majesty's Navy, for his part in the rescue of the ship's cargo. It is superbly engraved with scenes of the foundering ship and is without doubt one of the finest examples of engraved English silver from the second half of the 18th century. Its whereabouts had been unknown until it was consigned to Christie's New York for sale by a direct descendant of the original recipient, whose family had moved to Virginia around the turn of the century.

Victorian equestrian group of an Indian spearing a buffalo
By Charles Frederick Hancock, from a model by Raphael Monti
London, 1872
20½ in. (52 cm.) long
Sold 27.10.86 in New York for $41,800 (£29,230)
Sold in 1886 from the collection of Mary Jane Morgan, who presumably purchased it from Hancocks. The wife of
Charles Morgan, the railroad and steamship tycoon, she is said to have spent over $4,000,000 on art and jewels
before her death. Most of her silver was specially commissioned from Tiffany, much of it with Indian themes, and
this figure was one of the few pieces of European silver in the collection. The next lot in the 1886 sale was a
'carved ebonized pedestal for the above, made by Messrs. Herter Brothers', present whereabouts unknown.

Empire silver-gilt sucrier
By J.B.C. Odiot
Paris, 1809–19
12½ in. (31.5 cm.) high
Sold 12.5.87 in Geneva for
Sw.fr.286,000 (£116,735)

Objects of Art and Vertu

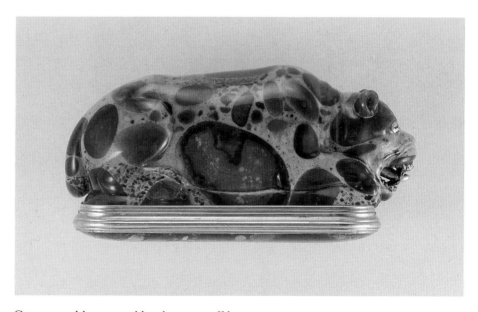

German gold-mounted hardstone snuff-box
Dresden, *c.*1750
3¾ in. (9.7 cm.) long
Sold 11.11.86 in Geneva for Sw.fr.74,800
(£30,800)

Above left:
George I heavy gold snuff-box
*c.*1715
3⅛ in. (8 cm.) long
Sold 17.12.86 in London for £15,400 ($21,853)

Above:
Louis XV jewelled gold snuff-box
By Daniel Gouers, with the charge and décharge of Hubert
Louvet
Engraved 'Gouers AParis'
Paris, 1732–3
3 in. (7.8 cm.) long
Sold 12.5.87 in Geneva for Sw.fr.275,000 (£112,244)

Left:
Swiss vari-colour gold and enamel singing-bird box
The movement by Rochat Frères
Geneva, *c.* 1820
3 in. (7.9 cm.) long
Sold 11.11.86 in Geneva for Sw.fr.82,500 (£33,530)

Frederick the Great jewelled gold-mounted hardstone snuff-box
Berlin, *c.*1755
4 in. (10 cm.) long
Sold 11.11.86 in Geneva for Sw.fr.1,870,000 (£763,265)
Record auction price for a snuff-box

German documentary gold and silver-gilt mounted, enamel and rock-crystal centre-piece
By Reinhold Vasters
Aachen, *c.* 1870–90
The stand 8¼ in. (22 cm.) wide; the vase 5¾ in. (13.3 cm.) high
Sold 17.12.86 in London for £35,200 ($49,949)

Oval bust-length miniature of King
Edward VII
By Downey
3 in. (7.6 cm.) long
Sold 17.3.87 in London for £8,800
($13,957)
The property of John Phillips, Esq.

Gold-mounted riding whip
32¼ in. (82 cm.) long
Sold 17.3.87 in London for
£7,700 ($12,212)

These items were presented to Alice Keppel by King Edward VII. They
then passed to her daughter Violet (Mrs Denys Trefusis) and were bequeathed
by her to the vendor.

Right centre:
Birmingham two-handled
mug painted after J.E.
Nilson (1721–88)
*c.*1765
3¼ in. (8 cm.) high
Sold 18.3.87 in London for
£2,310 ($3,690)
From the Mullens
Collection

Two Birmingham white
ground beakers
*c.*1760
3⅛ in. (8 cm.) high
Sold 18.3.87 in London for
£2,310 ($3,690)
From the Mullens
Collection

Birmingham casket, the
cover painted with *Pour
garder l'honneur d'une
belle…c'est trop peu de Pierrot
pour faire sentinelle*, after
Cochin the Younger after
Watteau
*c.*1755
7⅝ in. (19.2 cm.) long
Sold 18.3.87 in London for
£27,500 ($43,918)
From the Mullens
Collection

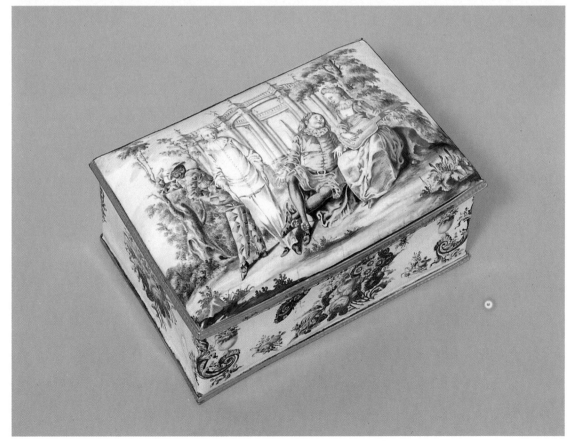

SAMUEL COOPER
Barbara Villiers, Countess of Castelmaine and Duchess of Cleveland
Signed with monogram and dated 1664
On vellum
Oval, 3¼ in. (8.3 cm.)
Sold 26.11.86 in London for £38,500 ($54,786)
Record auction price for a work by the artist

HENRY BONE, R.A.
Henry VIII after Hans Holbein
Signed and dated 1823
Enamel
Rectangular, 13¾ in. (35 cm.) high
Sold 17.3.87 in London for £52,800 ($83,741)
Record auction price for a work by the artist

Right:
LOUIS MARIE AUTISSIER
Marie-Amélie Thérèse, Duchess of Orléans
Signed and dated 1820
Oval, $2\frac{5}{8}$ in. (6.5 cm.) high
Sold 17.3.87 in London for
£11,000 ($17,446)

Far right:
JOHN SMART
A Young Girl
Signed with initials and
dated 1804
Oval, 3 in. (7.6 cm.) high
Sold 17.3.87 in London for
£14,300 ($22,680)

Right centre:
GEORGE CHINNERY
Portrait of an Officer of the Royal Horse Artillery
Signed on the reverse and
dated 1794 with the address
Sackville Street
Oval, $3\frac{1}{2}$ in. (8.9 cm.) high
Sold 17.3.87 in London for
£16,500 ($26,169)

Right:
JOHN SMART
Portrait of an Officer of the 5th Madras Native Infantry
Signed with initials and
dated 1794 and I for India
Oval, 3 in. (7.7 cm.) high
Sold 17.3.87 in London for
£13,200 ($20,936)

Far right:
ABRAHAM DANIEL
Portrait of Master T. Keighley
Guilloche surmounted by a
blue and white enamel
plaque enhanced with the
initials TK in rose-cut
diamonds
Oval, 3 in. (7.6 cm.) high
Sold 17.3.87 in London for
£13,200 ($20,936)

Porcelain from the Russian Imperial Porcelain Factory

ALEXIS DE TIESENHAUSEN

Throughout its existence (1744-1917) one of the main characteristics of the Imperial Porcelain Factory was the high quality of the painting and decoration on the porcelain. The development of styles during the reigns of Catherine II, Nicholas I and Alexander III did not detract from the high standard of execution.

This characteristic, together with the new fashion for collecting Russian art explains the high prices fetched by porcelain in specialized Russian Works of Art sales held in London and New York this season. For example, a covered cup and saucer, c.1760, which sold at auction in the 1960s for the sum of 240 guineas, made £8,800 in April 1987. The cup is painted with the coat of arms and crest of Count Rumiantsev Zadunaiski and the saucer gilt with his interlaced initials within a trophy of arms. It is interesting to note that the Hermitage has only one teacup from this service in its collection. The trophy of arms is similar to one that appears on a service made for Prince Dolgoruki-Crimski. Both Count Rumiantsev and Prince Dolgoruki fought in the Turkish War in the 1760s, and the similarity in the services suggests that they were part of a special order from Catherine the Great to award to heroes of that war.

Further examples of fine quality porcelain made during the 18th century are the two cups, saucers and spoons, which, according to Alexander Popov, come from Catherine the Great's private service. Each cup is painted with the profile of Catherine the Great on a burgundy ground within a circular gold ciselé frame embellished with ribbon-tied laurel leaves, and each saucer is painted with central ciselé gold cypher of the Empress on similarly coloured ground. One of these cups and saucers was sold for £15,400 by Christie's in April 1987.

During the reign of Nicholas I the Imperial Porcelain Factory produced important vases reproducing Old Masters on the sides. A pair of monumental two-handled campana vases was sold in London for £60,500 in April 1987. The vases are painted in the Dutch style, with huntsmen on horseback standing with hounds in extensive landscapes, in square panels (one painting after Wouwerman), one panel signed by the factory painter N. Kornilov, who worked during the reigns of Alexander I, Nicholas I and Alexander II.

The Raphael Service was the largest and most important porcelain service produced during the reign of Alexander III (1881–94), and illustrates the last period of the Imperial Porcelain Factory. The designs were originally derived from Raphael frescoes in the loggias of the Vatican and were reproduced in the Winter Palace during the reign of Catherine the Great. They probably served as a direct source of inspiration for the service. A set of twelve dinner plates was sold in New York last April for $31,900, proving that interest in Russian porcelain flourishes on both sides of the Atlantic.

Corner plates:
Four from a set of
eight Alexander III
imperial porcelain
soup-plates from the
Raphael Service, each
marked with a gilt
overglaze imperial
cypher
By the Imperial
Porcelain Factory, St.
Petersburg
Dated 1884, 1892 and
1894
Sold 29.4.87 in New
York for $18,700
(£11,354)

Remaining plates:
Eight from a set of 12
imperial porcelain
dinner-plates from the
Raphael Service, each
marked with a gilt
overglaze imperial
cypher
By the Imperial
Porcelain Factory, St.
Petersburg
Period of Alexander III
and Nicholas II
Dated 1886, 1890,
1891, 1892, 1899 and
1903
Sold 29.4.87 in New
York for $31,900
(£19,369)

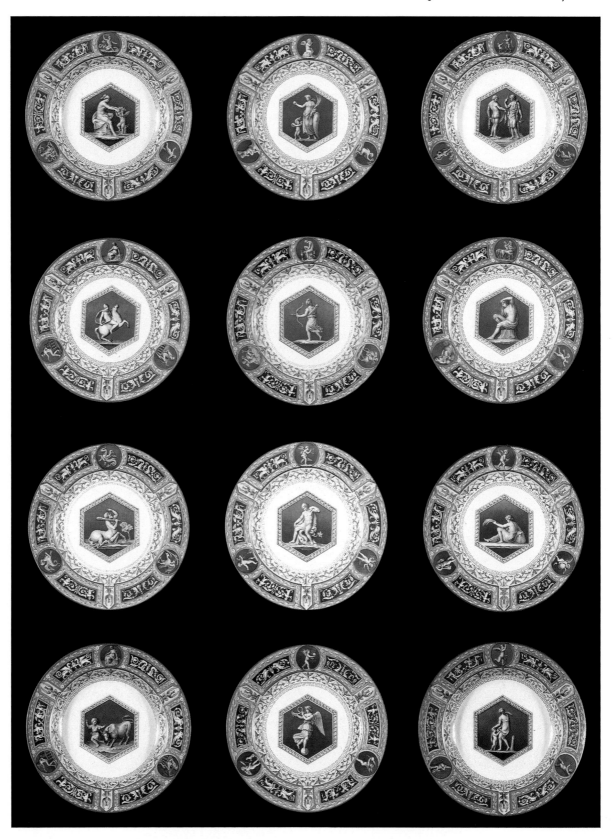

Far left:
Imperial porcelain covered cup and
saucer, the cup painted with the coat of
arms and crest of Count P.A.
Rumiantsev-Zadunaiski
By the Imperial Porcelain Factory, St.
Petersburg
Period of Elizabeth I, *c.*1760
3¼ in. (8.3 cm.) high with cover
Sold 8.4.87 in London for £8,800
($14,168)

Left centre:
Imperial porcelain covered cup, saucer
and spoon, the cup with a profile of
Catherine the Great *en grisaille*
By the Imperial Porcelain Factory, St.
Petersburg
Period of Catherine II
Sold 8.4.87 in London for £15,400
($24,794)

Above left:
Imperial porcelain covered cup, saucer
and spoon, the cup with a profile of
Catherine the Great *en grisaille*
By the Imperial Porcelain Factory, St.
Petersburg
Period of Catherine II
Sold 8.4.87 in London for £12,100
($19,481)

Far left, above and below:
Two porcelain plates painted with
military scenes of the Imperial Guard
Preobrajensky regiment
By the Imperial Porcelain Factory, St.
Petersburg
Period of Nicholas I
Dated 1823 and 1832
Sold 8.4.87 in London for £8,800
($14,168)

Left, above and below:
Two porcelain plates painted with
military scenes of the Imperial Guard
Dragoon regiment
Period of Nicholas I
Dated 1830 and 1833
Sold 8.4.87 in London for £5,500 ($8,855)

Ormolu-mounted malachite desk set
1830–40
12 ½ in. (31.8 cm.) wide
Sold 16.10.86 in London for £5,500 ($7,909)

Silver table-lighter formed as an elephant
Marked Fabergé, worked by Julius Rappoport, St. Petersburg
c. 1890
4¼ in. (10.7 cm.) long
Sold 13.5.87 in Geneva for Sw.fr.126,000 (£51,209)

Gold-mounted jewelled hardstone carving of a flower study
By Fabergé, worked by Henrik Wigström, St. Petersburg
1908–17
2¾ in. (7 cm.) high
Sold 13.5.87 in Geneva for Sw.fr.143,500 (£58,571)

Jewelled guilloché enamel three-colour
miniature photograph frame
Marked Fabergé, worked by Victor
Aarne, St. Petersburg
1899–1903
2¼ in. (5.8 cm.) high
Sold 12.11.86 in Geneva for
Sw.fr.37,400 (£15,487)

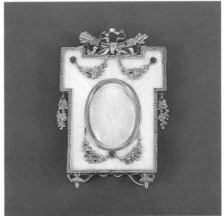

Jewelled two-colour gold presentation
brooch
By Fabergé, worked by August
Hollming, St. Petersburg, No. 2999
c.1900
2 in. (5 cm.) long
Sold 13.5.87 in Geneva for
Sw.fr.20,900 (£8,531)

Silver-gilt niello icon of Saints Feodor and Paraskeva
Signed by the Brothers Popov, Viliki Ustyug; assaymaster
Alexei Torlov, Moscow
1773
11¾ in. (30.1 cm.) high; 10½ in. (26.5 cm.) wide
Sold 12.11.86 in Geneva for Sw.fr.63,800 (£26,419)

Works of Art

18th-century English marble bust of a negro
By Francis Harwood
Signed and dated 1758
26¾ in. (68 cm.) high
Sold 9.4.87 in London for £99,000 ($159,588)

White marble portrait bust of Lord Byron
By Bertel Thorvaldsen, Danish
Signed
c. 1818–19
19½ in. (49.5 cm.) high
Sold 13.6.87 in New York for $275,000 (£171,875)
From the collection of the Troy Public Library

Louis XVI marble bust of Madame la Marquise de Gestas
By Augustin Pajou
Signed and dated 1775
29⅛ in. (74 cm.) high
Sold 17.6.87 in London for £35,200 ($56,320)

Painted plaster bust of
Thomas Jefferson
By Jean Antoine Houdon,
French
With applied red wax seal
inscribed 'ACADEM ROYALE DE
PEINTURE ET SCULPT HOUDON
SC'
28¾ in. (73 cm.) high
Sold 29.5.87 in New York
for $2,860,000 (£1,682,353)
Record auction price for a
portrait bust and for a piece
of pre-20th-century
sculpture

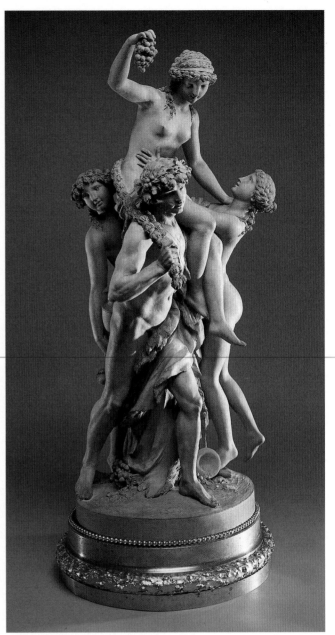

French terracotta maquette of Admiral de Tourville
By Joseph Marin
Early 19th century
16⅜ in. (41.5 cm.) high
Sold 9.4.87 in London for £15,400 ($24,825)

Terracotta group of a Bacchant and three Bacchantes
By Claude-Michel, called Clodion, French
Signed and dated 1800
25 in. (63.5 cm.) high
Sold 13.6.87 in New York for $352,000 (£220,000)

Venetian marble relief of
Mucius Scaevola
By Giovanni Maria Mosca
Early 16th century
13½ × 8¼ in.
(34.5 × 21 cm.)
Sold 7.7.87 in London for
£104,500 ($167,200)
Sold by order of the trustees
of the 10th Duke of Leeds
will trust

Florentine gilt bronze statuette of Mars
By Giambologna
Monogrammed 'I.B.'
16th century
15½ in. (39.4 cm.)
Sold 17.6.87 in London for £660,000
($1,056,000)

Opposite:
Anglo-Italian bronze relief of the
temptation of Adam and Eve
By Francesco Fanelli
Early 17th century
10½ × 8½ (27 × 21.5 cm.)
Sold 10.12.86 in London for £46,200
($65,882)
From the Wernher Collection at Luton
Hoo

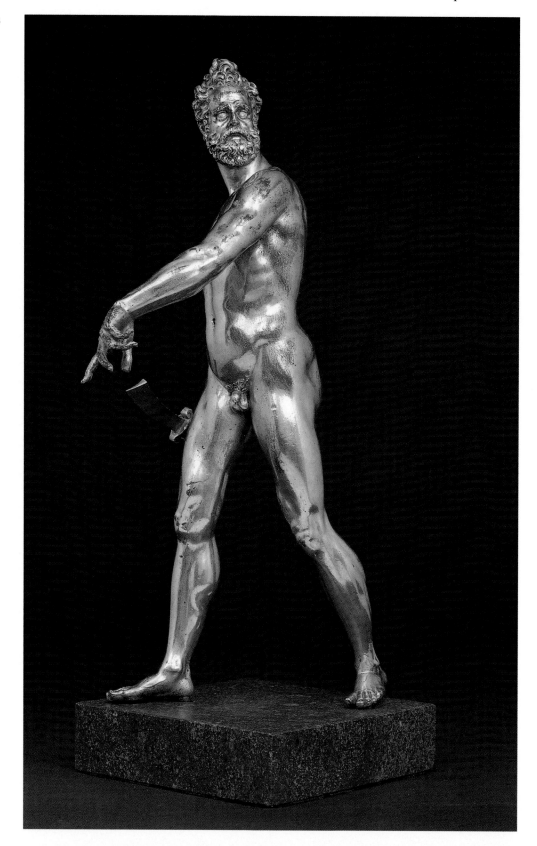

Byzantine processional cross (back view)
10th–11th century
22¾ × 15 in. (58 × 38.5 cm.)
Sold 9.4.87 in London for £330,000 ($531,960)

Limoges enamel crozier head of the Annunciation
Inscribed on both sides 'AVE MARIA GRA PLEM'
Mid-13th century
11 in. (28 cm.) high
Sold 7.7.87 in London for £70,400 ($112,640)

Bronze relief *Amor Caritas*
By Augustus Saint-Gaudens, American
Inscribed 'AMOR CARITAS' and 'AUGUSTUS SAINT GAUDENS
MDCCCXCVIII' and 'IN MEMORY OF NANCY LEGGE WOODE HOOPER
MDCCCXIX–MDCCCXCVIII'
1898
Dark green patina
39⅞ in. (101.3 cm.) high
Sold 5.12.86 in New York for $160,000 (£113,155)
From the collection of the Unitarian Society, Fall River,
Massachusetts

Bronze group depicting *Europa and the Bull*
By Carl Milles, Swedish
Inscribed 'Carl Milles' and 'Herman Bergman Fud.'
*c.*1921–6
Rich red-brown green patina
31 in. (78.8 cm.) high; 24½ in. (62.2 cm.) wide
Sold 5.12.86 in New York for $165,000 (£116,691)

French bronze figure of the
'Cheval Turc'
Cast from a model by Antoine
Louis Barye
Mid-19th century
$15\frac{1}{4} \times 11\frac{5}{8}$ in. (38.5 × 29.5 cm.)
Sold 14.5.87 in London for
£49,500 ($82,170)

English bronze statue of physical
energy
By George Frederick Watts
Late 19th century
Sold 29.1.87 in London for
£27,500 ($42,130)

Austrian marble figure of Diana
By Victor Tilgner
Signed and dated 1896
50 in. (127 cm.) high
Sold 29.1.87 in London for £55,000 ($84,260)
Record auction price for a work by the artist

American Carrara marble lifesize figure of Pandora
By C.B. Ives
Signed 'C.B. Ives Fecit. Romae. 1858'
67 in. (170 cm.) high
Sold 22/24.9.86 at Callaly Castle in Northumberland for
£24,200 ($35,090)

Right:
One of four oak open
armchairs
By Bell & Coupland,
Preston
Early Victorian
Sold 29.1.87 in London for
£7,700 ($11,797)

One of a pair of oak pedestals
Designed by William Burges
1853
43 in. (109.5 cm.) high
Sold 27.5.87 at Great Tew Park in
Oxfordshire for £22,000 ($35,684)

Below:
Ebony and marquetry
octagonal library table
By Edward Holmes Baldock
Early Victorian
29½ in. (75 cm.) high;
58 in. (147.5 cm.) wide
Sold 25.9.86 in London for
£7,700 ($11,096)

Mahogany bed
By Mathias Ginsbach, with
sculptured decoration by
Auguste Rodin
1882
64¼ in. (163 cm.) high;
60 in. (152 cm.) wide;
90¼ in. (229 cm.) long
Sold 1.2.87 in Monaco for
F.fr.1,110,000 (£119,612)

Continental neo-classic
patinated bronze and
ormolu-mounted mahogany
bed
Early 19th century
71 in. (177.5 cm.) wide;
104½ in. (262.5 cm.) long
Sold 13.6.87 in New York
for $104,500 (£65,313)

Right:
Egyptian solid gold snake bracelet
Romano-Egyptian
150g. weight
Sold 10.12.86 in London for £17,600
($24,992)

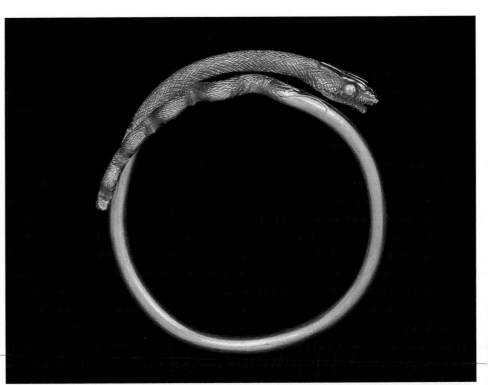

Above:
Red jasper syncretistic statuette of Tueris
6th–4th century BC
2¾ in. (7.5 cm.) high
Sold 10.12.86 in London for £13,200
($18,744)

Gold medallion of Gordian
III, 10 aurei, on gold snake-
headed chain
242 AD, the chain late
3rd–early 4th century AD
The medallion 2 in.
(5.2 cm.) diameter; the
chain 21½ in.
(52.5 cm.) long
Sold 10.7.87 in London for
£99,000 ($158,400)

Opposite:
Blue and white glazed
composition pectoral
Early Dynasty XIX
4¼ × 3½ in. (11 × 9 cm.)
Sold 10.12.86 in London for
£10,450 ($14,839)

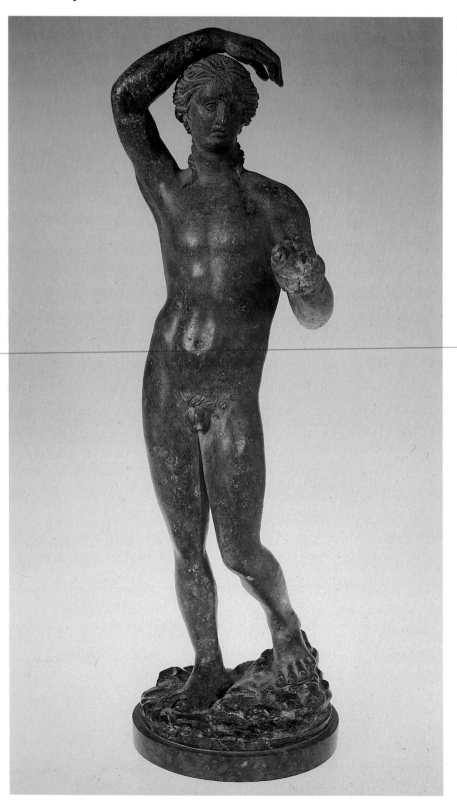

Bronze figure of Apollo
1st–2nd century AD
22 in. (56 cm.) high
Sold 10.7.87 in London for £46,800 ($74,880)

Marble cuirassed bust of the
Emperor Septimius Severus
After 200 AD
34¾ in. (88 cm.) high
Sold 10.7.87 in London for
£220,000 ($352,000)
Formerly at Marbury Hall

Classical Sculpture formerly at Marbury Hall, Cheshire

CHRISTINE INSLEY GREEN

The sale of fourteen items of sculpture on 10 July 1987 fetched the record sum of £1.5 million, individual items breaking one record after another. Thus was the interest in classical sculpture, so intermittently manifest since the sale of Hope sculpture at Christie's in 1917, revived in a brief twenty minutes of excited bidding.

The provenance of the Hon. James Smith Barry and Marbury Hall accounted for much of the interest. However, the lack of restoration since the 18th century (apart from the recent removal of period restorations on the equestrian figure) and the fact these pieces had remained unseen by scholars for the most part of this century were added bonuses.

The Hon. James Smith Barry visited Rome between 1771 and 1776. He was a close friend and pupil of the elder great English collector Charles Townley, with whom he travelled. This was the period when the major English sculpture collections were being formed. Thomas Jenkins and Gavin Hamilton resided in Rome and were agents for such collectors, Jenkins affording handsome credit to the young and as yet untitled Barry.

The Townley archive holds records of Barry's purchases: 'Bust of Antoninus Pius large life £60' (this piece was sold by Christie's for £33,000); 'Bust of Mar Aurelius £80' (sold for £99,000) and 'Bust of Sept Severus £50' (sold for £220,000). 'Head of Juno £20' possibly refers to the Empress Livia, which sold for £154,000.

At the same time that Barry was purchasing sculpture for Belmont and eventually Marbury Hall, great Italian collections formed in the 16th and 17th centuries were being disbanded. Such a one was the collection of Ciriaco Hasdrubal Mattei, housed in the Villa Mattei on the Caelian Hill in Rome, and which his bankrupt heir, Giuseppe, was forced to sell. Pope Clement XIV, who controlled the antiquities' market, selected thirty-four important pieces which would eventually stand in the Vatican Museum. The rest came on the market. Barry bought the 'Bacchante' or Maenad, which sold for £242,000, the highest price paid at auction for a piece of classical sculpture. He also acquired the figure of Apollo for £400. This sold at Christie's for £110,000.

Since the papal control of antiquities was so strong, Gavin Hamilton resorted to his own excavations. One of the sites at Tor Colombaro on the Via Appia yielded the equestrian figure restored as 'Paris/Amazone'. Hamilton sold it to Jenkins, who intended to sell it to Lord Shelburne, but eventually Barry bought it for £300. This sculpture fetched £198,000. Barry purchased another figure restored as 'Paris/Herdsman' for £200, and this sold for £159,500.

These sculptures were brought back to England, first to Belmont and then Marbury Hall, where they were seen by Dallaway, the Comte de Clarac, Waagen and Michaelis, who observed they were displayed in too dark surroundings. They then fell into obscurity. The house was sold in 1936 and some of the sculptures appeared on the London market, fetching sometimes less than their original purchase price. Marbury Hall was demolished in 1956. The fourteen sculptures which appeared on the market on 10 July had remained in the family, and were the last substantial portion. It was therefore gratifying that, after more than two centuries, the passion of the Hon. James Smith Barry for collecting classical sculpture should finally have been rekindled in Christie's Great Rooms.

Greek marble statue of an equestrian huntsman
Roman, *c.*1st–2nd century AD
28 in. (71 cm.) high; 35 in. (89 cm.) long
Sold 10.7.87 in London for £198,000 ($316,800)
Formerly at Marbury Hall

Right:
Parian marble portrait bust
of the Empress Livia
Roman, late 1st century
BC–early 2nd century AD
19¾ in. (50 cm.) high
Sold 10.7.87 in London for
£154,000 ($246,400)
Formerly at Marbury Hall

Opposite far left:
Greek marble statue of a
maenad or the Muse Thalia
Roman, 2nd century AD
5 ft. 8 in. (172 cm.) high
Sold 10.7.87 in London for
£242,000 ($387,200)
Formerly at Marbury Hall

Opposite left:
Thasian marble statue of a
herdsman restored as Paris
Roman, 2nd century AD
5 ft. 8 in. (174 cm.) high
Sold 10.7.87 in London for
£159,500 ($255,200)
Formerly at Marbury Hall

Owo ivory bowl, for use in Ifa
divination
17th–18th century
7 in. (18 cm.) high
Sold 29.6.87 in London at
South Kensington for
£27,500 ($44,000)
Collected on the Benin Punitive
Expedition of 1897 by a member
of Colonel Egerton's force, and
sent for sale by a descendant

North-west Coast wooden
raven rattle
Early 19th century
14¾ in. (38.3 cm.) long
Sold 29.6.87 in London at
South Kensington for
£22,000 ($35,200)

Pair of Yoruba wooden twin
figures *ere ibeji* from Efon
Alaye, Nigeria
Probably by a member of
the Adshina carving house
Late 19th century
12 in. (30.4 cm.) high
Sold 29.6.87 in London at
South Kensington for
£16,500 ($26,400)

Pair of *ibeji* from Oro
10¼ in. (26 cm.) high
Sold 29.6.87 in London at
South Kensington for
£4,180 ($6,688)

Pair of Tonga wooden clubs with whale-ivory inlay
18th–19th century
41 in. (104 cm.) and 42 in. (107 cm.) long
Sold 29.6.87 in London at South Kensington for £13,200
($21,120) and £3,740 ($5,984) respectively

These clubs were deposited with the Methodist Church Overseas Division (Methodist Missionary Society) by the Rev. Frederick Langham. He was born in Tasmania in 1833 and was sent to Fiji in 1857, where he served in Bau, the royal islet of 'King' Cakobau. Langham was much admired by the Fijians, to whom he was devoted, and much consulted by Cakobau, who probably gave him the clubs. He served as Chairman of the District of Fiji from 1875 until his retirement in 1895, when he went to England to revise the Fijian Bible.

Ceramics and Glass

Meissen cylindrical tankard
Painted with Chinoiseries by Johann
Gregor Höroldt
c. 1728
4¼ in. (10.5 cm.) high
Sold 29.6.87 in London for £17,600
($28,160)

Right:
One of a pair of Meissen
Chinoiserie two-handled
beakers and saucers
*c.*1728
Sold 10.11.86 in Geneva
for Sw.fr.71,850
(£29,216)

Below:
One of a pair of Meissen
celadon fond sake bottle-
vases
1730–5
12¼ in. (31 cm.) high
Sold 11.5.87 in Geneva
for Sw.fr.88,000
(£35,620)

Above:
One of a pair of Meissen yellow-ground soup-cups
and two-handled deep saucers
*c.*1735
The saucers 7 in. (18 cm.) wide
Sold 11.5.87 in Geneva for Sw.fr.99,000 (£40,080)

Left:
Meissen armorial Chinoiserie teabowl and saucer
From the Clemens August service
Painted by C.F. Herold
*c.*1735
Sold 10.11.86 in Geneva for Sw.fr.60,500
(£24,693)

THE CHRISTIAN VI SERVICE
Meissen royal armorial tea service painted and gilt with the royal arms of Denmark, crowned and surrounded by the chain of the order of the Elephant, the four pieces of form with Chinoiserie vignettes, the cups with the monogram of Christian VI and with landscape panels in shaped quatrefoil cartouches of *Laub-und-Bandelwerk* in puce, iron-red, Böttger-lustre and gold, and with *indianische Blumen* c.1730
Sold 1.12.86 in London for £303,600 ($433,237)
Record auction price for any service
This service remained in the Danish Royal Collection until 1795 when it was included in a list of items saved from the disastrous fire at Christiansborg castle and transferred to Rosenborg. In 1797, it was offered in the sale of salvaged effects from Christiansborg and acquired by the ancestors of the vendor. At the time of that sale, the service consisted of two slop-bowls, a teapot, two sugar-basins, four two-handled chocolate-cups, eighteen teabowls and saucers. Of these, one slop-bowl has disappeared, one sugar-basin is on the international art market, and four teabowls and one saucer are missing.

Vienna commedia dell'arte group of
Scaramouche and Pulcinella
*c.*1750
5¾ in. (14.5 cm.) high
Sold 29.6.87 in London for £8,800
($14,080)

Capodimonte (Carlo III) group of three figures
Modelled by Giuseppe Gricci, probably representing a doctor and youthful assistant
attending to a patient
*c.*1750
6 in. (15 cm.) high
Sold 30.3.87 in London for £18,700 ($75,117)

Pair of documentary
Vincennes white hunting
groups *La Chasse au
Sanglier* and *La Chasse au
Loup*
Modelled by Jean
Chabry, after Oudry
*c.*1752
12½ in. (32 cm.) wide
Sold 6.10.86 in London
for £93,500 ($133,985)

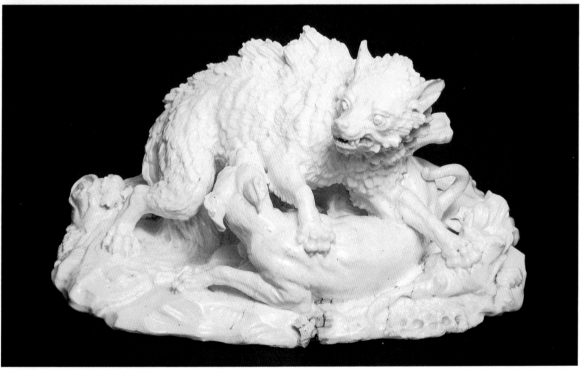

Deruta blue and gold lustre dish
Painted with Hercules lifting the
giant Antaeus from the ground
*c.*1520
16 in. (40.5 cm.) diameter
Sold 29.6.87 in London for
£27,500 ($44,000)

Raeren grey and blue salt-glazed
bulbous krug
The central coat-of-arms dated
1595
11¾ in. (30 cm.) high
Sold 17.12.86 in Amsterdam for
D.fl.32,480 (£9,842)

Lyons istoriato deep dish
Decorated in the Italian manner with Moses receiving the tablets on Mount Sinai
*c.*1580
17³/₄ in. (45 cm.) diameter
Sold 30.3.87 in London for £24,200 ($38,793)

Böttger brown stoneware cylindrical tankard and hinged cover
c.1715
8½ in. (21.5 cm.) high
Sold 29.6.87 in London for £19,800 ($31,680)

Würzburg baluster coffee-pot with domed cover
c.1775
9½ in. (24 cm.) high
Sold 30.3.87 in London for £14,300 ($22,923)

Böttger rectangular teapot
and cover
Painted in *Schwarzlot*
enriched in gilding by Ignaz
Preissler
*c.*1720
6 in. (15 cm.) high
Sold 29.6.87 in London for
£37,400 ($59,840)

Chantilly kakiemon
square box and cover
*c.*1740
9¾ in. (25 cm.) high
Sold 9.10.86 in
London for £16,500
($23,645)

Pair of Vincennes
two-handled small
seaux in the Meissen
style
*c.*1752
$5\frac{1}{2}$ in. (13.5 cm.)
wide
Sold 6.10.86 in
London for £10,450
($14,860)

Sèvres two-handled
bleu nouveau and
Louis XVI ormolu
jardinière
1784
$20\frac{1}{2}$ in. (52 cm.) wide
Sold 6.10.86 in
London for £28,600
($40,670)

Vienna (Dupaquier) rectangular casket
and liner in a contemporary fitted
leather box
*c.*1728
6½ × 4¾ in. (16.5 × 12 cm.)
Sold 29.6.87 in London for £22,000
($35,200)

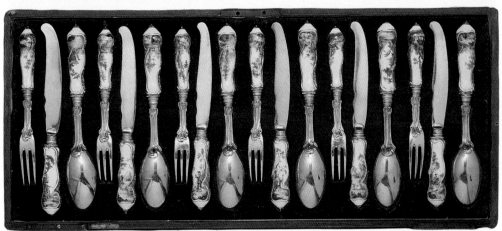

Six from a set of 12 Meissen porcelain-handled knives, forks and spoons, painted with *Jagd*
subjects
*c.*1750
Sold 30.3.87 in London for £22,000 ($35,266)

Documentary Wrotham slipware dated tyg
By Nicholas Hubble
Moulded with the date 1656 and the initials NH
6½ in. (16.5 cm.) high
Sold 23.2.87 in London for £8,800 ($14,124)

Staffordshire 'Thin Man' toby-
jug of Ralph Wood type
c.1780
9¼ in. (23.5 cm.) high
Sold 1.6.87 in London for £6,050
($10,104)

Above, clockwise:
Staffordshire saltglaze baluster jug
*c.*1760
6½ in. (16.5 cm.) high
Sold 1.6.87 in London for £1,100 ($1,837)

Staffordshire saltglaze scratch-blue baluster
puzzle-jug
*c.*1755
7¾ in. (19.5 cm.) high
Sold 1.6.87 in London for £3,300 ($5,511)

Staffordshire saltglaze large baluster jug
*c.*1760
9 in. (22.5 cm.) high
Sold 1.6.87 in London for £1,760 ($2,940)

Staffordshire saltglaze baluster chocolate-pot and
cover
*c.*1755
8¾ in. (22 cm.) high
Sold 1.6.87 in London for £10,450 ($17,452)

Staffordshire saltglaze baluster jug
*c.*1750
5¼ in. (13.5 cm.) high
Sold 1.6.87 in London for £462 ($772)

Staffordshire saltglaze globular teapot and cover
*c.*1750
5 in. (13 cm.) high
Sold 1.6.87 in London for £660 ($1,103)

Left:
Documentary Bristol
white figure of Lu
Tung-Pin
From the factory of
Benjamin Lund
Marked 'Bristol 1750'
in relief on the reverse
7 in. (17.5 cm.) high
Sold 20.10.86   in
London for £19,800
($28,156)

Chelsea group of two goats
Painted in the workshop of William
Duesbury
raised red anchor mark
*c.*1751
6½ in. (16.5 cm.) wide
Sold 20.10.86 in London for £9,900
($14,108)

Chelsea 'Crawfish' salt
After a silver original by Nicholas Sprimont
Painted in the London workshop of William
Duesbury
1745–9
5 in. (12.5 cm.) wide
Sold 20.10.86 in London for £14,300
($20,378)

Far left:
Chelsea decagonal plate
c.1752
7¾ in. (17.5 cm.)
diameter
Sold 20.10.86 in London
for £1,760 ($2,508)

Left centre:
Chelsea silver-shaped
plate
1750–2
9 in. (23 cm.) diameter
Sold 20.10.86 in London
for £4,400 ($6,270)

Left:
Chelsea fluted
saucer-dish
c.1752
7 in. (18 cm.) diameter
Sold 20.10.87 in London
for £6,820 ($9,719)

Chelsea peach-shaped cream-jug
c.1750
4¼ in. (11 cm.) wide
Sold 20.10.86 in London for £4,620 ($6,584)

Chelsea octagonal fable-
decorated teabowl and
saucer
Painted in the manner of
Jefferyes Hammet
O'Neale
c.1752
Sold 20.10.86 in London
for £4,620 ($6,584)

Chamberlain's Worcester blue-ground botanical part dessert-service comprising two rectangular two-handled centre-dishes, two shaped oval dishes, two square dishes, four shell-shaped dishes, six plates
Script marks
*c.*1820
Sold 1.6.87 in London for £16,500 ($27,555)

Coalport botanical part dessert-service comprising four oval two-handled sugar bowls with covers and two stands, four shaped oval dishes, four shell-shaped dishes, three square dishes and 32 plates
*c.*1800
Sold 27.10.86 in New York at Christie's East for $48,400 (£33,611)

Staffordshire chamber-service comprising five oval two-handled footbaths, five two-handled vases, two two-handled circular vases, two chamber-pots, six oviform jugs, five rectangular divided toothbrush-dishes and a rectangular soap-dish

Sold 27.5.87 at Great Tew Park in Oxfordshire for £17,732 ($25,269)

From the collection of the late Eustace Robb

According to an inscription in a photograph album at Tew, this extensive group of chamber-ware was reputedly intended for Napoleon's use at Longwood, the house on the island of St. Helena provided for the exiled Emperor by the British. It was not delivered, the story goes, because the decoration was thought to resemble too closely a victor's laurels. Though not described in detail in George Bullock's account it seems highly probable that these pieces are part of the large quantity of bedroom china invoiced by Bullock in 1817. Several of the bedrooms were supplied with a 'Chamber Service complete bordered' at £3. 3s. but the exact quantity received at Tew was the subject of numerous detailed exchanges between Matthew Boulton's and George Bullock's clerks. (See p. 200)

Opposite:
South Netherlands engraved winged goblet
*c.*1660
11 in. (27.5 cm.) high
Sold 2.6.87 in London for £6,050 ($10,134)

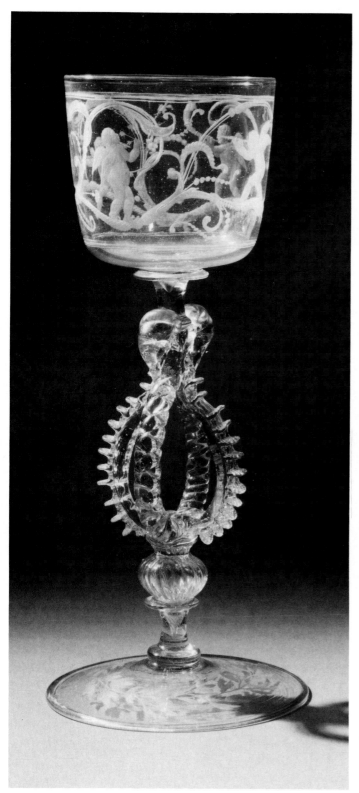

Above:
A pair of Beilby opaque-twist wine-glasses
*c.*1765
6¾ in. (17 cm.) high
Sold 2.6.87 in London
for £1,540 ($2,580) each

Above centre:
Beilby opaque-twist
firing-glass
*c.*1765
3¾ in. (9.5 cm.) high
Sold 2.6.87 in London
for £2,860 ($4,791)

Left:
Stipple-engraved wine-
glass, the ovoid bowl
decorated with a horse
courant in a meadow,
flanked by two trees and
with buildings in the
distance
By David Wolff
The Hague, 1780–90
6 in. (15.5 cm.) high
Sold 25.11.86 in London
for £4,400 ($6,200)

The 'Breadalbane' Amen
Glass, the bowl engraved in
diamond-point with a crown
above the royal cipher of King
James VIII, the letters JR direct
and reverse and with the figure
of 8 worked into the
monogram at the base, below
the word AMEN, the reverse
with the four verses of the
Jacobite anthem
Inscribed to James's younger
son: 'To His Royal Highnefs
Prince Henry Duke of ALBANY
and YORK'
1745–50
8 in. (20 cm.) high
Sold 25.11.86 in London for
£28,600 ($40,298)
Record auction price for an
amen glass

Opposite right:
Viennese transparent-
enamelled Ranftbecher
Inscribed in gilt on the
reverse 'Leur union est
notre force'
*c.*1830
4½ in. (11 cm.) high
Sold 25.11.86 in London for
£5,280 ($7,440)

Right:
Netherlands turquoise
serving-bottle
2nd half of the 17th century
7½ in. (19.5 cm.) high
Sold 2.6.87 in London for
£2,420 ($4,054)

Far right:
Netherlands turquoise
serving-bottle
2nd half of the 17th century
7 in. (18.5 cm.) high
Sold 2.6.87 in London for
£2,750 ($4,607)

Right centre:
Viennese transparent-
enamelled topographical
Ranftbecher
Attributed to Anton
Kothgasser
Inscribed in gilt on amber
panel 'Vue du Bain de
Joseph devant le Frauenthor
à Baden'
*c.*1830
4¾ in. (12 cm.) high
Sold 25.11.86 in London for
£4,950 ($6,975)

Far right:
Viennese gold-ground
enamelled Ranftbecher
Attributed to Anton
Kothgasser
Inscribed 'La Cathedrale de
St. Etienne à Vienne'
*c.*1830
4¼ in. (11 cm.) high
Sold 25.11.86 in London for
£4,620 ($6,510)

Far left:
Baccarat snake weight
3¼ in. (7.9 cm.) diameter
Sold 25.11.86 in London for £3,300
($4,650)

Left:
Baccarat faceted double-overlay
patterned millefiori weight
3 in. (7.8 cm.) diameter
Sold 2.6.87 in London for £4,180
($7,002)

Far left:
Clichy yellow pompom-dahlia weight
2¾ in. (7 cm.) diameter
Sold 2.6.87 in London for £7,700
($12,898)

Left:
Clichy pansy weight
2¾ in. (7 cm.) diameter
Sold 2.6.87 in London for £8,800
($14,740)

Far left:
Baccarat spaced concentric millefiori
weight
3 in. (7.8 cm.) diameter
Sold 2.6.87 in London for £3,850
($6,449)

Left:
St. Louis pink pelargonium weight
2½ in. (6.5 cm.) diameter
Sold 2.6.87 in London for £1,760
($2,948)

Oriental Ceramics and Works of Art

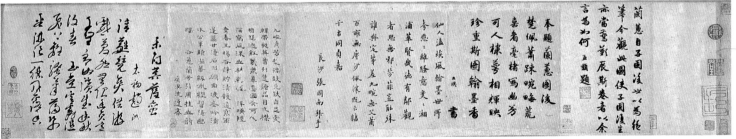

ZHAO MENGFU (1254-1322)
Spring and Autumn Orchids (Lan Hui Tu) and six colophons
Inscribed 'Wang Yuanzhang, my old friend's son, is going to Shaoyang. I executed this ''Lan Hui Tu'' as a ''farewell'' gift.'
Signed 'Ziang'
Handscroll, ink on paper
10⅛ × 41¾ in. (25.7 × 106.1 cm.)
Sold 1.12.86 in New York for $363,000 (£254,380)
Record auction price for a Chinese painting

Large gilt and polychromed
wood figure of Guanyin
Song Dynasty
68 in. (172.8 cm.) high
Sold 2.12.86 in New York for
$120,000 (£84,093)

Sancai glazed figure of a
caparisoned horse
Tang Dynasty
27¼ in. (69.2 cm.) high
Sold 2.12.86 in New York
for $160,000 (£112,124)

Grey pottery figure of a
horse and groom
Late Six Dynasties/early
Tang Dynasty
The horse and groom
25¾ in. (65.5 cm.) high
Sold 4.6.87 in New York for
$572,000 (£400,841)
Record auction price for an
unglazed Tang Dynasty
figure

Export blue and white jar
*c.*1580
14¼ in. (36 cm.) high
Sold 23.10.86 in
Amsterdam for D.fl.58,000
(£17,846)

Opposite:
Blue and white dinner
service comprising 322
pieces
Qianlong
Sold 23.10.86 in
Amsterdam for D.fl.197,200
(£60,676)

Ming green dragon bowl
7¾ in. (19.6 cm.) diameter
Sold 13.1.87 in Hong Kong for
HK$715,000 (£63,274)

Ming Wucai octafoil cylindrical box
and flat cover
4¼ in. (11 cm.) diameter
Sold 13.1.87 in Hong Kong for
HK$440,000 (£38,938)

Opposite:
Inset:
Pair of jade navette-shaped
stones forming a brooch
The jade stones approx.
1 in. (2.5 cm.) long; the
diamond weight approx.
9 carats in total
Sold 13.1.87 in Hong Kong
for HK$275,000 (£24,336)

Jade necklace of 73 beads
Approx. ³⁄₁₆–⅛ in.
(3–8 mm.) diameter
Sold 13.1.87 in Hong Kong
for HK$990,000 (£87,610)

Opposite far left:
Green jade figure of
Guanyin
Late Qing Dynasty
17 in. (44 cm.) high
Sold 13.1.87 in Hong
Kong for HK$506,000
(£44,778)

Opposite left:
Cizhou brown and
white calligraphic vase
Jin Dynasty
15 in. (38 cm.) high
Sold 8.6.87 in London
for £99,000 ($161,073)

Pair of inlaid bronze mask and ring handles
Warring States/Western Han Dynasty
The masks 3¾ in. (9.5 cm.) diameter; the rings 3½ in. (9 cm.) diameter
Sold 9.12.86 in London for £60,500 ($85,668)

Ding Yao bottle
Northern Song Dynasty
9¾ in. (25 cm.) high
Sold 8.12.86 in London for
£66,000 ($93,258)

Yuan blue and white broad baluster jar
*c.*1350
13 in. (33 cm.) diameter
Sold 8.6.87 in London for £154,000 ($250,558)

Pair of export models of
standing hawks
Qianlong
11 in. (28 cm.) high
Sold 15.6.87 in London for
£18,700 ($30,612)

One of a pair of red, green
and yellow lacquer table
chests
17th century
9¾ × 9½ × 7 in.
(24.5 × 24 × 18 cm.)
Sold 8.6.87 in London for
£41,800 ($68,009)

A selection of armorial porcelain
From the estate of Carsten Faurschou sold 19.11.86 in London for £170,709 ($242,407)

Korean Ceramics from the Collection of Robert Moore

SEBASTIAN IZZARD

The sale on 16 October 1986 of Robert Moore's collection of Korean ceramics, a carefully chosen selection of 180 pieces representing the Korean ceramic tradition, was a rare opportunity for a coterie of private collectors from America, Europe, Japan and Korea, as well as museums and the international trade, to add to their collections.

A private collector with an exceptional eye for Japanese and Korean art, Moore's first purchase was a cup stand and cover from the Silla period, which he bought in a wholesale decorative arts department store in San Francisco for $9.95. Following this he assembled his ceramics over a twenty-five year period. Armed with a sure eye and a love of the hunt, Moore built a collection that was remarkable for its scope and for the number of fine pieces.

In addition to representative examples of prehistoric and Silla dynasty tomb ceramics, he found a well-rounded group of Koryo dynasty celadons of the 12th and 13th centuries, which included an exceptional barbed cup and matching stand, and a rare and important group of Yi dynasty pieces, one of the more important groups of these types of ceramics in the West.

The unaffected and robust charm of early Yi dynasty (15th/16th century) Punch'ong stonewares was recognized by Japanese connoisseurs early on and the best collections are either in Korea or in Japan. Moore's collection boasted several important examples, such as a very fine Punch'ong bottle, decorated in sgraffito style with boldly drawn floral designs, and a bale-form bottle, decorated in *hakeme-e* style iron slip with floral scrolls.

Among the Yi ceramics most prized by Japanese collectors are the iron-slip decorated porcelain storage jars of the 17th century, of which the Moore collection held three examples. The finest was Moore's favourite piece. The well-shaped, robustly potted jar, decorated with a single dragon chasing its tail, exemplified for him the spontaneous, unsophisticated and honest nature of the Korean potter.

Moore's collection also contained fine examples of the blue and white porcelain wares from kilns established in the 18th century and patronized by the Confucian upper classes. One of these, a storage jar decorated with a pair of dragons chasing each other through clouds, was thought to be one of the finer extant examples of its type and fully justified its record price when it sold to the Cleveland Museum of Art.

Blue and white storage jar
Yi Dynasty
18th century
$15\frac{1}{2} \times 12$ in. (39.4×30.5
cm.)
Sold 16.10.86 in New York
for $88,000 (£61,197)
From the collection of
Robert Moore
Record auction price for a
Korean work of art

Nio

WILLIAM TILLEY

Kongo Rikishi is the traditional guardian of Buddhist temple gates, charged with preventing the entry of demons and other evil influences. A powerful muscular figure of great size and frightful aspect, Kongo Rikishi, literally 'vajra-wielding strongman', guards both sides of the outer gate of Nio-mon of the larger Buddhist temples, and appears as an image on each side of it. For this reason Kongo Rikishi is popularly called Nio, or Two Kings, yet although there are two figures in contraposition they are, in Buddhist conception, but one, the union of spiritual and material forces.

Like much else in Japanese Buddhism, the Nio have an ancient Indian origin and derive from the Hindu gods Indra and Brahma, Indra being the most celebrated character in the Rig-Veda, governing the weather and dispensing rain, and Brahma known in Hindu tradition as the Creator.

Looked at facing the gate, the right-hand figure represents the masculine principle; known as Kongo, he has an open mouth enunciating the mantra 'Om' and holds aloft a tokko, a type of vajra or Buddhist thunderbolt.

The left-hand figure with closed mouth and holding a club is known as Missaku and represents the female principle. In common usage the two figures are known, from their colouring, as Aka-oni and Aoi-oni, or Red devil and Green devil.

The oldest Kongo Rikishi images in Japan date from 711 and guard the Chomon of the Horyu-ji, while the largest are those at the Nandaimon of the Todaiji at Nara, 26 feet tall and carved by Unkei and his pupils in the Kamakura period, 1185–1393.

Although the Horyuji figures are a form of stucco, most Nio figures are, like those at Todai-ji, carved from cypress wood built up in several sections, a technique called yosegi-zukuri which gave the carver more latitude than the earlier ichiboku-zukuri or single-log style.

To protect them from constant touching by the devout the Nio sculptures are usually enclosed in cages, which does not prevent their being spattered with pellets of chewed paper thrown by pilgrims hoping to have some desire granted. Waraji or straw sandals are often hung in front of these cages as votive offerings by people who wish to become tough-footed pedestrians, especially at the temple of Kannon at Asakusa.

At the Nichiren temple at Minobu the afflicted sit for hours reciting the Lotus Sutra, 'Namu Myoho Renge Kyo', until at last the eyes of the statues (usually inlaid in rock-crystal) appear to move, and the devotees collapse in a state of hypnosis or hysteria, albeit sometimes cured.

The pair of cypress wood figures of Nio sold by Christie's in New York on 22 April 1987 from the collection of Michael J. Collins, realized $352,000 (£216,749), a world record auction price for any Japanese work of art. Dating from the first half of the 14th century, they have, with the passing of the years, lost most of their original colouring and also the fragile carving representing the narrow, diaphanous, celestial scarf usually found with these figures.

Despite this, and a small amount of restoration, they rank among the finest Japanese sculptures ever to appear in the West.

Pair of guardian kings
Late Kamakura, Nambokucho
1st half of the 14th century
53 1/4 and 53 1/2 in. (135 and 136 cm.) high respectively
Sold 22.4.87 in New York for $352,000 (£216,749)
From the collection of Michael J. Collins
Record auction price for a Japanese work of art

Ritual bronze bell
Yayoi period
c. 2nd century
9⅜ in. (23.8 cm.) high
Sold 22.4.87 in New York for
$126,500 (£77,894)

Bronze mirror
Tumuli period
c. 5th century
8⅛ in. (21 cm.) diameter
Sold 22.4.87 in New York for $44,000 (£27,094)

Koto Tachi blade
Signed 'Nobufusa saku'
Late 12th or early 13th century
27 in. (68 cm.) long
Sold 4.12.86 in New York for $132,000
(£92,697)
Record auction price for a Japanese sword

Kawari-Kabuto
Momoyama or early
Edo period
Late 16th or early 17th
century
Sold 22.4.87 in New
York for $35,200
(£21,675)
Record auction price
for a Japanese helmet

Kakiemon hexagonal jar and domed cover
Enpo/Jokyo period
1673-87
12½ in. (32 cm.) high
Sold 9.3.87 in London for £60,500 ($95,227)
An inventory taken at Hampton Court in 1696 mentions 'coloured jars of six squares', which Soame Jenyns of the British Museum interprets as the hexagonal jars later known as 'Hampton Court' vases. This appears to be one of the very few perfect examples known.

Ko-Imari oviform jar
Late 17th century
13½ in. (34 cm.) high
Sold 23.6.87 in London for
£60,500 ($96,800)

TOSHUSAI SHARAKU
Oban tate-e
An *okubi-e* portrait of the actor Segawa Tomisaburo II in the
role of Yadorigi, from the play *Hana ayame bunroku Soga*
15¼ × 10¼ in. (38.7 × 25.9 cm.)
Sold 22.4.87 in New York for $143,000 (£88,055)
From the collection of the late Werner Schindler
Record auction price for a print by the artist

KUNISADA
Oban tate-e
An *okubi-e* portrait of the actor Onoe Matsusuke II as the
carpenter Rokusaburo, from the play *Mijikayo Ukina no
Chirashigaki*. From the series *Oatari Kyogen no uchi*.
14¾ × 10 in. (37.1 × 25.6 cm.)
Sold 15.12.86 in London for £24,200 ($34,510)
Record auction price for a print by the artist

KITAGAWA UTAMARO
Oban tate-e
Three-quarter-length portrait of a
beauty holding a fan decorated with
a *kiri* leaf crest, from the series *Fujin
sogaku juttai* (Ten Types of Feminine
Physiognomy)
15 × 9¾ in. (38.4 × 25 cm.)
Sold 22.4.87 in New York for
$187,000 (£115,148)
From the collection of the late
Werner Schindler
Record auction price for a Japanese
print

Four-case Koma School Inro
Signed 'Koma Kyuhaku saku'
19th century
Sold 4.12.86 in New York for $30,800
(£21,630)
From the collection of Carl A. Kroch

Three-case Inro
Signed 'Kanshosai'
19th century
Sold 4.12.86 in New York for $13,200
(£9,270)
From the collection of Carl A. Kroch

Momoyama period Christian host box or pyx (Seiheibako)
Late 16th century
3¾ in. (9 cm.) high
4¼ in. (11 cm.) diameter
Sold 23.6.87 in London for £24,200 ($38,720)
Host boxes are one of the rarest forms of Namban art, for their function and design was of such significance to the Christian community that they became an obvious target for destruction when the persecution began. Very few are known to have survived.

Noh costume, Karaori
Late Edo period
Sold 18.11.86 in London for £18,700 ($26,386)
Record auction price for a kimono

Lacquer cabinet inlaid in
Shibayama style
Late 19th century
85 × 53¼ × 17¼ in.
(216 × 135 × 44 cm.)
Sold 23.6.87 in London for
£44,000 ($70,400)

Tibetan gilt copper figure of Buddha
The figure 16th century; the base late 18th century
Figure 11$\frac{1}{2}$ in. (29 cm.) high; base 4 in. (10 cm.) high
Sold 16.6.87 in London for £6,600 ($10,673)

Gandhara grey schist figure of Buddha
2nd–3rd century
21½ in. (54.5 cm.) high
Sold 16.6.87 in London for £6,380
($10,317)

Gandhara grey schist figure of a
Bodhisattva
2nd–3rd century
25 in. (63.5 cm.) high
Sold 16.6.87 in London for £8,800
($14,229)

Mesopotamian polychrome
lustre bowl
9th–10th century
11 in. (27.5 cm.) diameter
Sold 21.11.86 in London for
£1,980 ($2,785)

Ottoman tortoiseshell, ivory
and mother-of-pearl inlaid
wood scribe's chest
Early 17th century
22 in. (56 cm.) wide
Sold 16.6.87 in London for
£7,150 ($11,562)

Qur'an
Persia, Qajar, 10 Safar AH 1188 (22 April 1774)
Folio 12 × 8 in. (30.5 × 20.3 cm.)
Sold 21.11.86 in London for £49,500 ($69,647)
A highly important royal Qur'an of superb quality, prepared for Sultan Fath 'Ali Shah

Qur'an
Mulla Fathulla: Tafsir Mulla Fathullah
Kashmir, 20 Ramadan AH 1246 (22 April 1831)
Folio 9 × 5½ in. (22.9 × 14 cm.)
Sold 16.6.87 in London for £22,000 ($35,200)

River Scene
Lucknow or Murshidabad, *c.*1770–80
Overall 18½ × 24½ in. (47 × 62.2 cm.)
Sold 16.6.87 in London for £7,700
($12,320)
After 1800, renderings of daily life or
studies of the crafts and trades and castes
of India became increasingly common,
being produced for the British community
of the area

Illustration to the Anwar-i-Suhayli
Mughal, *c.*1570–80
Overall 8½ × 5¾ in.
(21.5 × 14.5 cm.)
Sold 16.6.87 in London for £7,700
($12,320)

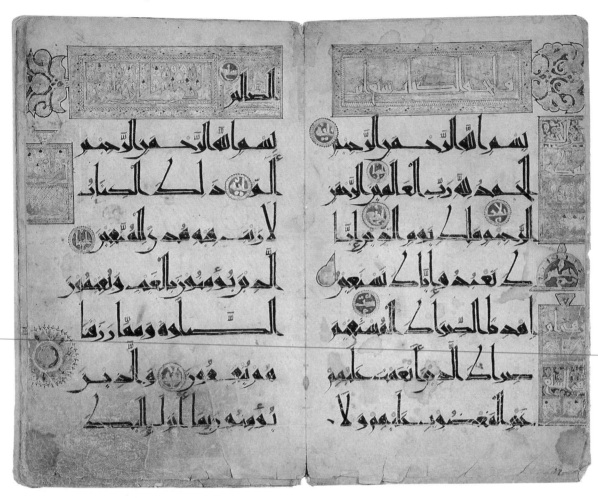

Qur'an section
Persia, late 11th or 12th century
Folio 14½ × 9¼ in. (36.7 × 23.5 cm.)
Sold 16.6.87 in London for £16,500 ($26,400)

Modern Decorative Arts

Les Amis de toujours
Bronze and ivory figure cast and carved from a model
By Demêtre Chiparus
25 in. (63.5 cm.) high
Sold 15.4.87 in London for £22,000 ($35,530)

Carved and acid-etched blowout table lamp
By Gallé
18 in. (46 cm.) high
Sold 15.4.87 in London for £44,000 ($71,060)

Pâte-de-verre table lamp
By G. Argy-Rousseau
16 in. (41 cm.) high
Sold 13.6.87 in New York for $40,700 (£24,666)
Record auction price for pâte-de-verre

Internally decorated engraved
and applied glass vase
Engraved 'Daum Nancy'
13¾ in. (35 cm.) high
Sold 26.9.86 in London for
£55,000 ($78,540)

Verrerie parlante vase
By Gallé
16¼ in. (41.5 cm.) high
Sold 17.12.86 in London for £52,800
($74,924)

Triple cameo glass table lamp
By Gallé
31 in. (79 cm.) high
Sold 1.2.87 in Monaco for F.fr.266,400
(£28,707)

Opposite right:
Silver-plated clock with
original key
Designed by Josef
Hoffmann; executed by the
Wiener Werkstätte
*c.*1913
9⅛ in. (23 cm.) high
Sold 13.6.87 in New York
for $60,500 (£36,666)

Opposite far right:
Burr walnut, ivrene,
enamel, silver-plated, agate
and mother-of-pearl mantel
clock
Designed by Josef Urban
for the Paul Hofner
Restaurant, Vienna 1906
22⅝ in. (60 cm.) high
Sold 13.12.86 in New York
for $44,000 (£30,344)

'Wisteria' leaded glass and
bronze table lamp
By Tiffany Studios
Stamped 'Tiffany Studios
New York 22525'
The shade 18 in. (46 cm.)
diameter; overall 27½ in.
(70 cm.) high
Sold 13.6.87 in New York
for $110,000 (£66,666)

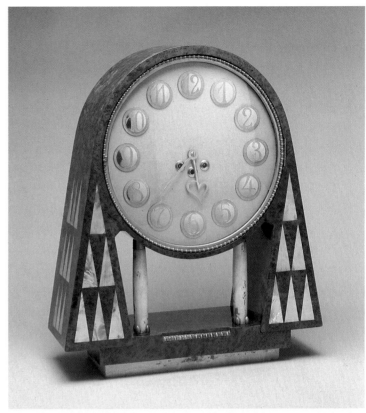

Five-piece pewter coffee and tea service
Designed by Josef Maria Olbrich; executed by E. Hueck
c. 1904
The coffee pot 10 in. (25.5 cm.) high; the pewter and wood tray 22¼ × 15 in. (56.5 × 38 cm.)
Sold 13.12.86 in New York for $37,400 (£25,793)

Black stained limed oak buffet
Designed by Josef Hoffmann; executed by the Wiener Werksätte
84½ in. (214.4 cm.) high; 129½ in. (328.6 cm.) wide; 18¼ in.
(46.3 cm.) deep
Sold 26.9.86 in London for £38,500 ($54,978)

Opposite:
JEAN DUPAS
French 1882–1964
Nude upon Rearing Horse
Signed and dated 1920
Oil on canvas
42¾ × 35 in. (108.6 × 88.9 cm.)
Sold 13.12.86 in New York for $82,500 (£56,896)
Jean Dupas was one of France's foremost artists
during the Art Deco period. A student of Albert
Besnard, he was awarded a gold medal at the Salon
des Artistes Français in 1922 and also won the Prix
de Rome. He is perhaps best known for his work at
the 1925 Paris Exhibition and on the ocean-liner
Normandie (1932).

Palisandre and giltwood table
By Jacques-Emile Ruhlmann
*c.*1928
Inscribed 'Sculpté pour la Famille
Ducharne / Ruhlmann Le
Bourgeois 1929'
29 in. (73.7 cm.) high; 37 in.
(94 cm.) diameter
Sold 13.12.86 in New York for
$28,600 (£20,141)

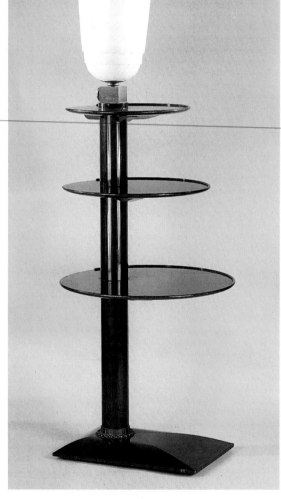

Gilt bronze mounted
macassar ebony low
table
By Jacques-Emile
Ruhlmann
20½ in. (50 cm.)
high; 27½ in.
(70 cm.) diameter
Sold 1.2.87 in
Monaco for
F.fr.177,600 (£19,138)

Standing lamp and display stand combined
By Jacques-Emile Ruhlmann
72½ in. (184 cm.) high
Sold 1.2.87 in Monaco for
F.fr.555,000 (£59,806)

Bronze, marble and ivory
coiffuse
By Armand-Albert Rateau
c.1920–2
Stamped 'A.A. RATEAU INUD'
twice and 'PARIS 1211 343C'
60½ in. (153.7 cm.) high;
35½ in. (90.2 cm.) wide;
20¾ in. (52.7 cm.) deep
Sold 28.3.87 in New York
for $110,000 (£68,750)

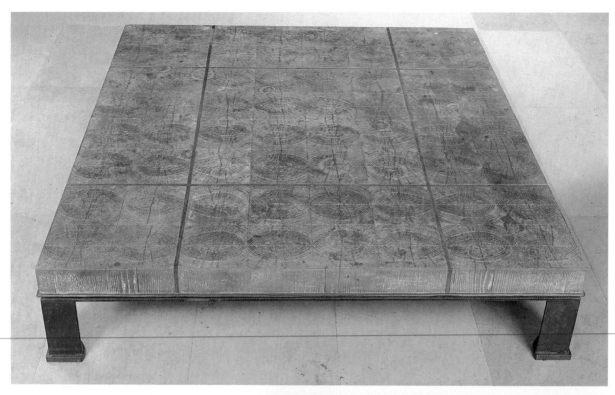

Coffee table
By Paul-Dupré Lafon
1948
13½ in. (34.5 cm.) high; 62½ in. (159 cm.)
square
Sold 1.2.87 in Monaco for F.fr.333,000
(£35,884)
Record auction price for a work by the artist
Paul-Dupré Lafon (1900–71) was an interior
designer who, along with Ruhlmann and
Leleu, worked in the best French tradition of
luxurious modernism. In his work he liked to
employ rare and exotic materials, and was
fortunate in finding clients who could afford
his style. In 1948 he was asked to refurbish a
splendid villa at Ste. Maxime near St.
Tropez on the Côte d'Azur. This coffee table
is one of the pieces from this commission.

Articulated nest of tables
Designed by Pierre Chareau
c.1924
21¾ in. (55.2 cm.) high; 24¼ in. (62.2 cm.)
wide; 15 in. (38.1 cm.) deep
Sold 13.12.86 in New York for $18,700
(£13,169)

Oak dining-table and eight chairs
Designed by Frank Lloyd Wright; probably executed by Matthews Brothers Furniture Co., for the George Barton House of the
Darwin D. Martin Complex, Buffalo
c. 1903
The table top 60 × 54 ¼ in. (152.4 × 138.4 cm.); the chairs 46 in. (116.8 cm.) high
Sold 20.6.87 in New York for $594,000 (£368,944)
Record auction price for any piece of 20th-century furniture

Copper and mica table lamp
By Dirk van Erp
*c.*1910
25½ in. (64.8 cm.) high
Sold 20.6.87 in New York
for $71,500 (£44,409)
Record auction price for a
work by the artist

Opposite right:
Nine-drawer chest
Designed by Frank Lloyd
Wright; probably executed
by John W. Ayers Co., for
the Francis W. Little
House, Peoria, Illinois
*c.*1902
70⅛ in. (178.1 cm.) high;
22⅞ in. (58 cm.) wide;
27⅜ in. (69.5 cm.) deep
Sold 20.6.87 in New York
for $264,000 (£163,975)

Opposite far right:
Oak high-back spindle side
chair
Designed by Frank Lloyd
Wright for the Ward W.
Willits House, Highland
Park, Illinois
*c.*1901
56¼ in. (63.5 cm.) high
Sold 12.12.86 in New York
for $198,000 (£136,551)
Record auction price for a
20th-century chair

Above:
Aluminium armchair
By Gerrit Thomas Rietveld
1942
27³⁄₄ in. (70.3 cm.) high
Sold 21.5.87 in Amsterdam for D.fl.156,600 (£46,059)

Above right:
The 'Berlin' chair
By Gerrit Thomas Rietveld
1923
39¹⁄₄ in. (99.8 cm.) high
Sold 21.5.87 in Amsterdam for D.fl.197,200 (£58,000)
Record auction price for any piece of 20th-century Dutch furniture

Right:
The Red-Blue Chair
Designed by Gerrit Thomas Rietveld and made by G.A. van de Groenekan
1919
34 in. (86.2 cm.) high
Sold 21.5.87 in Amsterdam for D.fl.162,400 (£47,765)

Above:
Stoneware jug
By Hans Coper
Impressed 'HC' seal
*c.*1952
14 in. (35.6 cm.) high
Sold 18.12.86 in London for £38,500 ($54,632)

Left:
Tall 'hour-glass' vase
By Hans Coper
Impressed 'HC' seal
18 in. (45.5 cm.) high
Sold 23.6.87 in London for £18,700 ($29,920)

1950s Italian Glass

DAN KLEIN

1950s Italian glass is brightly coloured, uninhibited and exciting. It is easy to enjoy and disarmingly seductive. When it was new it was sold in department stores or gift shops more or less as a household article. Those who bought it then and still possess it today are astounded to find that they now own a rare collector's item. Of course, not every piece of 1950s Italian glass has enjoyed this fate, which makes one curious as to why one piece is worthy of a museum showcase, while another, which to the untrained eye looks almost identical, is dismissed as unworthy of artistic comment.

Venice and Murano have been famous for glass since the 17th century, but for two hundred years, from the mid-18th century to the mid-20th century, Venetian glassmakers did little more than trade on past glories, catering above all for the tourist industry. It took the dynamic personality of Paolo Venini to combat some of the staleness in Venetian glassmaking. Over a span of two decades he brought new life to the industry, and it is a measure of his achievement to observe that since his death at the end of the 1950s Venetian glass has once more had to resort to plagiarism and repetition.

Paolo Venini was not a Venetian. He had been a Milanese businessman before coming to Venice in 1921, and he brought with him a broadmindedness and a degree of artistic sophistication that was badly needed in the glass industry. In Venice he found the most talented glassblowers in the world stubbornly content with the traditional exhibitionism of long-established virtuoso techniques. After a brief partnership with Capellini, a Venetian glassmaker, Venini set up on his own.

Most 20th-century Venetian glass, thin blown and decorated with senseless frills, is notable mainly for its lack of taste. Paolo Venini encouraged a radically modern approach. He was not a glassmaker himself but was passionate about glass and about design in general, and he asked friends from Milan, top designers like Carlo Scarpa and Fulvio Bianconi, to turn their minds to the problem of designing glass. These men were impervious to the small-minded jealousies of the Venetian glass world and, for the first time in hundreds of years, their freedom of design allowed the industry to breathe and move forward again. They invented new techniques such as *pezzato* (patchwork), *murrhina* (mosaic) and *battuto*, based on the ancient Venetian traditions and talents yet at the same time providing a much needed modern language for glass.

Many other Venetian glassmakers followed Venini's lead, and the 1940s and particularly the 1950s were highly inventive periods. During these years a dying craft was turned into a modern decorative art form. What attracted most attention were the new shapes and new colours. The shapes were more asymmetric than before, less bound by tradition. There were such modern classics as the 'Fazoletto' or folded handkerchief vase, and the series of 'Valva' vases designed by Flavio Poli for Seguso. Apart from Venini, the best known firms working in the modern idiom were Seguso, Barovier, Salviati, Fratelli Tosi, Fontana Arte and AVEM. Technique was still the most important factor in Venetian glassmaking, and allowed for exhibitionism as never before. Many of the techniques have a quality of wizardry about them, and the glory of these pieces is shared by technicians and designers alike. Almost none of the famous designers of the period made their own designs. This job was entrusted to the Venetian glassblowers, and the magic of 1950s Italian glass lay in their lung power and sleight of hand.

The more complicated vases were expensive to produce and were made in smaller numbers. In a few instances unique pieces were made, usually for a special occasion such as for one of the Milan Triennale exhibitions. There is still argument among collectors as to what is a good piece, and this is reflected in the unpredictable prices realized for Italian glass of this period. Nobody is quite sure why one piece should be worth over £60,000 while another is unsaleable. These pieces were not conceived as works of art, and they are often poorly documented. But research is being done, and a number of books on the subject are scheduled to appear. It should prove to be one of the richest periods in the history of glass.

Lancet II
Designed by Timo
Sarpaneva; executed by
Iittala
1957
11 in. (28 cm.) high
Sold 1.2.87 in Monaco for
F.fr.199,800 (£21,530)

Pâte-de-verre bowl
By Diana Hobson
1986
Sold 27.1.87 in London for £1,540
($2,340)

Vase
Designed by Fulvio Bianconi; executed by Venini, Murano, Italy
11 in. (27.5 cm.) high
Sold 23.6.87 in London for £61,600 ($98,560)
Record auction price for a post-war glass

Arms and Armour and Modern Sporting Guns

Cased single-trigger over-and-under flintlock pocket pistol
By Joseph Egg, London
c. 1820
6 in. (15.3 cm.) overall
Sold 18.3.87 in London for £15,400 ($24,594)

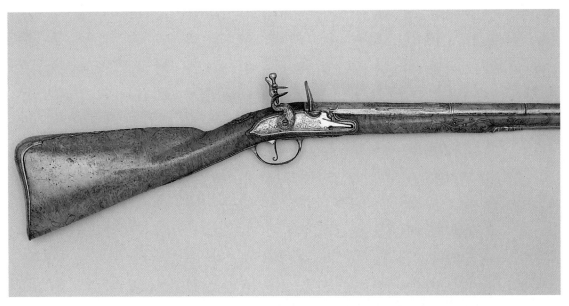

French flintlock
fowling-piece
By Bertrand Piraube, Paris
Dated 1681
48¼ in. (122.6 cm.) barrel
Sold 18.3.87 in London for
£13,200 ($21,081)
Bertrand Piraube, personal
gunmaker to Louis XIV, was
granted *logement* in the
Galleries du Louvre on 25
January 1670, and held his
appointment until about
1724. He is generally
recognized as the most
distinguished of the French
gunmakers of the classical
Louis XIV period, and is well
represented in most
important royal and
princely armouries.

Rare French gunstocker's casket
Attributed to the unidentified maker of the stocks of a very small group of
early 17th-century French wheel-lock firearms
Early 17th century.
7½ × 4¼ × 3½ in. (19 × 11 × 9 cm.)
Sold 29.10.86 in London for £19,800 ($27,958)
Previously sold by Christie's at Hamilton Palace in 1882 for 123 gns.

Pair of French over-and-under flintlock pistols
By Le Page *Arquebusier de l'Empereur à Paris*
Dated 1805
12 in. (30.5 cm.) overall
Sold 29.10.86 in London for £33,000 ($46,596)
Traditionally held to have been made for Napoleon I, and acquired by Colonel Basil Charles Boothby after the Battle of Waterloo
Exhibited in H.M. Armouries, Tower of London, 1962–85

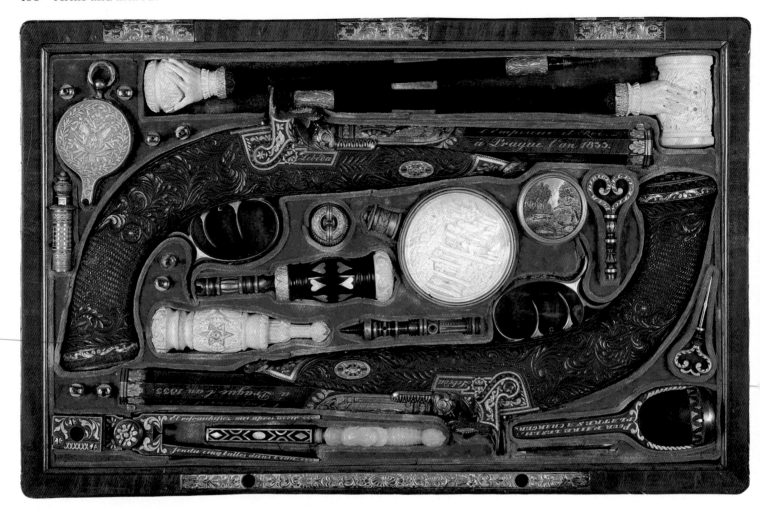

Pair of Bohemian royal percussion target pistols
By Anton Vincent Labeda, Prague
Dated 1833
14 in. (35.5 cm.) overall
Sold 29.10.86 in London for £49,500 ($69,894)
Probably made for the 1st Duke of Cambridge, Viceroy of Hanover (1774–1850)

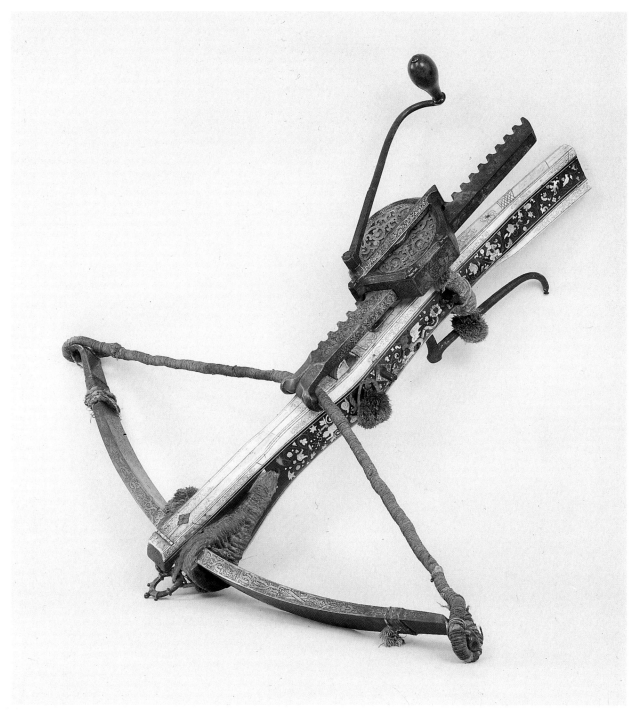

German sporting crossbow, with its original cranequin
c. 1610
33 and 19½ in. (84 and 49.5 cm.) respectively
Sold 18.3.87 in London for £66,000 ($105,402)
Record auction price for a crossbow

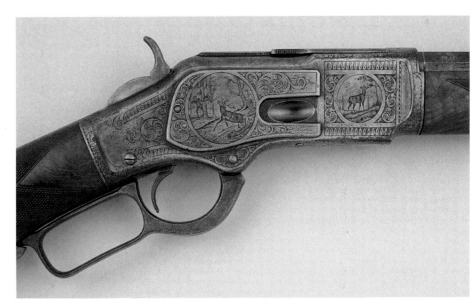

Winchester .44(W.C.F.) Model 1873 presentation sporting rifle, engraved by J. Ulrich
Produced in 1884
24⅜ in. (62 cm.) barrel
Sold 21.11.86 in New York at Christie's East for $27,500 (£19,470)
The presentation inscription reads: 'Presented to George P. Bissell, Colonel 25th Regt. C.V., by members of the Regiment at the Regimental reunion, April 14, 1884, as a slight testimonial of affection for their old commander'

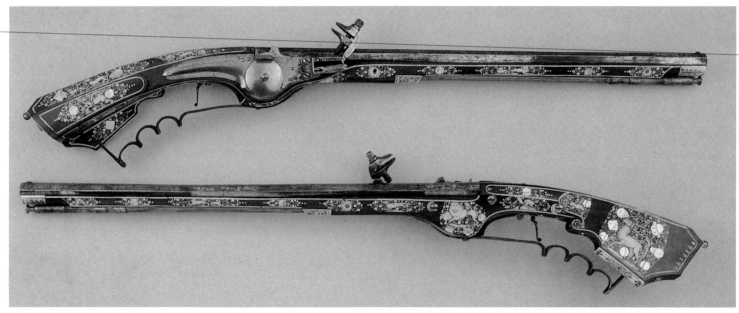

Pair of Teschen long wheel-lock rifled holster pistols
By Georg Kurland
c.1630
28⅜ in. (72 cm.) overall
Sold 20.11.86 in New York at Christie's East for $37,400 (£26,479)
Originally in the Saxon Electoral Armouries, Dresden

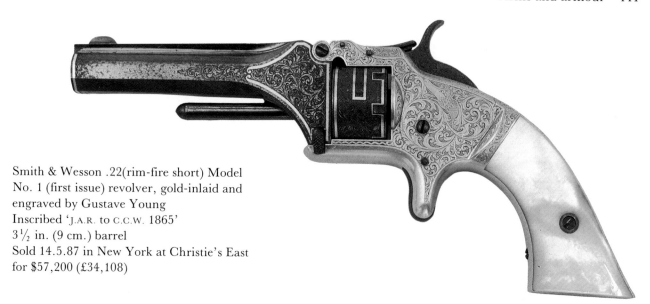

Smith & Wesson .22(rim-fire short) Model
No. 1 (first issue) revolver, gold-inlaid and
engraved by Gustave Young
Inscribed 'J.A.R. to C.C.W. 1865'
3½ in. (9 cm.) barrel
Sold 14.5.87 in New York at Christie's East
for $57,200 (£34,108)

Colt .45 Single-Action Army revolver, serial number 1
Produced in 1873
7½ in. (19 cm.) barrel
Sold 14.5.87 in New York at Christie's East for $242,000 (£144,305)
From the estate of Charles L. Bricker
Record auction price for an American firearm
The Colt Single-Action Army revolver, the 'Peacemaker', may be said to epitomize the culture of the Western
Frontier and total production of the model exceeded 300,000. Thus, the romantic appeal of 'No. 1' is apparent.

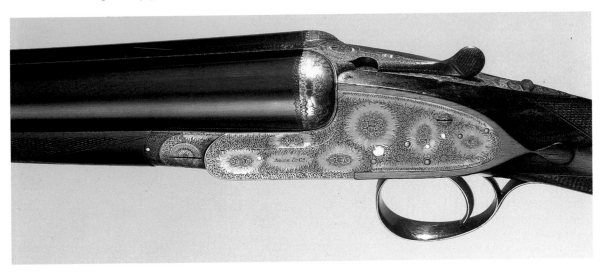

Pair of sidelock ejector 16-bore d.b. single-trigger guns
By Boss, London
Built in 1930
Sold 26.11.86 in London for £19,800 ($28,314)

Over-and-under sidelock ejector 12-bore d.b. single-trigger gun
By Boss, London
Built in 1922
Sold 26.11.86 in London for £17,050 ($24,381)

Self-opening sidelock ejector 12-bore d.b. gun, chiselled and gold-encrusted by K.C. Hunt
By J. Purdey, London
Completed in 1971
Sold 25.3.87 in London for £22,000 ($35,640)
Record auction price for a British modern sporting gun
A distinctive feature of the gun's decoration is the incorporation of astrological symbols relating to the lady for whom it was built. The eagle and phoenix, encrusted in gold on the underside of the gun, allude to characteristics associated with the sign of Scorpio, and the stock is inlaid in gold with a zodiacal scorpion.

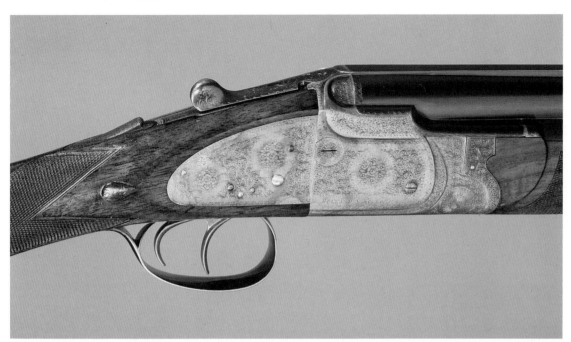

'Badminton' over-and-under backlock ejector 12-bore d.b. gun
By Holland & Holland, London
Commenced in 1947 and completed in 1951
Sold 15.7.87 in London at South Kensington for £6,600 ($10,652)
The gun is believed to be the only over-and-under version of the 'Badminton' model ever built by Holland & Holland

Pair of self-opening sidelock ejector 12-bore d.b. guns
By J. Purdey, London
Built in 1928 and rebarrelled in 1952
Sold 15.7.87 in London at South Kensington for £26,400 ($42,609)

'Royal' sidelock
ejector .240
(Holland's Magnum
Flanged) d.b. rifle
By Holland &
Holland, London
Built *c.*1937
Sold 15.7.87 in
London at South
Kensington for
£15,400 ($24,855)

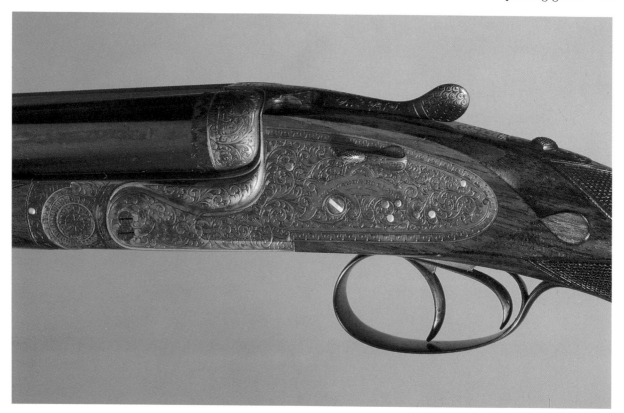

Detachable-boxlock
ejector .318 d.b.
single-trigger rifle
By Westley Richards,
Birmingham
Built *c.*1920
Sold 15.7.87 in
London at South
Kensington for £5,500
($8,877)

Horsley 1863 Patent snap-action 8-bore d.b. bar-in-wood hammer gun
By T. Horsley, York
Built in 1889
Sold 26.11.86 in London for £3,850 ($5,505)
The gun has the distinctive pull-back action-lever of Horsley's 1863 Patent, but uses a Purdey double-bolt rather than the single-bite bolt of Horsley's original design

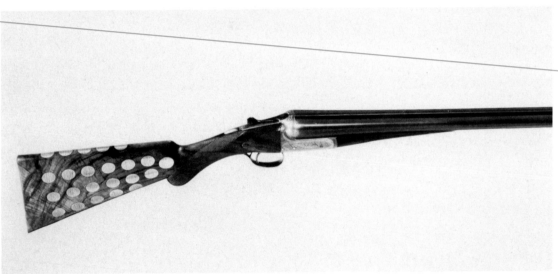

The Percy Stanbury 'Championship' boxlock ejector 12-bore d.b. single-trigger pigeon-gun
By Webley & Scott, Birmingham
Built c.1921
Sold 15.7.87 in London at South Kensington for £3,300 ($5,326)
The late Percy Stanbury was in the England International Team for 26 years and the stock of his gun is inlaid with 45 inscribed silver ovals recording many of his successes in competitive shooting between 1926 and 1953. In his own words, he used the gun 'for everything', from skeet to wildfowl. It follows that the gun is much worn and the price it achieved reflects the respect and affection in which Mr Stanbury was held by the shooting community.

Stamps

U.S.A. 1861 letter from New York to San Francisco carried by the Pony Express
Sold on 25.3.1987 in New York for $165,000 (£102,680)
From the Louis Grunin Collection

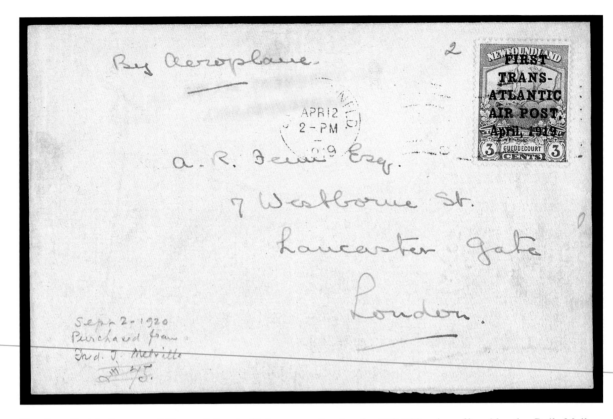

Sw.fr.14,625
(£5,850)

Sw.fr.90,000
(£36,000)

Sw.fr.73,125
(£29,050)

Newfoundland: Attempted Trans-Atlantic flight competing for the £10,000 prize offered by the *Daily Mail*. Lieut. Henry G. Hawker (pilot) and Lieut.-Commander K. Mackenzie Grieve (navigator), left St. John's on 18 May 1919, in the Sopwith bi-plane *Atlantic*. They crashed west of the Azores, the crew being saved by a Danish vessel, the plane and the mail being salvaged by the s.s. *Lake Charlotville*. The envelope is endorsed 'Sep. 2 1920 Purchased from Fred J. Melville £75'.
Sold 25.6.87 in New York $8,800 (£6,235)

The Isleham Collection

This was probably the last of the great stamp collections, for the owner had tried, and very nearly succeeded, in finding one example of each stamp issued between 1840 and 1940. The collection was started in 1910 and steadily enlarged until the owner's death in 1974.

The disposal of the collection was spread over six sales:

30 October 1986	United States Possessions	New York
30 October 1986	British North America	New York
6 November 1986	Near and Far East	Zurich
11 March 1987	British Empire	New York
12 March 1987	Latin America	New York
13 May 1987	Europe and Colonies	Zurich

The total realized for the collection was £1,600,132 ($2,439,138).

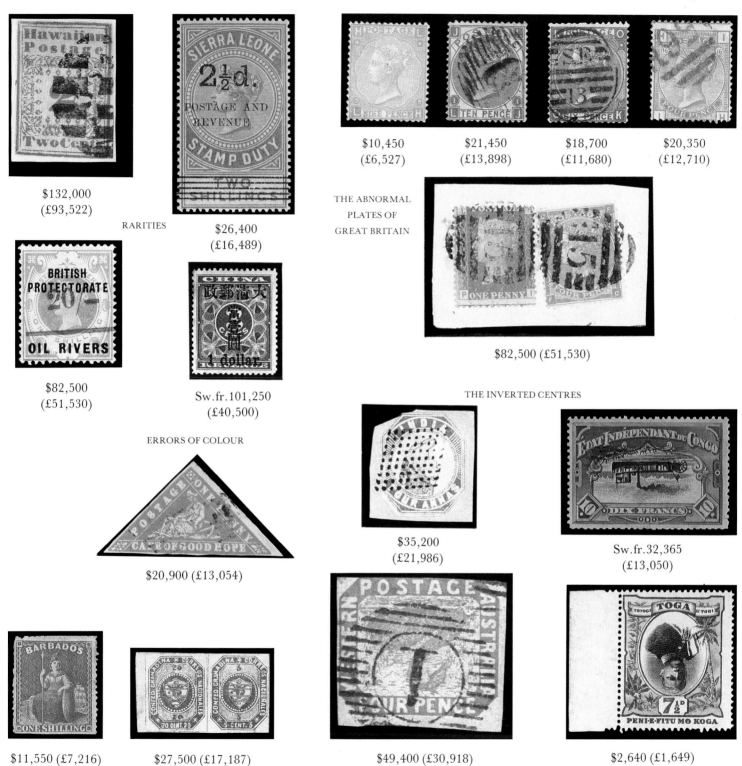

$132,000
(£93,522)

RARITIES

$26,400
(£16,489)

$10,450
(£6,527)

$21,450
(£13,898)

$18,700
(£11,680)

$20,350
(£12,710)

THE ABNORMAL
PLATES OF
GREAT BRITAIN

$82,500 (£51,530)

$82,500
(£51,530)

Sw.fr.101,250
(£40,500)

ERRORS OF COLOUR

THE INVERTED CENTRES

$35,200
(£21,986)

Sw.fr.32,365
(£13,050)

$20,900 (£13,054)

$11,550 (£7,216)

$27,500 (£17,187)

$49,400 (£30,918)

$2,640 (£1,649)

The 20 lots on these facing pages realized £480,581 ($728,153)

Stamps and Postal History sales held during the year in London, Bournemouth, Zurich and New York provided an auction turnover of £9,300,664, an increase of 46.9% on the previous season.

LONDON

Of the fifty-one auctions held during the season, sixteen were held in London. There were four sales of Great Britain. The first contained the collection formed by Robert Cole between 1839 and 1841; his penny black on 6th May wrapper made £8,800 ($12,700). The November sale included the *Rainbow* collection of early colour trials and die proofs – the 38 lots realized £165,984 ($253,733). In the same auction, the late S.W. Southwood's collection of surface-printed stamps included a mint block of six of the 1884 5s., which sold for £2,200 ($3,492), and the King Edward I.R. Official 6d. SPECIMEN which fetched £2,640 ($4,190).

Great Britain 1840 Southgate's caricature of the Mulready, envelope used from Bangor to Holywell, March 1841
Sold 19.5.87 in London for £4,950 ($7,174)

Great Britain March 1840 die proof
Sold 25.11.86 in London for £16,500 ($23,913)

February saw a mint pair of the 1891 £1 green fetch £2,860 ($4,540) and a die proof of the 1913 Seahorses sold for £2,750 ($4,365). In May the collection of illustrated envelopes formed by Herman Herst Jun. proved very popular.

Illustrated is one of the attractive caricatures of the original Mulready sheets. A Mulready 2d. lettersheet bearing two penny reds used in 1844 fetched £2,640 ($3,826) and the same price was paid for a used Fores' caricature. A lovely hand-painted envelope used from Jersey in 1865 showing four envelopes overlapping made £1,430 ($2,072). The collection of Oxford and Cambridge College stamps formed by the late A.R. Tucker fetched £8,119 ($11,767), the Selwyn 1882 ½d. on an envelope bringing £1,760 ($2,551).

The total for the four sales was £561,217 ($926,008).

There were three of the ever popular Postal History Auctions, which realized £253,429 ($418,158). Among the larger properties was the late Eric Buckley's collection; in this collection an 1839 letter from Guildford with Universal 4d. Post handstamp brought £1,430 ($2,072) and the 1850 letter from Cape Coast Castle with a blue HASTINGS SHIP LETTER made the same price. In March, Robert Bagshawe's Antarctica made £20,290 ($32,206), and a 1903 envelope bearing the NATIONAL ANTARCTIC EXPEDITION 'Discovery' label brought £2,640 ($4,190). In the same sale a 1674 letter from St. Osyth with the post office publicity handstamp ESSEX POST GOES AND COMES EVERY DAY made £3,080 ($4,889). The May sale saw the collections of the late Kenneth Hodgson and A.R. Tucker sold. The 1681 letter from Farnham with the 'hot cross bun' brought £2,860 ($4,145), an 1850 Admiralty Experimental Balloon leaflet sold for £1,650 ($2,391), an 1849 PAID AT BELIZE made £1,870 ($2,740) and a China 1920 Peking to Tientsin airmail wrapper made £2,035 ($2,949).

India 1854 4 annas, fourth printing, block of four
Sold 11.9.86 in London for £6,050 ($8,768)

Lagos 1874 registered envelope to England
Sold 14.4.87 in London for £1,650 ($2,391)

There were nine British Empire sales, which brought £1,253,429 ($2,066,488). These included Jochen Heddergott's India, the late Lt. Col. D.M.C. Pritchard's Canada, the late S.W. Southwood's collection, the late Michael Burberry's New Zealand, William Mitchell's New South Wales, Lee Addison's Seychelles, Richard Bagshawe's Falkland Islands Dependencies, a distinguished sale of South Africa, the late Mark Strutt's Solomon Islands, D. Hammond-Giles's India, Donald Lowe's Jamaica, the late G. Philip Grabfield's Malta and V.F.N. Surtees's Antigua, Bahamas and St. Vincent.

ZURICH

There were thirteen auctions in Zurich, which realized Sw.fr.5,287,190 (£2,158,037) and included the two Isleham sales described earlier.

In November, the best properties included a further portion of the late F.T.K. Caröe's Denmark. A mint corner copy of the Thiele 2 R.B.S. fetched Sw.fr.51,750 (£20,700), and the 1871 money letter bearing the 1867 3sk. and 8sk. used with 1870 4sk. and two 48 sk. made Sw.fr.45,000 (£18,000).

Denmark 1871 money letter from Løgstør to Copenhagen
Sold 4.11.86 in Zurich for Sw.fr.45,000 (£18,000)
From the F.T.K. Caröe collection of Denmark

A small Postal History sale had letters addressed to the Duke and Duchess of Parma which sold for a total of Sw.fr.15,395 (£6,158). These included a letter from Philip II of Spain, 1557, which brought Sw.fr.2,025 (£810), and one from Charles IX of France, 1572, which realized Sw.fr.1462 (£585). A letter written by a captured slave from Algiers in 1674 made Sw.fr.2,475 (£990). A sale of proofs and essays included De La Rue ink trials at Sw.fr.14,883 (£5,993), 23 die proofs of the head of Queen Elizabeth at Sw.fr.14,569 (£5,827) and fifteen imperforate sets of 1937 Coronation issue at Sw.fr.20,841 (£8,336).

The Ricoy Guatemala made Sw.fr.79,369 (£31,748) and the Robert Meyersburg U.S.A. made Sw.fr.219,358 (£87,743). The Near and Far East sale included the Trudi Korzyn stock of Japan, a mint block of thirty 1871 100m. fetched Sw.fr.8,437 (£3,375) and the 1874 20s. on laid used Sw.fr.9,000 (£3,600). In the Isleham collection, the Shanghai 1866 1c. on laid unused fetched Sw.fr.32,625 (£13,050). The Howard Selzer collection of Malaya made Sw.fr.204,755 (£81,902).

In May, the collection of Military Mail formed by Dr E.H. Mayer made Sw.fr.112,365 (£44,946), a 1775 envelope signed 'Geo. Washington' bringing Sw.fr.6,570 (£2,700). The first portions of the Brabant Belgian Congo sold for Sw.fr.209,042 (£83,617), an 1884 letter with CONGO RIVER and an Angola 100r. made Sw.fr.8,437 (£3,375).

The fine collection of the classic stamps of Switzerland formed by Professor H.H. Landau made a total of Sw.fr.809,308 (£372,372). Sw.fr.49,500 (£19,800) was paid for a Zurich 1843 4 rappen on envelope. The same price was reached for an 1849 Vaud 4c. on envelope. The top price was Sw.fr.51,750 (£20,700) for a Zurich 1850 Winterthur 2½ rappen used with a Rayon I 5r. on an 1851 envelope. The bisected Strubeli 20c. on an 1862 letter and the bisected seated Helvetia on an 1867 letter both brought Sw.fr.22,500 (£9,000).

Geneva 1848 5c. large eagle
with red 3
Sold 13.5.87 in Zurich for
Sw.fr.27,000 (£10,800)

Switzerland 1850 Poste
Locale 2½ rappen
unframed cross
Sold 13.5.87 in Zurich for
Sw.fr.29,750 ($10,700)

The collection of China included the late Bernard E. Stoloff's studies and made Sw.fr.517,578 (£207,031). The 1879 3c. used on an envelope from Tamsuy to Shanghai brought Sw.fr.61,750 (£24,700). Sw.fr.28,125 (£11,250) was paid for the mint sheet of 1870 5 candereens, also the 1897 large 2c./2c. a used block of four, two stamps with the surcharge omitted. An envelope from the Peruvian Legation at Nagasaki bearing the Japanese 12 sen bird made Sw.fr.27,000 (£10,800).

BOURNEMOUTH

Twelve general sales were held selling some 12,500 lots for £1,652,107 ($2,725,977) on behalf of over a thousand vendors (25 were major named properties) to over a thousand buyers resident in 37 countries. Bournemouth is thus part of the international scene.

One lot realized £8,800, three lots realized over £4,000 (top £4,620), five over £3,000, ten over £2,000 and seventy-five over £1,000.

NEW YORK

The ten sales in New York were dominated by the four Isleham auctions and the wonderful collection formed by Louis Grunin of U.S. 1851–7 issues on covers, which was sold on 15 March for $1,500,279 (£937,674), every lot finding a buyer. Two envelopes are illustrated on this page, and one on p. 447.

Other six-figure lots were $121,000 (£75,419) for a marginal strip of three of the 1851 5c. red-brown on an 1857 letter from New Orleans, and $110,000 (£68,530) for an 1857 12c. black on cover cancelled with the blue oval PONY EXPRESS SAN FRANCISCO. The New York sales totalled $5,399,650 (£3,452,445).

U.S.A. 1861 patriotic envelope bearing two 1861 3c. and two 1857 12 c. from Boston to Vienna via England and Belgium
Sold 25.3.87 in New York for $12,650 (£7,872)

U.S.A. hand-drawn envelope from West Cambridge, Mass., to New York
Sold 25.3.87 in New York for $6,380 (£3,970)

Coins and Medals

The Victoria Cross awarded to General Sir Dighton Probyn for his services during
the Indian Mutiny
Sold with his Orders and Decorations 21.7.87 in London for £28,600 ($45,760)
Dighton Probyn, 1833–1924, was the epitome of the irregular cavalry officer;
flamboyant and reckless, he went on to command 'Probyn's Horse', which was
nicknamed in his honour. He accompanied the Prince of Wales on his first visit to
India in 1875-6, and became a close friend and adviser to the royal family for the next
50 years.

The Victoria Cross
awarded to Surgeon
William Maillard, Royal
Navy, for actions in
Crete, 1898
£13,200 ($21,120)

Naval General Service
Medal awarded to
Cornelius Carroll, who
fought on *The Victory* at
Trafalgar, aged 14
£1,430 ($2,288)

Military General Service
medal awarded to
Corporal J. Coates, 40th
Foot
£1,980 ($3,168)

Brazil, Order of the Rose, Star
£1,760 ($2,816)

Sweden, Order of the Seraphim, Star
£858 ($1,372)

Great Britain, Colchester
and Essex Bank, £10, 1884
£352 ($563)

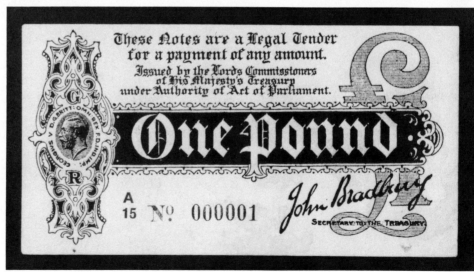

Great Britain, Treasury £1,
Bradbury first issue, 1914
£1,430 ($2,288)

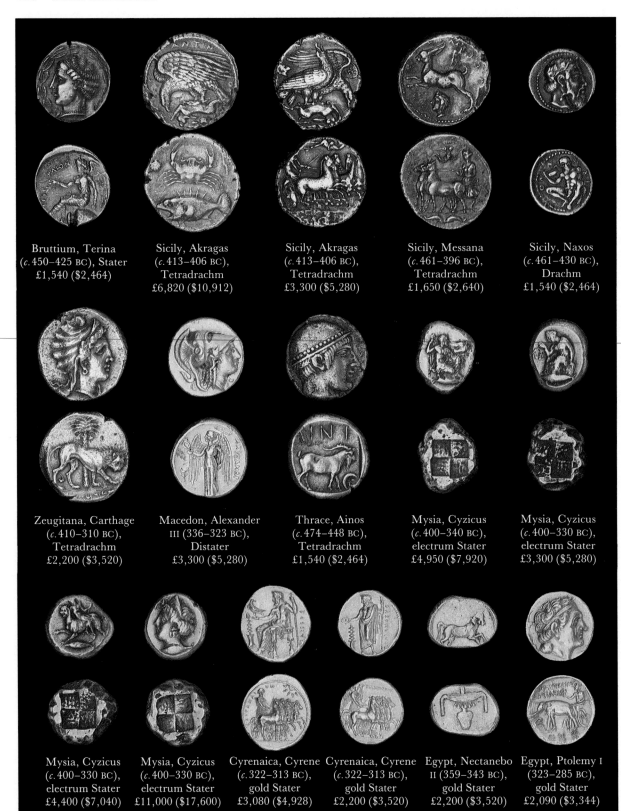

Bruttium, Terina
(c. 450–425 BC), Stater
£1,540 ($2,464)

Sicily, Akragas
(c. 413–406 BC),
Tetradrachm
£6,820 ($10,912)

Sicily, Akragas
(c. 413–406 BC),
Tetradrachm
£3,300 ($5,280)

Sicily, Messana
(c. 461–396 BC),
Tetradrachm
£1,650 ($2,640)

Sicily, Naxos
(c. 461–430 BC),
Drachm
£1,540 ($2,464)

Zeugitana, Carthage
(c. 410–310 BC),
Tetradrachm
£2,200 ($3,520)

Macedon, Alexander
III (336–323 BC),
Distater
£3,300 ($5,280)

Thrace, Ainos
(c. 474–448 BC),
Tetradrachm
£1,540 ($2,464)

Mysia, Cyzicus
(c. 400–340 BC),
electrum Stater
£4,950 ($7,920)

Mysia, Cyzicus
(c. 400–330 BC),
electrum Stater
£3,300 ($5,280)

Mysia, Cyzicus
(c. 400–330 BC),
electrum Stater
£4,400 ($7,040)

Mysia, Cyzicus
(c. 400–330 BC),
electrum Stater
£11,000 ($17,600)

Cyrenaica, Cyrene
(c. 322–313 BC),
gold Stater
£3,080 ($4,928)

Cyrenaica, Cyrene
(c. 322–313 BC),
gold Stater
£2,200 ($3,520)

Egypt, Nectanebo
II (359–343 BC),
gold Stater
£2,200 ($3,520)

Egypt, Ptolemy I
(323–285 BC),
gold Stater
£2,090 ($3,344)

Far left:
Hungary, gold 'Juden-medaille', 17th century
£1,045 ($1,672)

Left centre:
Elizabeth I (1558–1603), Sovereign of 30-shillings
£2,640 ($4,224)

Left:
Germany, Hamburg, Bank-Portugalöser of 10-Ducats, 1672
£4,620 ($7,392)

Far left and left:
Elizabeth I, oval silver plaque, by Simon de Passe
£8,800 ($14,080)

Left centre:
Massachusetts, Oak Tree Shilling, 1652
£1,870 ($2,992)

Far left:
Liechtenstein, Francis Joseph I, Ducat, 1778
£3,300 ($5,280)

Left centre:
Maryland, Lord Baltimore Sixpence, undated (1658)
£1,980 ($3,168)

Left:
Charles II, Hammered coinage (1660–2), gold Crown
£770 ($1,232)

Brazil, Pernambuco,
gold 12-Guilders siege
piece, 1645
£7,480 ($11,968)

Sommer Islands,
Sixpence, undated,
*c.*1616
£10,450 ($16,720)

Germany, Frankfurt,
Double Storm Ducat,
1710
£1,870 ($2,992)

George I, Half-
guinea, 1726
£460 ($736)

William IV, Sovereign, 1832
£660 ($1,056)

Elizabeth I (1558–1603),
Pound, m.m. key
£2,090 ($3,344)

James I (1603–1625),
Laurel, m.m. spur rowel
£2,200 ($3,520)

George II, Crown,
1743
£605 ($968)

George III, Octagonal
countermarked
Dollar, Santiago, 1743
£638 ($1,020)

Elizabeth I (1558–1603), Crown, m.m. 2
£3,740 ($5,984)

Austria, Maximilian I, Schauguldiner, dated 1479, struck in 1511
£3,520 ($5,632)

Dime, 1896
$2,200 (£1,375)

Panama-Pacific
2½-Dollars,
1915
$2,530 (£1,581)

Proof Cent,
1858
$3,190 (£1,993)

3-Dollars, 1878
$4,400 (£2,750)

Louisiana
Purchase,
1-Dollar, 1908
$2,145 (£1,340)

5-Dollars, 1819
$47,300 (£29,562)

1-Dollar, 1868
$3,520 (£2,200)

Half-Dollar, 1896
$3,300 (£2,062)

Proof 10-Dollars,
1907
$42,900 (£26,812)

Sicily, Syracuse
(c. 385–380 B.C.),
Decadrachm
$24,200 (£15,125)

Pattern Metric 20-Dollars, 1879
$9,460 (£5,912)

All sold in New York

Kellogg and Co. 50-Dollars, 1855
$63,800 (£39,875)

Falkland Islands,
£1, 1927
Sold 2.10.86 in
London for £825
($1,320)

New Zealand, Reserve
Bank £1
Sold 2.10.86 in
London for £187
($300)

Collectors' Sales

A collection of eighteenth-century fans
Sold 9.12.86 in London at South Kensington for a total of £12,650 ($17,914)

The Sale of Two Centuries

E.W. SWANTON

The sale by Christie's of 845 items belonging to the MCC, at Lord's on 13 April 1987, was a landmark in the world of cricket for several reasons. Throughout its history Marylebone Cricket Club has been ambivalent in its appreciation of the memorabilia of the game: the books and pictures, the implements, and all that can be generically classed as cricketana. Although many objects, including paintings, predate the foundation of MCC in 1787, the Club's sole possessions almost a century later were two pictures, one of them admittedly by Frances Hayman.

MCC was fortunate at this point in the interest taken in all things artistic by Sir Spencer Ponsonby-Fane, a man steeped both in the public service and in cricket. He was private secretary in turn to Palmerston, Clarendon and Granville at the Foreign Office. It was he who brought back from Paris the treaty that ended the Crimean War. All his life he fostered a deep love of the game. Ponsonby-Fane, Treasurer of MCC for thirty-six years from 1879 until his death in 1915 aged 91, acquired pictures and drawings, persuaded his friends to donate, and commissioned works on MCC's behalf. With the expansion of the game more and more objects of historical importance found their way to Lord's.

As to a library, a gift of books was accepted from a Capt. H.B. Sutherland in 1893. Even so, the Committee decided there was no need for a library 'at present' – in the age-old dismissive phrase of committee minutes. It was the generous and unfettered offer of her husband's library in 1944 by Lady Cahn, widow of Sir Julien, the furniture millionaire (who had himself acquired most of it by purchase from F.S. Ashley-Cooper), that put MCC in almost fortuitous possession of the most complete collection in the world at that time. MCC has since provided itself with the most worthwhile of the mass of cricket writing. Even so it needed a degree of pressure in appropriate directions to secure, only two years ago and for the first time in its history, a library building worthy of its contents.

Although the pictorial side of MCC's heritage after its tardy start reflects, as I have remarked, a rather more creditable story, here again the initiative during most of the Club's existence came from one man, Ponsonby-Fane. The first professional curator was appointed only forty years ago. In future, it is safe to say, the importance of the artistic and literary side of our possessions will be more respectfully regarded by even the more philistine elements of the membership seeing that by the auction sale of 'selected objects' from the *reserve* collection MCC is richer by £290,000.

Hence, of course, this article. It should perhaps be explained to readers that this item in MCC's 1987 bicentenary programme was far from a selling-off of the family silver, to borrow the late Earl of Stockton's phrase. Over the course of time much more material had been bequeathed or presented to the Club than it had room to show. Accordingly the Committee approved the proposal of the Arts and Library Sub-Committee under Mr T.M.B. Sisson's chairmanship that a sale should take place. Rather than allow things to gather dust in the basement below the Long Room, why not offer them to a public with a keen taste for cricketana of all kinds and

The founders of *I Zingari* (the gypsies), the oldest wandering cricket club: J.L. Baldwin (in the wheelchair), Sir Spencer Ponsonby-Fane (left) and his brother, the Earl of Bessborough. Painted in 1897

The MCC sale at Lord's, 13.4.87. Colin Cowdrey (centre left) in discussion with Jim Swanton (centre); Tim Rice sits in the row behind (right)

at the same time create a fund in order to keep the main collection in good order and repair, and to be in a position to acquire any such desirable item as came on to the market in future? The expectation hovered around £100,000. Christie's thought that might be on the low side, yet they were surprised as well as gratified by the result, and at the end of an eleven-hour non-stop sale their team of auctioneers – nine in all – had found a buyer for every one of the 845 objects in the catalogue. It was said to be Christie's longest day ever.

So what went for what? Well, the pattern was set right away when Henry Wyndham, of MCC and Christie's, and no stranger to the new ball, totted up £1,000 or more for each of four watercolours by Frank Reynolds which first appeared in the 1922 summer number of *Punch*. This was some three times above the mean of the estimates. Soon a small 18th-century painting showing a curved bat attracted a bid of £6,500; and Eleanor Hughes D'Eath's 18th-century copy, after R.A. Cotes, of a boy, Lewis Cage, at the wicket commanded £10,000. This proved to be the top score of the day. The purchaser was Christopher Ondaatje, a Canadian investment banker, who still turns out, according to the *Independent*, for the Old Blundellians. Portraits of youthful cricketers had great appeal. A portrait by John H. Chandler, after John Russell, of Henry St. Clair in a landscape holding bat and ball and with dog at his side fetched £5,500.

Printed cotton handkerchiefs, as always, were popular. Without offering any normally on display, the Club was willing to part with a commemorative handkerchief in purple, framed with the Laws of the Noble Game and depicting a game at the White Conduit Club at Islington, just prior to MCC's foundation. This went for £7,000 to the syndicate who are constructing the Bradman Museum at Bowral, Sir Donald Bradman's birthplace. Occasionally something like a bargain was snapped up – for instance a handkerchief of the 1882 Australian team, edged with their twelve portraits, sold for £500. Generally speaking, the earlier the date the higher the price.

Bats and balls of every age, description, size and weight were offered in profusion. The oldest bat, from the mid-18th century, and much the heaviest at 51lb. 5oz., which was made of oak, curved and bowed with humped back (a rather ridiculous-looking object), was sold for £5,000. Others of slightly later date, including one stamped with the ducal coronet of Buccleuch and almost black, also attracted lively attention. The autographing of bats was common in W.G. Grace's day; a Gunn and Moore signed by him realized £1,500. Balls were less popular, although the one used in the first Test wherein South Africa beat Australia went for £750.

A few of the objects on view were as bizarre as some of the prices realized, none more so than the cream wool tennis shorts labelled 'P.F. Warner' which went for £140. They had been unearthed by the Curator, Stephen Green, from a dark corner of the courts.

When all is said and done, the personality which dominated the proceedings was that of W.G. Grace, the man who, in a career spanning over forty years (1865–1908), did much more than anyone to transform a country pastime into the national summer game. This was evident from the start of the sale when a pen and ink caricature of W.G., black-bearded and sun-hatted, estimated at £100 to £120, realized £1,000. A series of pen and ink sketches by Harry Furniss went for £3,000, and a crude pen and ink likeness in a frame carved with wickets, bats and balls for £2,200.

The best-known photogravure of Archibald Stuart Wortley's painting of W.G. at the wicket, signed by subject and artist, went for ten times more than its recent market price of £200. W.G. scored four figures in all his first six innings: the forty-odd items in which he featured added up to £24,030. Needless to say, numerous remembrances of W.G. remain to decorate the pavilion and the Memorial Gallery.

For the final lot or two the President of MCC, Colin Cowdrey, took the rostrum, coming in last with more confidence no doubt than when at Lord's, a quarter of a century earlier, he had arrived No. 11 at the wicket in a Test against West Indies, with four balls to go, his broken arm in plaster, and three results possible. The answer then was a draw. This time a handsome victory was already in the bag. Yet everyone was too weary to enjoy the full culminating irony. The head and skin of a tiger shot on an MCC tour of India went for £2,000. The marksman was C.S. Marriott, an admirable bowler but one of the worst batsmen ever to put on pads for England. (He is one of the few men in history who have taken many more wickets than they scored runs.) That tiger must have been as sleepy as everyone who had sat for so many hours, weighing up and bidding for what the Chairman of Arts and Library succinctly described as 'an attractive rag-bag of oddments from the pavilion basement'.

If an amateur prediction is worth anything I would say that, although the publicity and cachet of the MCC sale exalted many of the prices to artificially high figures, the market for cricketana has been given a lift which may continue to be felt even when prices stabilize. Cricket surely, and all appertaining to it, has a continuing fascination for its devotees which few other sports can match.

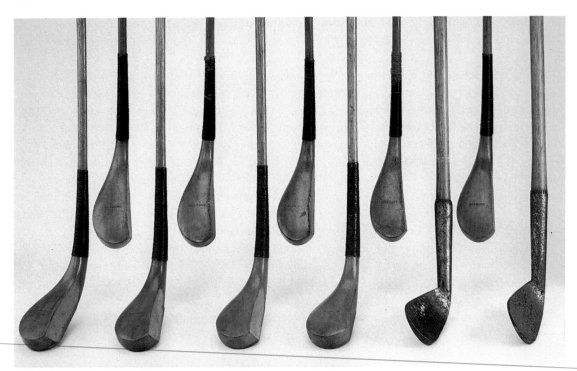

Group of scared-head clubs and two blacksmith-made track irons
By Jackson of Perth
c. 1830 and c. 1820
Sold 15.7.87 in Glasgow for a total of £53,735 ($85,976)
The clubs, the property of His Grace the Duke of Atholl, were discovered in a hallstand in the attic of Blair Castle

Group of cricket bats, balls and miniature bats
Sold 13.4.87 at Lord's Cricket Ground for a total of £11,858 ($19,187)

Above:
Four-room 'mystery' house
1897
Sold 3.3.87 in New York at Christie's East for
$15,400 (£9,891)

Above right:
Six-room 'mystery' house
Late 19th century
Sold 3.3.87 in New York at Christie's East for
$13,200 (£8,478)
From the Mary B. Rhoads Collection
These two houses are from a series of
remarkable commercial doll's houses hand-
crafted in the late 19th century. They are called
'mystery' houses because their exact origin is
unknown; however, they were probably
produced in the North-east, possibly in
Massachusetts. The price of the four-room
house in 1897 was listed at $33.

Right:
Painted wooden doll's house simulating a
Venetian Pallazio
German, late 19th century
43 in. (109 cm.) wide
Sold 5.12.86 in London at South Kensington for
£3,520 ($4,999)
From the collection of the late Lore
Höllersberger

Important Needlework at Christie's South Kensington

SUSAN MAYOR

On 23 June 1987, Christie's South Kensington held what will probably turn out to be the needlework sale of the century. Needlework collectors clamoured to view and to buy. Never had they had such choice both in terms of quality and quantity. The sale of 245 lots was packed with rarities and these realized nearly £1 million. In no other sale had comparable needlework realized such high prices or been sold in such quantities.

This remarkable English collection had been started at the turn of the century, probably in about 1907, and had been largely unexhibited for many years. The Edwardian period saw the dispersal of many family collections and the creator of this collection was thus in an enviable position of being able to purchase many fine objects from the collections of Lord Abingdon, Sir John Ramsden, Bt., Sir William Lawrence, Bt., Percival Griffiths and Talbot Hughes.

Collectors were amazed by what they saw when they arrived to view the collection at South Kensington, where it filled the Hangar Saleroom and was arranged against terracotta-coloured linen walls. It was as if they were viewing an imaginary sale of the 1920s, with part of several collections dispersed at that time all amalgamated into one unbelievable sale. For almost a week the saleroom looked like a museum – indeed many of the items had been loaned to museums over the years.

As predicted, Admiral Sir William Penn's purse was the star lot, fetching £55,000. Sir William (1621–71) was Pepys's official superior at the Navy Office. Pepys describes him variously as, 'a hypocritical rogue and a jovial companion, fond of his glass and telling a good story or singing a song, quite uninterested by any puritanical scruples'. His Quaker son of the same name (1644–1718) founded Pennsylvania in 1682. It is said that when he thanked Charles II for naming Pennsylvania after him, the King replied, 'I named it after the jolly fellow your father'. The purse is certainly a charming piece: the embroidery really captures the Admiral's twinkling smile, Penn's coat of arms is embroidered inside, and it has an impeccable provenance.

But the most sought-after pieces were the mid-17th-century examples which included much raised or stump work. The enchanting mirror illustrated here fetched £36,200. It may even have been worked by the Admiral's daughter Margaret, as it bore the initials M.P. in seed pearls. The brightest casket also had raised work on the doors and made £27,500. There were two extraordinary three-dimensional pieces of raised work: *Rebecca at the Well* which made £19,800 and *The Judgement of Solomon* which fetched £15,400, despite being a little worn. Even the enchanting little picture of the lady under an arbour with a frog at her feet, which measured only 8 × 12 in., realized £16,500, more than £1,000 per square inch. The very jolly cushion worked with the *Story of Bathsheba* also fetched £16,500.

There were various different types of needlework in the sale all of which commanded great interest. First came the novelties such as the charming revolving tape measure disguised as a spray of dog roses, the vellum tape of which is inscribed: 'Take this small present at my hand and your servant to command Mary Hanney, 1687'; this fetched £2,320. Then came the rare

Needlework mirror, the bevelled plate set in a panel of raised or
stump-work enhanced with sequins, mica and seed pearls
English, mid-17th century
24 × 19¾ in. (61 × 50 cm.)
Sold 23.6.87 in London at South Kensington for £36,200
($57,920)

The Penn Family Purse,
depicting Admiral Sir William
Penn (1621–70) standing between
a globe and his dog, Port, all
embroidered; reverse worked with
his coat-of-arms
English, mid-17th century
8¼ × 6 in. (21 × 15.2 cm.)
Sold 23.6.87 in London at South
Kensington for £55,000 ($88,000)

group of 17th-century English book bindings – one was even late 16th-century. These drew great
interest. The top price was £14,300 for a copy of the *Book of Common Prayer* bound in ivory satin
and worked with allegories of Hope and Charity and which was finally bought by a book collector after great competition from an English needlework collector. The 16th-century valances
were very rare; the example which fetched the most at £17,600 was worked with an *Allegory
of Time and Abundance*. But even later embroidery sold exceptionally well, the charming games
box enclosing four small embroidered boxes of counters, *c.*1730, fetched £14,300 and the large
and naïve picture worked with the *Finding of Moses* fetched £10,980.

This remarkable sale will surely set new standards in an increasingly competitive field.

Above left:
Needlework mirror case
English, *c.*1660
12 × 10 in. (30.5 × 25.4 cm.)
Sold 12.5.87 in London at South Kensington for
£13,200 ($21,860)

Above:
Cantonese embroidered cover and two cushion
covers
*c.*1900
96 × 86 in. (243.7 × 218.3 cm.)
Sold 17.2.87 in London at South Kensington for
£2,200 ($3,351)

Left:
Embroidered workbag
English
With the initials I.S., the date 1669, and the age
of the embroideress – 10
18¹⁄₂ × 24 in. (47 × 61 cm.)
Sold 12.5.87 in London at South Kensington for
£8,250 ($13,662)

Ball dress of pink, blue, green and grey striped silk
*c.*1869
Sold 20.1.87 in London at South Kensington for £1,430 ($2,170)

Evening dress of saffron yellow muslin
*c.*1830
Sold 20.1.87 in London at South Kensington for £440 ($668)

Mantle of mushroom-coloured silk
*c.*1820
Sold 20.1.87 in London at South Kensington for £353 ($536)

Dress of pale blue and gold striped satin and gold ribbed silk
Labelled 'Josephine G. Egan'
*c.*1876
Sold 12.5.87 in London at South Kensington for £2,640 ($4,372)
From a collection of dresses made for the King Family, of the King Ranch, Texas

Above:
Bisque bonnet-headed baby doll
Marked 'JDK 12'
15 in. (38.1 cm.) high
Sold 14.5.87 in London at South Kensington for
£7,150 ($11,869)

Above right:
Clockwork musical automaton magician
Probably by Vichy, Paris
*c.*1880
25 in. (63.5 cm.) high
Sold 9.12.86 in London at South Kensington for
£7,700 ($10,927)

Above far right:
Bisque-headed clockwork musical automaton
conjuror
Probably by Decamps, head by Jumeau
Late 19th century
16 in. (40.6 cm.) high
Sold 23.10.86 in London at South Kensington
for £2,420 ($3,459)

Left:
Vladimir, a bisque-headed
bébé with closed mouth
Stamped in red 'DEPOSSE
TETE JUMEAU'
27 in. (68.6 cm.) high
Sold 9.7.87 in London at
South Kensington for
£6,600 ($10,560)
This doll was given to
Miss Ellen West, governess
to the children of the Duke
and Duchess of Edinburgh,
as a leaving present in
*c.*1900

Snow White and the Seven Dwarfs
Evil witch by her boiling cauldron dipping the apple in poison
1937
Gouache on two full celluloids applied to a master background
12¹⁄₂ × 16 in.
(31.8 × 40.6 cm.)
Sold 1.11.86 in New York at Christie's East for $30,800 (£21,953)
Record auction price for a celluloid

Left:
Mickey Mouse Presenting a Bouquet to Minnie Mouse
By Walt Disney
Signed
Pen, black ink and watercolour
3¹⁄₄ × 4¹⁄₄ in. (8.2 × 10.8 cm.)
Sold 26.2.87 in London at South Kensington for £1,760 ($2,693)
Accompanying letter from the vendor stated 'This drawing and autograph was done for me by Walt Disney when he visited Grosvenor House, Park Lane, London, where my father, V.G. Samaden was working as Head Waiter…*c.*1940'

c. 4 in. scale Foden type twin-cylinder overtype
two-speed steam lorry, Registration No. 911 FRF
Built by A. Groves, Watford
1937
36½ × 88 in. (92.5 × 223.5 cm.)
Sold 8.8.86 in London at South Kensington for
£5,500 ($7,788)

Exhibition standard model of the 3-cylinder
compound surface condensing vertical reversing
marine engine fitted to the Cunard Liner
SS *Servia*
Modelled by Thomas Lowe
1907
14½ × 12½ in. (37 × 31 cm.)
Sold 8.8.86 in London at South Kensington for
£4,400 ($6,512)

Exhibition standard 5 in. gauge model of the Great Western Railway Armstrong Class 4-4-0 locomotive and tender No. 14, *Charles Saunders*
Built by P.J. Rich, Rhiwderin
14 × 62 in. (35.5 × 157.5 cm.)
Sold 8.8.86 in London at South Kensington for £11,220 ($15,888)

Exhibition standard 1:75 scale fully planked and rigged model of the French 60-gun man-of-war
Le Protecteur
Built by P.M. di Gragnano, Naples
*c.*1760
31 × 38 in. (78.5 × 96.5 cm.)
Sold 8.8.86 in London at South Kensington for £5,500 ($8,140)

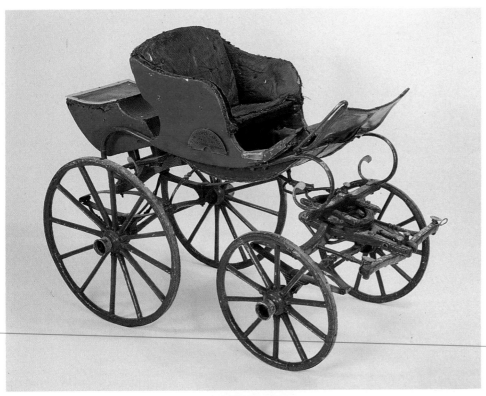

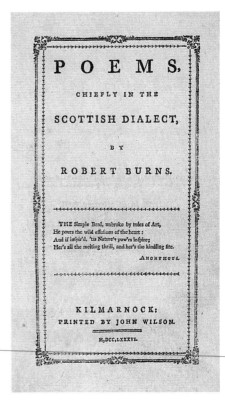

Above:
Miniature phaeton with single-seat body
The brass plates engraved 'TOM THUMB'S CARRIAGE, PASSED BY H.M. BRITISH CUSTOMS'
25 in. (63.5 cm.) high;
41 in. (104.1 cm.) long;
27 in. (68.6 cm.) wheel base
Sold 12.12.86 in London at South Kensington for £3,190 ($4,529)
This diminutive carriage is believed to be a relic from a European tour of the showman P.T. Barnum's most famous midget, General Tom Thumb

ROBERT BURNS
Poems
First edition, (Egerer 1)
John Wilson, Kilmarnock, 1786
8½ × 5 in. (21.2 × 12.5 cm.)
Sold 15.4.87 in Glasgow for £9,900 ($15,989)

Three-quarter length portrait of Queen Victoria
Inscribed 'Victoria RI 1889'
11½ × 9¼ in. (29.2 × 23.5 cm.)
Sold 26.2.87 in London at South Kensington for £1,210 ($1,845)

Wheel of Life zoetrope
By London Stereoscopic Company
12 in. (30.5 cm.) diameter
Sold 19.3.87 in London at South Kensington for
£1,870 ($2,792)

Above:
Leica M2 camera
No. 1142451; Leica
250 Reporter Model
GG camera No. 150185;
Leica 1 camera
No. 47958; Replica
Ur-Leica camera
Sold 16.7.87 in
London at South
Kensington for
£2,420 ($3,872);
£3,960 ($6,336);
£4,400 ($7,040);
and £1,100 ($1,760)
respectively

Leica 1 camera No. 176
Sold 16.7.87 in London at South
Kensington for £10,450 ($16,720)

Right:
George Knight & Co. Cosmorama table-top
stereoscope; Achromatic table stereoscope
No. 2308 by Smith, Beck and Beck; and
Zeiss Ikon twin-lens Contaflex camera
Sold 15.1.87 in London at South
Kensington for £935 ($1,396); £825
($1,232) and £605 ($903) respectively

Tonneau III, No. 7212
By Bing
c. 1903
10 in. (25.4 cm.) long
Sold 30.7.87 in London at
South Kensington for
£12,100 ($19,360)

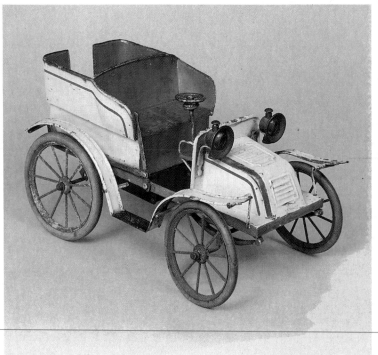

Bahamas Police Band comprising European director,
cymbalist, four trombones, two saxaphones, two French
horns, four trumpets, two side drums, four clarinets, two fifes,
a euphonium and a bassoon
Britains, set No. 2186
Post-war
Sold 11.12.86 in London at South Kensington for £2,200
($3,124)

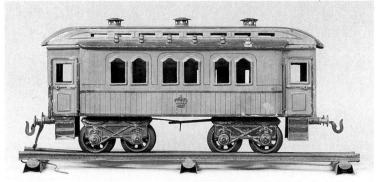

Gauge 1 'Kaiser Train' twin-bogie passenger coach
By Bing
c. 1902
Sold 2.10.86 in London at South Kensington for £1,045 ($1,501)

HMS *Barfleur*
By Märklin
*c.*1924
35 in. (89 cm.) long
Sold 29.1.87 in London at
South Kensington for
£20,900 ($32,019)

Clockwork tinplate Nassau-
class battleship
In original wooden crate
bearing Märklin trade label
39 in. long
Sold 19.5.87 in Glasgow for
£11,550 ($19,301)

Amounderness Local Militia
(Lancashire) uniform
Early 19th century
Sold 1.5.87 in London at South
Kensington for £5,280 ($8,739)

Officer's scarlet coat, possibly
Royal Lancashire Militia
c.1778–83
Sold 1.5.87 in London at South
Kensington for £1,100 ($1,821)

24⅝ in. Polyphon hall clock
98½ in. (250 cm.) high
Sold 3.7.87 in London at South Kensington for £10,500
($16,800)

Edison fireside phonograph, Model A No. 28672
Sold 3.7.87 in London at South Kensington for £900
($1,440)

24-key barrel-organ, No. 8863
By Gavioli & Co., Paris
20 in. (50.8 cm.) wide
Sold 3.7.87 in London at South Kensington for £2,600
($4,160)

Edison class M electric phonograph
50½ in. (127 cm.) high
Sold 16.4.87 in London at South Kensington for £7,700 ($12,451)
Presented by Colonel Gouraud to H.M. Stanley on the occasion of his
wedding in 1890

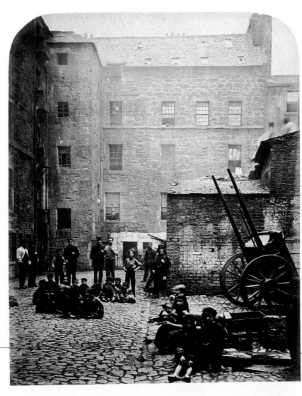

THOMAS ANNAN
Old Closes and Streets of Glasgow
One from a set of 31 albumen prints
1868
Seven approx. 12 × 15 in.
(30.5 × 38.1 cm.); the remainder
approx. 11 × 9 in. (28 × 23 cm.)
Sold 30.10.86 in London at South
Kensington for £16,500 ($23,122)

ALFRED STIEGLITZ
The Flat-Iron
Large format photogravure on
vellum
*c.*1903
12⅞ × 6½ in. (32.7 × 16.5 cm.)
Sold 11.11.86 in New York for
$8,800 (£6,129)
From the collection of the
Museum of Modern Art, New
York

D.O. HILL and R. ADAMSON
Bonaly Towers
From the album *Memorials of Bonnie
Bonaly*, containing 27 calotypes
1849
Each approx. 8 × 6¼ in. (20 × 16 cm.)
Sold 30.10.86 in London at South
Kensington for £18,700 ($26,218)

CARLETON E. WATKINS
Yosemite Valley from the 'Best General View'
From the album *Yosemite*, containing 26 mammoth-plate albumen prints
*c.*1867, printed before 1876
Each approx. 16½ × 20½ in. (42 × 52 cm.)
Sold 30.4.87 in London at South Kensington for £30,800 ($51,005)

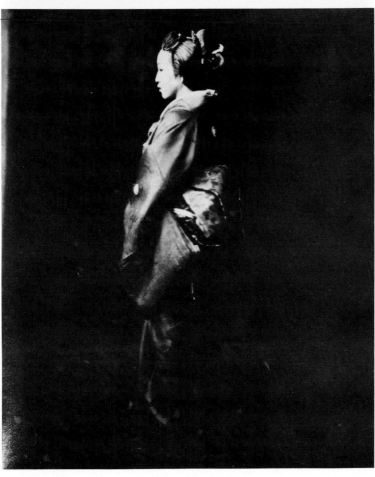

Left:

JOHN THOMSON, L.F. FISLER, E. RUSFELDT, W. SAUNDERS and others
Photographs of China and its inhabitants
One from an album of 69 photographs and five composite
panoramas, albumen prints
Of varying size
c. 1860–75
Sold 30.10.86 in London at South Kensington for £8,200
($11,497)

Below:

FELICE BEATO, F.C. GOULD and others
Japanese landscape, Samurai Warriors and military life
One from an album of 99 individual photographs, one two-print,
one three-print and one five-print panorama, albumen prints
Of varying size
c. 1864
Sold 30.10.86 in London at South Kensington for £15,400
($21,591)

Left:

FELICE BEATO
The Simonoseki Campaign and others
One from an album of 53 individual photographs, one two-
print, one four-print and one five-print panorama, albumen
prints
1864
Of varying size
Sold 30.10.86 in London at South Kensington for £11,000
($15,422)

Right:
MAN RAY
Seated Nude
Stamped 'Rue Campagne-
Première' on the reverse
Solarized gelatin silver print
1934
$11\frac{1}{2} \times 9\frac{1}{8}$ in.
(29.2 × 23.2 cm.)
Sold 11.11.86 in New York
for $10,120 (£7,048)

Far right:
EDWARD WESTON
Portrait of Margrethe with Fan
Inscribed 'Loaned by Mrs.
Rae Davis Knight' in pencil
Platinum print
1914
$9\frac{1}{4} \times 6\frac{1}{2}$ in.
(23.5 × 16.5 cm.)
Sold 11.11.86 in New York
at Christie's East for
$26,400 (£18,385)

Right:
ALFRED CHENEY JOHNSTON
*Study of Caroline Nunder,
Ziegfeld*
Gelatin silver print
*c.*1926
$12\frac{1}{2} \times 10\frac{1}{2}$ in.
(32.7 × 26.7 cm.)
Sold 11.11.86 in New York
for $4,400 (£2,927)
Record auction price for a
photograph by the artist

Far right:
MAN RAY
Dos Blanc
Gelatin silver print, *c.*1926
$11\frac{1}{2} \times 8\frac{7}{8}$ in.
(29.2 × 22.5 cm.)
Sold 11.11.86 in New York
for $28,600 (£19,917)
Record auction price for a
photograph by the artist

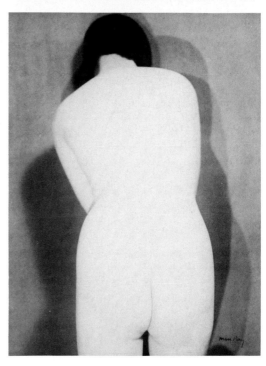

Bugattis and Ferraris in Monaco

PETER HAWKINS

The Bugatti and Ferrari auction in Monaco on 26 May was our first motor-car sale in the principality. Timing and location were carefully chosen in line with our international policy of offering the most advantageous conditions to our vendors. The date fell just after the finish of the historic Mille Miglia rally in Brescia, and only days before the Monaco Grand Prix. The sale took place in the Grand Salon of the Loews Hotel, situated yards from the Grand Prix circuit, and was not without its challenges for our staff. The cars had to enter and leave by the front steps of the hotel, and this was only possible between four and six o'clock in the morning. Also, they all had to be out of Monaco the next day, as the day after was the first day's practice for the Grand Prix. Entries for the sale arrived from Europe, America and New Zealand: appropriately two came directly from the Mille Miglia, still wearing their competition numbers for the event.

The theme chosen for the sale was Bugattis and Ferraris, two of the most distinguished marques in the history of motoring, both exceptional in their performance and the beauty of their design. It was the first sale ever of its type and one of the finest motor-car auctions ever held. Public response was highly enthusiastic and the cars were sold before a larger audience than we have ever enjoyed in Monaco.

The European auction record for a motor was beaten three times, and the total for the sale, over £4 million, was in itself a European record for a motor-car auction. First to beat the record of £440,000 (paid for a Bugatti) was a 1958 Ferrari 250 Testa Rossa at F.fr.8,880,000 (£901,320), only to be followed 15 lots later by another Ferrari, a 1963 4-litre 330 GTO Berlinetta (one of only three ever built) at F.fr.9,268,500 (£940,752). The last lot in the sale, a unique 1932 Bugatti type 54 two-seater then sold for F.fr.5,550,000 (£563,325). Despite competition from the United States and Japan, all three were acquired by European collectors. International press comment after the sale credited us with a bold and highly successful operation.

1963 4-litre Ferrari 330 GTO Berlinetta
Chassis No. 4561 SA
Engine No. 4561 SA
Sold 26.5.87 in Monaco for F.fr.9,268,500 (£940,752)
'In the closing stages of the race there was a brief moment of excitement when Parkes was in the new 4-litre GT Ferrari in second place and...it was seen that Bonnier was closing up on the Ferrari. But it did not last for long; in spite of the rain Parkes opened out the big V12 Ferrari when his pit gave him the news and he just motored away...' (Denis Jenkinson, *Motor Sport*, London, July 1962)

1958 3-litre Ferrari 250 Testa Rossa
Chassis No. 0736 TR
Engine No. 0736
Sold 26.5.87 in Monaco for F.fr.8,880,000 (£901,320)
'The new Vee-12 3-litre 'Testa Rossa' cars, so called because of their red-painted cylinder heads, had gone very well…it was quite clear that they were going to go just about as quickly as the larger cars of previous years…' (Mike Hawthorn, World Champion Driver, 1958)

1932 4.9-litre Bugatti type 54 two-seat roadster
By Bachelier, London
Chassis No. 54205
Engine No. 5
Sold 26.5.87 in Monaco for F.fr.5,550,000 (£563,325)
'Let it suffice that over here this Bugatti is unique, in its very conception, wherein lies half its appeal, in the carefully constructed body and its equipment, and in the beauty of its finish…' (William Boddy, *Motor Sport*, London, 1936(?))

1960 3-litre Ferrari 250 GT SWB Competizione Berlinetta
Chassis No. 1807 GT
Engine No. 1953
Sold 26.5.87 in Monaco for F.fr.3,330,000 (£338,002)
'...a really comfortable Grand Touring car with good brakes, a super engine and crisp gearbox...quite difficult to fault, in fact...'
(Stirling Moss – forthcoming book on his cars and his racing career)

Wine

Half-bottle 1784 Château d'Yquem (detail)
Wheel-engraved with the initials 'Th. J.' for Thomas Jefferson
Sold 4.12.86 in London for £39,600 ($56,391)

An Eventful Season for Wine

MICHAEL BROADBENT, M.W.

A season of great activity and considerable variety, several new record prices, promotional sales on behalf of the Portuguese and two leading Bordeaux châteaux; and a festival of St. James's to celebrate a couple of Christie anniversaries. All this hard on the heels of the departure of our principal King Street wine auctioneer, the introduction of a buyer's premium on wine and an office move.

TWO NOTABLE RECORDS

On 4 December 1986 the star item in an already star-studded sale of Finest and Rarest Wines was a bottle of Château d'Yquem, vintage 1784, bearing the engraved initials of Thomas Jefferson. The price: £39,600 ($56,391), a world record for any white wine. The bottle, purchased by a buyer who not altogether successfully tried to escape a posse of reporters and cameramen, is still in London but will shortly find a resting place in the cellars of the *premier grand cru* château in Sauternes that gave it birth, alongside the original cellarbooks and ledgers detailing despatches and sales to Jefferson.

Another Jefferson relic, this time an exceptionally rare half-bottle of Château Margaux of the same vintage – and from the same collection unearthed in a Paris cellar – was the centre of attention at our Fine and Rare Wine Sale at VINEXPO in Bordeaux. It was bought for F.fr.198,000 (approx. £19,800) by Marvin Shanken of M. Shanken Communications Inc., New York. Mr Shanken is the most important wine journal publisher in North America. His empire includes *The Wine Spectator* and two trade orientated magazines, the glossy *Market Watch* and the statistic-packed *Impact*. The half-bottle, stored since the sale in the historic cellars at Château Margaux, was recorked by the cellarmaster and myself on 20 August and hand-carried to New York on Concorde on 2 September. It will have pride of place in the Shanken *Vinothèque*.

£19,800 – a world record price for a half-bottle – would not, perhaps, have come as all that much of a surprise to the owners of Château Margaux at the time or indeed to Jefferson himself. 1784 was one of the most renowned vintages of the 18th century, and *very* expensive. In Jefferson's own words, quoted from two letters, both dated 'Paris Feb. 15 1788', one addressed to his shipping agent, the other to a friend to whom he was selling some of his precious stock, 'This is indeed dear, being three livres a bottle, but it is Château Margau [sic] of the year 1784, bought by myself on the spot [in 1787] and therefore genuine... It is one of the best vintages which has happened in nine years, and is of one of the four vineyards which are admitted to possess exclusively the first reputation. I may safely assure you therefore that, according to the taste of this country [France] and of England there cannot be a better bottle of Bordeaux. It cost me at Bordeaux three livres in bottle, ready packed. This is very dear, but you say you do not limit me in price.'

Half-bottle 1784 Château
Margau (sic)
Sold 26.6.87 at VINEXPO in
Bordeaux for F.fr.198,000
(£19,800)

Dutch silver corkscrew
Sold 3.4.87 in London for
£605 ($966)

OTHER MAJOR WINES AND HIGH PRICES

Authentic bottles of old vintages of Lafite are always in demand, particularly if checked and recorked at the château. The 1832, recorked by the *maître de chai* in 1986, recapsuled, relabelled, but of course with the original wine in the original bottle, sold for £3,520 ($5,013) on 4 December 1986, and a magnum of the same vintage for £4,840 ($7,744) on 4 June 1987. A magnum of the 1848 in the same sale sold for £4,070 ($6,512).

Also in December, a half-bottle of 1727 Rüdesheimer Apostelswein from the famous Bremen Ratskeller, the deeply arched cellars below the Town Hall in Bremen, realized £715 ($1,019), a record price for this wine. A half-litre of Tokay Essence of the fabulous 1811 fetched a fraction more: £748 ($1,066). The 'comet vintage' was probably the most perfect ever recorded in Europe. This particular wine came originally from the cellars of 'the Princely Family of Bretzenheim which became extinct in 1863', according to Berry Bros.' label. The wine was 'walled up during the Hungarian revolution of 1849, rediscovered in 1925' and shipped by Berry Bros. in that year. Tokay Essence is probably the longest living of all wines. The 1811 is still good. I know: I once bought, and drank, a bottle.

Another perfect-to-drink old wine, the 1858 Mouton-Rothschild, was bought by an American dealer on 4 December 1986. In a rare double-magnum, it commanded £11,110 ($15,821).

Believed to be unique, a jeroboam of Château Pétrus 1945, one of the greatest post-war clarets, sold for £7,920 ($11,277). Coincidentally, exactly the same price was paid for another rare jeroboam, Château d'Yquem of the perfect 1937 vintage.

PRIVATE CELLARS

Although a large amount of wine emanating from private cellars in the United Kingdom flows unceasingly through our salerooms, it has been very noticeable that the largest and most complete 'pristine' – untouched, unmoved – cellars come from France. Outstandingly the best recent single collection from France filled an entire morning's sale on 2 April 1987. The stock, consisting entirely of top growths of Bordeaux and Burgundy, vintages roughly from 1898 to 1926, came from a cellar near Biarritz. Virtually all were first growths or equivalent and an exceptionally large number in *grand format* bottles, for example the 1926 Lafite was represented by two jeroboams and fifteen magnums as well as over four dozen standard-size bottles. There was also Mouton in four jeroboams and seventeen magnums, Latour in five jeroboams and twelve magnums, Margaux in three jeroboams and five magnums – and so forth.

The levels were quite remarkable for the age of wine although many labels were bin-soiled, not unusual in old cellars. They sold for a total just short of £143,000 ($226,655).

SPECIAL SALES

The third sale of the season, entitled 'Fine Wine in St. James's', was held on 11 October 1986 to celebrate the 20th anniversary of the newly formed wine department. As the 11th was a Saturday, and the autumn of 1986 also happened to be the 220th anniversary of the foundation of Christie's, we decided to turn it into a complete wine event by inviting our equally old-established neighbours in St. James's to participate. The wine merchants were represented by Berry Bros. & Rudd, Christopher's (both founded in the 17th century), Fortnum & Mason (1707), Harveys of Bristol (1796), Hatch Mansfield (1802) and Justerini & Brooks (1749). Each had a stand, with an 18th-century backdrop, to dispense their wine. In addition, Paxtons (founded in 1797) presented rare cheese, Robert Lewis (1787) displayed cigars, and Hatchards of Piccadilly (1797) offered for sale a wide range of books on wine.

On 23 October we held an equally original event, this time to celebrate the 600th anniversary of the Treaty of Windsor. In the first place we had been approached by the Portuguese Trade Office to promote their little known but excellent table wines, but we expanded this idea to include the classic ports and madeiras. The port section featured the widest range of shippers and vintages ever offered, and also the greatest collection of old madeiras.

German wine *c.* 1725 in bocksbeutel (side view) Sold 4.6.87 in London for £594 ($950)

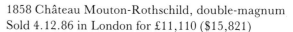
1832 Château Lafite
Sold 4.12.86 in London for £3,520 ($5,013)

1858 Château Mouton-Rothschild, double-magnum
Sold 4.12.86 in London for £11,110 ($15,821)

German wine c.1725 in
bocksbeutel (end view)
Sold 4.6.87 in London for
£594 ($950)

On 13 November 1986 the Woltner family, for whom we have organized several sales, disposed of an important quantity of wine from their former properties, the Châteaux La Mission Haut-Brion, La Tour Haut-Brion and the white Laville Haut-Brion; an unprecedented 48 vintages of the latter and 67 vintages of the renowned La Mission, ranging from 1888 to 1982.

Special promotional sales for two other leading châteaux were incorporated into two consecutive Fine Claret and White Bordeaux sales. The first, for the *1er cru classé* Sauternes, Climens, was on 21 May 1987 and consisted of 16 vintages especially shipped from the château for the sale, with of course a wide selection for the pre-sale tasting. The second was on 18 June for Château Calon-Ségur. Also still family owned, 26 vintages, ranging from a single bottle of 1895 to several dozen of the 1982, were shipped. Each sale was highly successful, all the lots were sold, and proprietors were pleased with both prices and publicity.

DEPARTMENTAL CHANGES

I try to avoid making the *Review of the Season* read like an end of term report, but I must record that 1986/7 started without the presence of the redoubtable Alan Taylor-Restell, who had resigned at the end of the previous season. After twenty years at Christie's, and prior to that with his family firm W. & T. Restell, Alan decided to put down his gavel and turn to another branch of the wine trade. Highly experienced, technically skilled and a familiar and respected figure in the rostrum, he is of course much missed. His departure necessitated some reorganization and, despite the pressure of extra autumn sales, the new administrative team managed to cope and now functions admirably.

Alan's departure coincided with the introduction of the 10% premium. We had been the odd-man out at Christie's (and Sotheby's) and fell into line at the same time as the premium came into force at Christie's South Kensington. Our new terms posed some small problems and uncertainties – how would our regular buyers react? – but, almost to a man, our clients have gracefully bowed to the inevitable.

No sooner had we mastered all these little problems than there was an office move. The department left the first floor overlooking Bury Street, and is now comfortably installed on the opposite side of Christie's, this time overlooking Duke Street. Although connected to the main salerooms, we now have our own entrance at 47 Duke Street, our own reception, complete suite of offices and a very light and airy tasting room. Visitors are most welcome.

OVERSEAS AND OTHER WINE SALES

The King Street team either provides the auctioneer for, or organizes, or both, all the wine sales conducted by the group: for the five sales in Chicago ($1,591,628 – total for last season), two each in Geneva and Amsterdam (totals Sw.fr.670,794 and D.fl.1,669,354 respectively).

Duncan McEuen has a leading hand in the European sales and conducts the increasingly successful monthly wine auctions at Christie's South Kensington, as well as three a year in the City of London and in Scotland.

SALES TOTALS

Converted to pounds sterling on the day of each sale, the total value of wine sold overseas by Christie's in 1986/7 was £2,179,179, the combined South Kensington, City and Scotland sales totalled £827,523 and the 26 main King Street wine auctions £5,324,061. Grand total sold at 53 wine auctions worldwide, £8,330,763.

Above:
'Fine Wine in St. James's'
A wine extravaganza held in
Christie's Great Rooms,
11.10.86

Above right:
Hatch Mansfield stand

Right:
Fortnum & Mason stand

Far right:
Harveys of Bristol stand

Christie's International Plc
Chairman: J. A. Floyd

EUROPEAN SALEROOMS

Head Office
Christie, Manson & Woods Ltd.
8 King Street, St. James's
London SW1Y 6QT
Tel: (01) 839 9060
Telex: 916429
Facsimile: (01) 839 1611
Chairman: The Hon. Charles Allsopp

South Kensington
Christie's South Kensington Ltd.
85 Old Brompton Road
London SW7 3LD
Tel: (01) 581 7611
Telex: 922061
Chairman: W.A. Coleridge

Scotland
Christie's & Edmiston's Ltd.
164-166 Bath Street
Glasgow G2 4TG
Tel: (041) 332 8134/7
Telex: 779901
Chairman: Sir Ilay Campbell, Bt.

Robson Lowe at Christie's
8 King Street, St. James's
London SW1Y 6QX
Tel: (01) 839 9060
Telex: 916429
Facsimile: (01) 839 1611

39 Poole Hill
Bournemouth
Dorset
Tel: (0202) 292740

Italy
Christie's (International) S.A.
Palazzo Massimo Lancellotti
Piazza Navona 114
Rome 00186
Tel: (396) 654 1217
Telex: 611524
Maurizio Lodi-Fé

Monaco
Peter Hawkins
Christie's Monaco S.A.M.
Park Palace
98000 Monte Carlo
Tel: (3393) 25 19 33
Telex: 489287

The Netherlands
Christie's Amsterdam B.V.
Cornelis Schuytstraat 57
1071 JG Amsterdam
Tel: (3120) 64 20 11   Telex: 15758
Cables: Christiart, Amsterdam
Harts Nystad
Facsimile: (3120) 640899

Switzerland
Christie's (International) S.A.
8 place de la Taconnerie
1204 Geneva
Tel: (4122) 28 25 44   Telex: 423634
Cables: Chrisauction, Geneva
Facsimile: (4122) 21 55 59
Hans Nadelhoffer

UNITED STATES OF AMERICA SALEROOMS AND REPRESENTATIVES

Christie, Manson & Woods International, Inc.
502 Park Avenue
New York, N.Y. 10022
Tel: (212) 546 1000
Telex: 620721
Cables: Chriswoods, New York
Facsimile: (212) 980 8163
President: Christopher Burge
Executive Vice Presidents: François Curiel,
Stephen S. Lash

Christie's East
219 East 67th Street
New York, N.Y. 10021
Tel: (212) 606 0400
Telex: 672-0346
President: J. Brian Cole

BEVERLY HILLS
Terry Stanfill
Russell Fogarty
Hillary Holland
342 North Rodeo Drive
Beverly Hills, Ca. 90210
Tel: (213) 275 5534
Telex: 6711872

BOSTON
Elizabeth M. Chapin
P.O. Box 2723
Cambridge, Mass. 02238
Tel: (617) 576 0400

CHICAGO
Frances Blair
Laura de Frise
200 West Superior
Chicago, Illinois 60610
Tel: (312) 787 2765

DALLAS
Carolyn Foxworth
7047 Elmridge Drive
Dallas, Texas 75240
Tel: (214) 239 0098

MIAMI
Hannah Shore
P.O. Box 331364
Coconut Grove
Florida 33233
Tel: (305) 445 1487

PALM BEACH
Helen Cluett
251 Royal Palm Way
Palm Beach, Fla. 33480
Tel: (305) 833 6952

PHILADELPHIA
Paul Ingersoll
Francis Gowen
Molly Wood
P.O. Box 1112
Bryn Mawr, Pa. 19010
Tel: (215) 525 5493

SAN FRANCISCO
Ellanor Notides
3516 Sacramento St.
San Francisco, Ca. 94118
Tel: (415) 346 6633

WASHINGTON
Nuala Pell
Joan Gardner
P.O. Box 25566
Washington, D.C. 20007
Tel: (202) 333 7459

REPRESENTATIVES

Great Britain and Ireland

Christie's in the City
Simon Birch, Peter Arbuthnot
56/60 Gresham Street
London EC2V 7BB
Tel: (01) 588 4424
     (01) 606 1848
Telex: 928637

Highland
John Douglas-Menzies
Mounteagle, Fern
Ross-shire IV20 1RP
Tel: (086283) 2866

Grampian
Lord Inverurie
The Stables, Keith Hall
Inverurie
Aberdeenshire AB5 0LD
Tel: (0467) 24366

Perthshire
Sebastian Thewes
Strathgarry House
Killiecrankie by Pitlochry
Perthshire PH16 5LJ
Tel: (079681) 216

Argyll
Sir Ilay Campbell, Bt.
Cumlodden Estate Office, Crarae
Inveraray, Argyll PA32 8YA
Tel: (0546) 86633

Edinburgh
Michael Clayton
5 Wemyss Place, Edinburgh EH3 6DH
Tel: (031) 225 4756/7

Ayrshire
James Hunter Blair
Blairquhan, Maybole, Ayrshire KA19 7LZ
Tel: (06557) 239

Northumbria
Aidan Cuthbert
Eastfield House, Main Street, Corbridge
Northumberland NE45 5LA
Tel: (043471) 3181

North-West
Victor Gubbins
Eden Lacy, Lazonby, Penrith
Cumbria CA10 1BZ
Tel: (076883) 8800

Yorkshire
Sir Nicholas Brooksbank, Bt.
Miss Sallyanne Sime
192 Huntington Road, York YO3 9BN
Tel: (0904) 30911

West Midlands
Michael Thompson
Stanley Hall, Bridgnorth
Shropshire WV16 4SP
Tel: (07462) 61891

Cheshire
Richard Roundell
Dorfold Hall
Nantwich, Cheshire CW5 8LD
Tel: (0270) 627024

East Midlands
The Hon. Lady Hastings
Mrs. William Proby
The Stables, Milton Hall
Peterborough PE6 7AA
Tel: (073121) 781

East Anglia
Richard Wills
Old Bank of England Court
Queen Street, Norwich NR2 4SX
Tel: (0603) 614546

Stuart Betts, M.C., F.G.A. *Consultant*
33 Constitution Hill, Ipswich IP1 3RL
Tel: (0473) 52308

Cotswolds
Viscount Ebrington
Rupert de Zoete *Consultant*
111 The Promenade, Cheltenham
Gloucestershire GL50 1PS
Tel: (0242) 518999

Hampshire & Wiltshire
Richard de Pelet
Tel: (0963) 70518

West Country
Richard de Pelet
Monmouth Lodge, Yenston
Templecombe, Somerset BA8 0NH
Tel: (0963) 70518

South Dorset & Solent
Nigel Thimbleby
Wolfeton House, Dorchester
Dorset DT2 9QN
Tel: (0305) 68748
and at:
39 Poole Hill, Bournemouth, Dorset
Tel: (0202) 292740

Cornwall
Christopher Petherick
Tredeague, Porthpean
St. Austell, Cornwall PA26 6AX
Tel: (0726) 64672

Devon
The Hon. George Lopes
Gnaton Estate Office, Yealmpton
Plymouth, Devon PL8 2HU
Tel: (0752) 880636

South-East
Tom Craig
Tel: (040376) 305

Sussex
Robin Loder
Leonardslee Gardens, Lower Beeding
Nr. Horsham, West Sussex RH13 6PP
Tel: (040376) 305

Kent
Christopher Proudfoot
The Old Rectory, Fawkham
Dartford, Kent DA3 8LX
Tel: (04747) 2854

Ireland
Desmond Fitz-Gerald, Knight of Glin
Glin Castle, Glin, Co. Limerick
Private Residence:
52 Waterloo Road, Dublin 4
Tel: (0001) 68 05 85

Northern Ireland
John Lewis-Crosby
Marybrook House, Raleagh Road
Crossgar, Downpatrick
Co. Down BT30 9JG
Tel: (0396) 830574

Channel Islands
Richard de la Hey
58 David Place, St. Helier, Jersey
Tel: (0534) 77582

Overseas

Argentina
Cesar Feldman *Consultant*
Libertad 1269, 1012 Buenos Aires
Tel: (541) 41 1616 or 42 2046
Cables: Tweba, Buenos Aires
Facsimile: (541) 311 1155

Australia
Sue Hewitt
298 New South Head Road
Double Bay, Sydney, 2028
Tel: (612) 326 1422   Telex: 26343
Cables: Christiart Sydney

Mrs Patricia Macdonald
103 Caroline Street, South Yarra
Victoria 3141, Melbourne
Tel: (613) 266 3715

Austria
Dr. Johanna Schönburg-Hartenstein
Kohlmarkt 4, 1010 Vienna
Tel: (43222) 63 88 12   Telex: 113265

Belgium
Janine Duesberg
Christie, Manson & Woods (Belgium) Ltd.
33 Boulevard de Waterloo, 1000 Brussels
Tel: (322) 512 8765 or 8830
Telex: 20380

Annette Van Thillo-Gérard
Arenbergstraat 1, 2000 Antwerp
Tel: (323) 233 2471

Brazil
Maria-Thereza de Azevedo Sodre *Consultant*
Av. Rui Barbosa 582, 22250 Rio de Janeiro
Tel: (5521) 551 1467   Telex: 213 4285

Canada
Murray Mackay
Christie, Manson & Woods
International Inc.
94 Cumberland Street, Suite 416
Toronto, Ontario M5R 1A3
Tel: (416) 960 2063   Telex: 06-23907

Denmark
Birgitta Hillingso
Dronningens Tvaergade 10
1302 Copenhagen K
Tel: (451) 32 70 75   Telex: 21075

Finland
Mrs. Barbro Schauman
Ulrikagatan 3 A, 00140 Helsinki
Tel: (358) 060 8212

France
Princesse Jeanne-Marie de Broglie
Laurent Prevost-Marcilhacy
Christie's France SARL
17 rue de Lille, 75007 Paris
Tel: (331) 42 61 12 47   Telex: 213468

Fabienne Albertini
2 rue Matheron
13100 Aix en Provence
Tel: (3342) 96 43 94

Hong Kong
Alice Yuan Piccus
3607 Edinburgh Tower, The Landmark
15 Queen's Road Central, Hong Kong
Tel: (852) 521 5396/7   Telex: 72014
Facsimile: (852) 527 1704

Israel
Mary Gilben
Christie's in Israel
6 Ben Zion Blvd.,   Tel Aviv 64285
Tel: (9723) 295211   Telex: 35770
Facsimile: (9723) 299171

Italy
Milan
Giorgina Venosta
Christie's (Italy) S.r.l.
9 via Borgogna, 20122 Milan
Tel: (392) 794 712   Telex: 316464

Turin
Sandro Perrone di San Martino
Corso Matteotti, 33, 10121 Turin
Tel: (3911) 548 819

Japan
Sachiko Hibiya
Ichibankan Bldg., B1
3-12, Ginza 5-chome
Chuo-ku, Tokyo 104
Tel: (813) 571 0668   Telex: 29879
Facsimile: (813) 571 5853

Luxembourg
Countess Marina von Kamarowsky
7 rue Pierre d'Aspelt, 1142 Luxembourg
Tel: (352) 452532

Mexico
P.O. Box 105-158
Mexico 11570
Tel: (525) 531 1686/1806

Norway
Ulla Solitair Hjort
Riddervoldsgt. 10b, Oslo 2
Tel: (472) 44 12 42

Portugal
Antonio M.G. Santos Mendonça
R. Conde de Almoster 44, 1° Esq.
1500 Lisbon
Tel: (3511) 78 63 83   Telex: 12839

South Africa
Cape Town
Mrs. Juliet J. Lomberg
14 Hillwood Road
Claremont, 7700 Cape
Tel: (2721) 712 676   Telex: 5-20414

Johannesburg
Harriet Gilfillan,
P.O. Box 650852, Benmore
Sandton 2010
Tel: (2711) 783 0303   Telex: 428751

Spain
Casilda Fz-Villaverde y Silva
Valenzuela 7, Madrid 28014
Tel: (341) 232 66 27   Telex: 46681
Cables: Christiart, Madrid

Sweden
Lillemor Malmström
Artillerigatan 29, 11445 Stockholm
Tel: (468) 620 131   Telex: 12916

Baroness Irma Silverschiold
Klagerups Gard, 230 40 Bara
Tel: (4640) 44 03 60

Switzerland
Maria Reinshagen
Christie's (International) A.G.
Steinwiesplatz, 8032 Zürich
Tel: (411) 69 05 05   Telex: 56093
Facsimile: (411) 251 04 71

Venezuela
Alain Jathiere
Apartado 88061, 1080 Caracas
Tel: (582) 343 751   Telex: 24950

West Germany
Jörg-Michael Bertz
Inselstrasse 15
D-4000 Düsseldorf 30
Tel: (49211) 4982986   Telex: 8587599

Jörg-Michael Bertz
Christiane Gräfin zu Rantzau
Wentzelstrasse 21, D-2000 Hamburg 60
Tel: (4940) 279 0866

Charlotte Fürstin zu Hohenlohe-
Langenburg
Residenzstrasse 27, D-8000 Munich 2
Tel: (4989) 22 95 39   Telex: 5218498

Monsieur Gèrald Van der Kemp, President d'Honneur of Christie's Europe, is based in our Paris Office.

Index